The
Paris
Baguette

Journals of a Protestant in Paris

The
Paris
Baguette

Lorelei M. Friesen

WinePressPublishing
Great Books, Defined.

© 2012 Photography: Sheena Friesen (p. 256), Rahela Markovic (p. 180, back cover author photo), John Svendsen (p. 274), Ron Wolf (p. 144) and Ron Friesen (pp. 13, 35, 58, 147, 253, 268).

WinePress Publishing (PO Box 428, Enumclaw, WA 98022) functions only as book publisher. As such, the ultimate design, content, editorial accuracy, and views expressed or implied in this work are those of the author.

These real-life stories have been written with the permission of the author's friends and family. Some names and locations have been changed to protect privacy.

ISBN 13: 978-1-4141-2046-1
ISBN 10: 1-4141-2046-X
Library of Congress Catalog Card Number: 2011922962

This book is dedicated to all who take the risk of being authentic and real in spite of the cost.

Contents

Acknowledgments

I WANT TO THANK:

Carol Anderson, who has been my champion and cheerleader. This book would not have been published without her resourcefulness, persistence and input.

Jane Wolf, one who is so much more than a friend, but also a lifelong mentor unafraid to gently address the darkness in my life, so I could experience God's accepting grace.

My husband, Ron, who courageously and consistently gives me the freedom to be who I am. My deep thanks to him for organizing what were scattered pieces of writing into a more organized whole.

Luanne Warren, for her encouraging friendship and her husband, Gerry, for his significant support of this project.

Ruth Dirks, Letha Quinn, and Erin van der Veen, who, in addition to Carol, Jane, Ron, and Luanne, provided many helpful suggestions on the manuscript.

The people of Trinity International Church of Paris. Because of our vulnerability in an unfamiliar culture, we were open to God and each other in unusual ways. Thank you for allowing me to write some of your stories. My life will be forever touched by the four years we spent together.

My brothers and sisters on the journey with me at LifePath, the support and recovery group ministry of Salem Alliance Church.

L'Été—
Summer 2004

August: Aliens in Paris

WE ARRIVED AT the remarkably ugly, dirty gray Aéroport Paris-Charles de Gaulle to a crowd of expectant faces from our new church, Trinity International Church of Paris. The faces contrasted markedly to the foreboding expression our daughter wore. Our choice had not been hers. We had uprooted her from a secure, familiar suburban life to an odd-feeling, urban apartment that echoed every foreign sound until the shipping container arrived six weeks later with the remnants of our American home.

Six hundred square feet and one bathroom would be an adjustment. Small things like door handles that were stationed too high and toilet flushers that pulled up out of the lid or down from the ceiling were a constant reminder that this was not home. Our fourteen-year-old's bedroom door slammed often to the tune of "You've ruined my life," accompanied by sobs.

Our family had landed in an alien, cosmopolitan world where stand-alone homes, Safeway®, Home Depot®, and Target® were fairytale material. Who would have guessed that Atac was a grocery store and not the local gun outlet? We were five-year-olds in an adult world without parents to guide us.

This was Paris. Our unplugged family wrapped up August by watching French broadcasts of the 2004 Summer Olympics as we sat on two stiff, 1950s kitchen chairs and one low beach lounger over which we fought. There was a distinct lack of American TV coverage and a noticeable addition of roundtable discussion by verbose French talking-heads. We were not in our native world.

School would be the first step to seeding our lives into this foreign soil, and it was bearing down on us with increasing speed. These are the scattered journals I kept as I struggled to live honestly in this new, unnatural world.

L'Automne—
Autumn 2004

September: French Lessons

I'VE HAD SOME surreal days when I was blissfully happy. I've thought, *Pinch me, I'm living in Paris!* I could actually see the Eiffel Tower downriver from the bridge close to our apartment. I've also had other, darker days when I longed to pinch someone else, or do something involving fists. There have been unbearable days of French immersion. Those who had studied Latin captured every nuance with disappointing speed while Ron and I struggled at the back of the pack, our brains twisting into tiny knots, our meager courage lost.

Each month we re-registered for our French class and each time there were only a few of us who continued from the previous session. For some incomprehensible reason we were joined by some new students with seven years of language study and fluent speech who needed only to fine-tune their writing skills. With these new imposters posing as French students, the teacher abruptly transitioned us from power walking on the beach to riding high-performance jet skis. Ron drowned while I waved from a buoy I clutched in desperation.

After a few months of increasing humiliation, depression set in. The French teaching style was not to our liking. Although we knew comparison would poison our tender grafting to a new culture, we indulged our wounded pride. In North America, new concepts were introduced and explained. Questions were answered before assigning exercise sheets, before prancing around the classroom with a red marker, scornfully exclaiming, "Noooo! Ooh-la-la, what can you possibly be thinking?" One glance from our professor could wither an orchard in heavy rain.

After three days of dismal guessing in the dark and multiple papers badly scarred by blood-red ink, the new grammar rule was handwritten on a blackboard in illegible chalk. Drowning students grabbed the life preserver desperately while the smug Latin speakers sprawled in their seats, bored.

Exhausted and pressured, Ron arrived in a dark blue funk one morning. Our well-coifed professor in her purple leather pants and matching jacket looked him over and asked how he was doing. Ron told her he was having a rough morning. From that point on, the prof picked on him repeatedly.

"Ron! What's the answer? You don't know? Oh-la-laaa." A few minutes later, the harassment would resume. "Ron? What's the problem here? Don't you know this? What's the matter with you?"

It went on and on. I was on the other side of the room. Still, I could see him dying, shrinking. My nails were extended, my hackles rising. How dare she shame my husband? I yanked my invisible leash. "Down girl, down," I whispered to my inner Rottweiler.

After a long hour of the prof's Pick-Pick-Slam game, Ron crossed his arms and fiercely responded, "Madame, je ne parle pas aujourd'hui. C'est tout. (Ma'am, I am not talking today. That's all.)." He stared her down in bitter silence. She baited him again and he glared back, white-hot. The game was finished.

That evening in the grocery store I noticed that even the dogs understood French better than we. But I had one sweet consolation: For the first time in my life I was thinking carefully before I finally spoke.

December: Tale of an Old Couple

ONCE UPON A time there were two very old people who decided they would learn a new language. Even though their brains were getting brittle in some places and soft in others, they moved to Paris and began to go to language school every day. To their dismay, some students had young, quick, pliable brains and others were Spaniards, Italians and South Americans who easily grasped this sister language. In time, these recycled students became quite discouraged and began to feel they would never grasp the secret key to speaking and understanding this new tongue. One could say they became Les Misérables.

Their French-fluent friends at church tried to encourage them. "Look at how much you've learned," they would say. "You probably know at least three thousand new words by now."

But the old woman, still somewhat adept at math, knew this figure left them with 297,000 more words to learn. At the current rate of twelve thousand words per year, she calculated that there were thirty more years to go. She, let alone her much older husband, would be dead by then.

So the aging woman came up with a fresh approach that would save years of hard work: speak English with a French accent. The basic principles, unlike French, were simple and straightforward:

Emphasize the last syllable of the last word in a phrase or sentence.

Zere are no "th" sounds in zis language; change all TH's to a Z or T.

Zere aren't any "h" sounds in French eizer, practice saying 'uge and 'appy.

All I's make an eee sound.

Speak weez pout-y leeps protrudeeng, as zoe you 'ave a collagen overload.

Zis steel took a leettle practeece, but zee new Paris-ites found it much faster and easier zan actually learning French, and best of all, she 'oped zee French would never guess zat she was actually an eegnorant Amereecan, who couldn't understand French.

Unfortunately, zee new plan only worked weez toureeests!

The couple felt old and disheartened with their studies. Not only that, they learned that integral people at their church were moving away—to Canada and to Hungary. Their shoulders stooped lower under this added weight. So upon coming home from school one dismal day, the old woman decided to use her "call-a-friend lifeline," while the old man preferred the "eat-a-baguette lifeline." Back in their home country, good friends learned the couple was discouraged and began to pray.

The next week the old couple noticed they were feeling younger again. Laughter returned to their language class just in time. The phone rang with friends from home on the other end. Other friends from Oregon and Alaska dropped by, cake mixes arrived from Canada, and even a drummer from Nepal materialized. Francophone friends at church reminded them that they had come far in only three months, and that the couple's expectations were perhaps a bit too high. The couple realized God was putting a finger on their over-charged perfectionism buttons.

With a sense of renewed vigor, the old couple decided to forge ahead by inviting three fellow students over for dinner. Unfortunately, no faith healers were available to lay hands on the roast beef the wife had prepared. It was a catastrophe. The meal would have been tastier had the husband's boots been marinated and served. Apparently, in France it is important to be able to read more on the label than just "viande bovine" (cow meat). The old couple concluded that language school was still a necessary ingredient. Shoot.

Le Printemps—
Spring 2005

March: The Music Scene

TODAY THE SUN lights my salon (living room) as I gaze out at the city set behind my wrought-iron Martha Stewart window boxes I bought at Kmart® a lifetime ago. The beauty of my balcony-garden and the warmth of the sunshine soften my heart. I've been musing on the past few years—the court case with our sliding-down-the-hill home, random jobs that materialized for Ron, and then the scattered pieces coming together to enable our move to France. Musing on the path that ultimately brought us here quiets my heart. Despite the language school torture, I feel sure we're meant to be in Paris.

Our fellow students and professors are curious about us. Each month the new students ask what we do and we tell them we're musicians. The next question is, "Where on the scene do you make your music?"

We reply, "The church."

This stops the questions and begins a pronounced silence. This lasts for a couple of weeks before the questions resume with, "Do you play the organ?" They think it's rather odd to hear that I play piano and sing, but when they hear that Ron plays the bass in church, it's always the same response. "That's bizarre! In the chapel? This cannot be."

We tell them we have an acoustic guitarist from Malaysia, an electric guitarist with Cambodian roots, a sax player from Germany, a drummer from Nepal, and singers from Belgium, Africa, and England. They are intrigued. They ask how we can do that in a church. We tell them to come and see.

Last week six people wandered upstairs to our little church, following the sounds of a live band on their way home from the Jardin du Luxembourg. Thirty more gathered on the sidewalk below our open windows. On the religious scene, pipe organs are regular; bands are irregular. What we do is seemingly something many in this, our new world, have never encountered. So we play on.

L'Été—
Summer 2005

June: Fresh French

FRENCH IS BEGINNING to take root, but I fake it regularly by saying "mmm," uttering polite chuckles, and working my eyebrows. We've learned to be cautious with the word "excited"—it only has one, sexually charged connotation in French. I'll now never forget to say, "I have hot," rather than "I am hot." That was embarrassing.

We knew we needed help reading our bills and our bank statements, so we should have gotten help reading a certain notice in our mailbox. Whether it was good news or bad news, we weren't sure. The day Ron stayed home from language school with a flu that caused him to pass out, crash to the bathroom floor, and cut open his forehead—that was the day they cut off our power. Turned out the notice had indeed been bad news. Ron managed to communicate via telephone with the electric company that all our bills were paid; they managed to communicate he had to get dressed, take a bus, and search for their office to rectify their mistake and get our power turned back on. Supper was late that night, but that's never an issue in France.

The best way to learn a language is to make friends with the natives. We've had quite a few delightful evenings with our

11

neighbors, those above and those below. The dinners have been fabulous gastronomic safaris and never less than five courses. We're the first ones to excuse ourselves at the groggy hour of one A.M., our heads fried from thinking in another language.

All of our conversations are in fast-flowing French, and our new friends continually amuse themselves by mocking my English sounds that aren't nasal enough, my "R" that doesn't roll in the back of my throat, and the three "ooo" sounds they claim are different. Yeah, right—ooo, ooo, and also ooo—one for above, another for below, and the last I forget. I need lip extensions to produce the identical triplets they claim are fraternal. Those who've mastered multiple languages prod, "Why can't you hear the difference? You're a musician; you're supposed to be able to hear that." At this, my middle school self wakes up, fully alert (she's a light sleeper), and whispers, "You're not a real musician; this proves you're a fake, fake, fake." So I feed her a few of her favorite French ginger cookies and beg her to go back to bed.

With our fresh French skills in hand, Ron and I politely asked for two baguette sandwiches at the award-winning bakery across the street from Genesis, our church's activity center near Châtelet, in the humming center of Paris. Ron ordered a Coke and I asked for Perrier; we were awarded one ice cube in each glass, a tribute to our English accents. We pushed our way back outside with a "pardon" here and there, and threaded our way down the sidewalk toward our favorite table snuggled in a corner far from the busy entrance.

As we enjoyed our quiet lunch, Ron and I noticed the owner/baker making his way toward us down the sidewalk, passing other tables, a disturbed look on his face. I wondered if we had unknowingly violated some cultural custom and we were about to be royally dressed down. He asked if we spoke French. "A little," we replied. He responded that his wife had "decided." I wondered what she had decided. I struggled to understand; I could tell he was distraught. Something terrible had happened. Had she left him a few days ago? I understood he lost her. I watched Ron respond; he caught on first. "Decided" wasn't decided—it was deceased. His pretty, young wife had unexpectedly died four days ago, leaving him with toddler twins, and here he was on the sidewalk, pouring out his terrible news. What do you say with such green language skills?

At dinner in the late evening, Sheena reminded us how difficult it is to find the right words to say, even in English. In his numb grief, this young man was searching for something; he probably didn't even know what. And what could we give his broken heart in our broken French?

Genesis, Trinity's Activity Center

L'Automne— Autumn 2005

October: Sheena's World

IN ANOTHER MONTH the sidewalk café season will be winding down. I sense from my perch by the kitchen window that the frosty air is calling for additional layers. Little poodles and tiny terriers are now sporting their knit wool coats. Does this make them dogs in sheep's clothing? From our sixth story nest I observe how many dogs on the sidewalk are off leash not too far from their owners and never straying into the street. It's impressive.

I see things from here that aren't written in the tour books, like the open garbage truck that passes regularly under my window. It collects carcasses from the butchers. It's very colorful, in a raw, red sort of way. I think I'll be a vegetarian.

Our kitchen observatory is a great place to sit and muse with Sheena when she arrives home from school in the late afternoon. She has made a complete, astounding about-face, having decided that the American School of Paris is where she wants to finish all four years of high school. She talks of working overseas someday and raising her own children in an international environment. The girl who once desperately pleaded to return to the secluded suburban world of Salem, Oregon, is now preparing to leave us. We helped shape her formidable wings—but what have we done?

I'm more worried about Sheena's school year than she is—geometry, chemistry, and algebra all in one year. How will this arts-oriented family handle the pathways of an unforgiving mathematical world? On a lighter side, volleyball tryouts are today, and Sheena is anxious to play. Volleyball assuaged the "You've ruined my life" syndrome last year. She was the only freshman who made the varsity team. It's strange for me to have a daughter with natural athletic talent. It's an unfamiliar, uncertain world.

It's good for Sheena to be so different from her musician parents, to have fallen so far from the apple tree. From the time she was little she asserted, "I'm not you and I'm never going to be you." It was her only defense against two powerful parents. So I knew it was good, in a sad, self-pitying kind of way. After all, deep inside I am quite fond of cloning.

There is one little piece of her mother that lives within her, though—Sheena is an unusual jock who seldom wears jeans. She loves to dress up in skirts and heels, and enjoys shopping arm in arm with her mom. It isn't the quality I would've picked to pass down to her, but at least it's evidence we're related.

Sheena continues to visit McDonald's® from time to time. She has mastered the skill of discovering America in Paris: The Gap®, Starbucks®, and Chicago Pizza Factory®, as well as Ben and Jerry's®, have all infiltrated resistant France. However, her European friends are slowly converting her. In North America, lunch was usually peanut butter and jelly sandwiches, mac 'n cheese, or possibly a pepperoni pizza. Here it's more likely that her friends will ask her if she prefers Roquefort, Chèvre, or Camembert cheese with her baguette. They make Caprese salads of tomatoes, water-packed mozzarella, olive oil, and fresh basil. Instead of soda, they drink Perrier® and compare the size of its sturdy gas bubbles to the fine bubbles of San Pellegrino®. Can these really be teenagers?

November: The First Soirée

It was our first big event, designed for the enjoyment of people who don't normally go to church. It featured the LF Jazz Trio—me and my piano, Ron on bass, and our drummer from Nepal.

That evening, a wonderful variety of people walked in off the street. One couple said they'd been looking for an Egyptian bar rumored to have great "sheesh" and found us instead. Another guest said he heard about us at the Louvre Museum from a fellow journalist, so the two of them plus another newsman came together. Our neighbors asked if there would be a "ceremony." We assured them of no sermon, just music. They came and stayed for the evening, tucking themselves under the stairs for the second set.

After playing many of my favorite jazz standards about love gained and lost, I told the audience I wanted to close the evening with two songs I wrote from my own spiritual journey. They were unusually quiet as I sang about God's reliable love.

When all was sung and done we were surprised by their warm response. One French girl asked if she could have a "warning" the next time this happened, because she wanted to come again. Our neighbors were very moved by the evening and invited us to enjoy Christmas Eve dinner with them.

Madame D., the friend they brought to the concert, had an extraordinary encounter that night with our friends from Salem who were in Paris on their way home from Russia. Madame D. wanted to know what they were doing there. Our friend Jane said she had been teaching recovering alcoholics and their families how to live in freedom. Madame D.'s eyes almost popped out of her head as she whispered that she'd been abstinent for ninety days.

"What do you think of the 12 Steps?" Madame D. quizzed my friend.

"I believe they are important biblical principles the church has lost. You know, Lorelei has gone to a 12-Step group."

"She has?" Madame D. was shocked. "Why?"

"Maybe you should get together with her and ask her yourself," my friend parried.

Following this surprising conversation, Madame D. came to tell me my friend Jane was "stupefying." It's unusual for intimate conversation to unfold so quickly in France. People are often rewarded with shame for their candor. Instead, Madame D. happened into a friendship I hope will always be seasoned by acceptance and grace.

L'Hiver—
Winter 2005–2006

December: Christmas Light

WE FELL INTO the Christmas season, losing our footing in the rush to put on our next event. It was too close to the last one. With such a small pool of musicians to pull from, preparations felt overwhelming. We wondered if there would continue to be non-churched, non-connected people curiously wandering in off the street.

How do we build meaningful bridges? How do we make ourselves available for further spiritual exploration without being salesmen who care only about "closing the deal?" The French are very suspicious of people who have these agendas—for good reason.

Additionally, how could we possibly have a Christmas soirée without creating an inviting ambiance with tiny white lights? Leaving Ron behind, I went to the hardware store, alone, to buy two white twig trees. I found the perfect pair, about nine feet tall. I figured there would be too many logical, male-type reasons why these trees weren't practical to transport to Genesis—rational grounds, like the possibility of removing the eyes of unsuspecting Métro passengers. Still, I bought them.

The trees were a little heavier than I expected and more awkward to carry with my bag of ornaments and lights. I couldn't decide which direction to cram the trees into the Métro—should the branches be snapped off on the way in or on the way out? I had only a brief, eighteen-second pause to maneuver into and stagger out of the two trains I needed to catch that day. After I stumbled into the first in a panicked hurry, I realized I had no way to open the door, trapped against the back wall as I was.

Though they may not smile at you, French people are very kind when you're in distress. When I was trying to exit, a fellow passenger opened the door for me and held back the passengers who attempted to rush in. Because the trees had become increasingly ponderous during the last forty-five minutes, they got caught halfway through a set of automatic doors on my way back up to the street. Ron just laughed at my foolish determination, and I got a workout without a gym or a shower, but Genesis was transformed by the magic of little white lights on trees.

With the Christmas season so full, it wasn't until January that Madame D. and I met for our first lunch alone together across the river from the Tour Eiffel. Quite the conversation took place. Had I ever had one like it before? She quizzed my faith without animosity, just a sincere desire to know how it worked for me. She told me when I sang my own songs that soirée night in November, she had realized I was human. She quoted to me the lyrics from that night two months earlier. I could hardly believe she had remembered them.

> I will trust your heart.
> I will trust your heart.
> When your face is invisible,
> Your footprints are unseen,
> When your hand's indiscernible
> And nothing is serene,
> Though we may feel far apart,
> I will trust your heart.
>
> I believe your heart is faithful.
> I believe your heart is good.
> I believe your heart is merciful,
> Though often it's misunderstood.[1]

A hunger lives in her heart; she's been diligently searching for decades. God wove events so we would find an apartment above her friends, and for these neighbors to bring her to our music soirée. Madame D. is warm and winsome; she has won my heart. May God win hers.

February: The Times

TOURIST TIME

I set aside some time to experience the normal "must-see-and-do" with our son Justin while he visited our side of the planet. We meandered through the Louvre and Carnavalet Museums, strolled the Marais, and ate crepes (he preferred the American style), sorbet (too healthy), and dark chocolate (heaven). Justin contentedly meandered through my favorite museum—the Marmottan, a private Monet collection in an intimate, historic mansion just a few stops away on our Métro line.

But it was The Dad who really knew how to introduce his son to Paris. Ron had a few hours free one Saturday afternoon, so he suggested checking out the Ferrari® dealership only three Métro stops away—a place every person in a helping profession needs to peruse. There they inspected Ferraris®, Maseratis®, and Bentleys®, restraining themselves from touching a Rolls Royce® with a price tag of 405,000 euros.

After that religious experience, they were strolling down the street when a man whipped past them, closely followed by another five in angry pursuit. My boys' curiosity drew them farther down the street, where they stood mesmerized. An enraged crowd charged out of a brasserie (bar), yelling and flailing their arms. Serious blood flowed from various body parts. Minutes later, the street was overrun by police with heavy riot gear, masks in place, shooting tear gas and overpowering the fist-fighters. More people came flooding out of the bar with their hands pressed against their eyes, the gas effectively persuading them to vacate the premises. The police battalion shoved bodies onto the street, roughly squatting on them—political correctness apparently was not an issue. The subdued rioters were herded efficiently into police buses standing nearby. Welcome to France—just before a soccer game.

Justin, finding the time with his dad more exhilarating than my museum expeditions, returned home with a cheerful, "Hey, Mom, Dad almost got us killed today!"

TEA TIME

I made real tea out of loose leaves in my black tea pot from Portland's Pearl District for Madame R., my neighbor, the other day, and there we sat having an intriguing conversation. At one point she turned to me, her eyes full of tears, and asked, "How can I have a faith like you?"

I responded, "You can start by just talking to God where you are; tell Him what you feel and think." I showed her a Psalm where David did just that.

Madame R. was emphatic. "I can't do that. God is like air…" and something else I didn't catch. My French is like erratic radio reception that comes in and out of the static.

So I suggested, "Then tell God you can't believe. Tell Him He isn't clear. You can even ask God to show Himself to you, because He will find you."

"Have you ever doubted?" she queried.

I began to unfold yet another chapter of my life story: my failings, my struggles with bitterness, and my doubts during the six years when our house was slowly sliding down a hill and we didn't know where Ron's next job would be. She listened to my broken French intently.

LUNCH TIME

I accidentally made lunch for Madame D., to whom I was first introduced on Christmas Eve by our neighbors, Madame and Monsieur R. I dread using my new language skills on the phone—it's the absolute worst, no facial cues, no hands, no chemistry.

Madame D. had intended to take me to a famous, historic café, but I misunderstood. She said she was inviting and coming to my apartment. I had no idea the use of the verb "invite" means one is offering to pay, so I had lunch ready for her when she arrived to take me out.

My faux pas was providential. Madame D. sat in our petite, private dining room with me for six hours while we talked of spiritual things "très profound."

After four hours, she said, "The major problem for me is that I can't believe in the resurrection. That is the central question; if I believe that, everything else falls into place."

Madame D. is an extremely bright, capable woman. So I hedged. "Let me see if I can get a hold of Ron; he loves this kind of stuff." No answer; he was in a Métro line without phone reception. So I tried to explain C.S. Lewis's provocative observation: Jesus is a liar, lunatic, or Lord.[2]

She turned the idea over and around in her mind, carefully examining it from a number of angles. I tried Ron again. He was waiting at the post office, now only six bodies from the front in a line that crept at the pace of France's celebrated escargot. He reassured me that resurrection discussions could wait a little longer. (Why does this remind me of the time I was in panicky labor, frantically waiting to go to the hospital while calm, methodical Ron finished his task?)

Madame D. was happy to wait. Since she's French, she knows you never leave a post office line once you've finally caught sight of the counter. We listened to Diana Krall, discussed jazz, and swapped childhood tales.

I learned of Madame D.'s great-aunt, whom she adored. The petite Mademoiselle D.'s life was ragged from the aftermath of a brutal divorce that never healed well. The doting auntie took my friend to the music store to introduce her to jazz, buy her records, and love her well. Madame D. explained that her great-aunt had a "personal relationship" with Jesus Christ, something unconventional in traditional France. The old auntie prayed that her great-niece would know God in the way she did and gave her books to read. The great-aunt had died twenty-three years earlier—yet heaven had saved her prayers.

Ron arrived in good time and found two books to read and discuss. Their conversation was relaxed and interesting. D. left at dinner time, reassured by Ron that it might not be pride that was stopping her from believing, as she suggested, but honest questions with which God was only too happy to give her the space to deal.

It was a few weeks later that we introduced Madame D. to a French software company CEO who goes to our church; I was trying to help her find a job. As our new friend marveled at how these complicated weavings of threads were coming together, Ron said, "Almost makes you want to believe there really is a God, doesn't it?"

She replied, "I just don't have the humility yet to accept this as the path laid out before me."

That's okay—it's a process, I thought.

Le Printemps— Spring 2006

March: Returns

RETURN OF OUR SON

OUR FAMILY SEEMS to be operating in reverse. Many families who live overseas go home when their children become young adults, to stand beside them while they find their legs and the lives that will be their own. Just as our son Justin was flying away from the nest, we abandoned him and left for France. Now, because our son was between job opportunities and feeling rather lost, we invited him to live with us for four months.

It has struck Ron and me repeatedly how good it is to live within proximity of each other again (six hundred square feet being fairly close proximity). The French think it is much more normal to have grown children at home—so we're fitting in better than ever. Justin is endearing himself to me with his fabulous cooking skills, ingratiating himself to his dad by helping with technical and construction-type projects, and winning the people at church with his ready laughter and the djembe he plays. He's discovered a new world, especially in grocery stores.

When you walk into the obsessively clean, organized grocery stores of North America without even the slightest hint of reeking cheese assaulting your nose, think of us here in France. The aisles of solid dairy in open refrigerators take a definitive toll on the air quality. At first I thought they were selling Justin's hockey socks, but it's the 365 varieties of cheese. Since Justin worked at a grocery store during high school, it's validating to see his astonishment at how these businesses operate here.

Loading docks seem non-existent. Delivery trucks park in two lane streets during any inconvenient hour of the day, tying up traffic in both directions and offering great entertainment. Angry horns are the obnoxious clue for us to run to the windows of our apartment observatory six stories above. A driver, oblivious to the fury around him, abandons his vehicle mid-street, sets the brake, and punches the hazard light button. He strolls between store and street as he leisurely goes about his business. Sometimes he even has enough time for a smoke.

RETURN TO THE STORE

Justin laughs at the empty shelves that would result in major hair-tearing at his former employer's grocery store. There's little concern here when raisins are gone. It may be days, weeks, or even months before they return, and this is not only because the French think a raisin is a waste of a good grape. It also occurs regularly with my obligatory fruit-and-fiber cereal and Sheena's favorite brown-and-serve bread. I've learned to squat down and search for hidden raisins behind dried bananas and peanuts on bottom shelves—until the entire shelving unit is removed for no apparent reason.

The best challenge occurred yesterday as Justin carried one shopping basket and I the second. As we headed to the notoriously slow checkout stands with the legendary lines, I remembered one more item. Justin went ahead to save us a place and I turned back to the bowels of the store. I had forgotten my son's gift: after years of working at Roth's grocery store, he now has an uncanny ability to deduce which line will be the fastest. It's almost a sixth sense.

By the time I returned, I was shocked to see Justin bagging the last of our groceries. I pushed ahead of the waiting clients like any confident European, explaining he was my son. However, the woman who was anticipating an eminent arrival at the cashier was less than pleased to see me. She rewarded my aggressive behavior with her own. I was sworn at, belittled, and told it was just too bad as she pushed her groceries forward, trying to eliminate the space on the belt where I struggled to set my groceries down. I was so happy—I could understand every nasty word she said! I just agreed with her, it really was too bad, and then thanked her with the standard line everyone says when someone does something very kind: "Merci beaucoup, Madame. C'est gentil." That was exhilarating! All the adrenalin rush of bungee jumping!

Some might say, "But Lorelei, what would Jesus do?" Unfortunately, I was wearing my What-Would-Peter-Do bracelet that day.

RETURN TO CONVERSATIONS

I had espresso with Madame D. last week. As we were chatting, I sensed something had changed. Finally, I took a breath and asked, "Madame D., do you believe in God now?"

She looked me straight in the eye and breathed a slow, drawn-out, "Oui."

I queried, "What about the resurrection?"

She raised her shoulders to her ears, lifted her eyebrows, and just stared at me with big, brown eyes.

"When did this happen?" I asked.

She told me it had happened fifteen days ago, after our last lunch together. She went downstairs to a brasserie, bought a cup of espresso, and experienced God's presence. She said her life had changed and I could see it in her face. I felt tears prick my eyes. What kind of dream am I living in that I am able to see someone taste God's goodness for the first time?

Two days later, the Mesdames and I lunched together again. Madame R. brought an extraordinarily tasty seafood tart as well as a gourmet salad. My, can that woman cook circles around Julia Child! Ron had assembled a collection of quotes on faith for them due to their earlier questions, and they were captivated by it. They were so taken with his collection that they pushed their lunch aside and studied the quotations intently. I asked Madame D. if she could translate them.

After reflecting for a moment she turned her head and looked up to say, "No, there are too many concepts in very few words. Besides, I read much more carefully in English."

April: School, Strikes, and More

DYING TO KNOW

Ron and I returned to language school last month. I walked late into class one day and heard the teacher say that we would be debating whether we were for or against "Le Tennessee." She divided us into two groups and told my group that we were against it. My classmates began to complain. They were all for Le Tennessee, so how could they think of any "anti" arguments? They didn't want to be against Le Tennessee. I thought, *Tennessee? It's controversial now? Is this about banning country music? Or perhaps I am for Kentucky? What is 'Le Tennessee'?"*

At first my Costa Rican acquaintance was no help. In response to my question, she just continued to repeat, "You know, Le Tennessee, Le Tennessee." I shook my head; I didn't understand. Finally she said to me in English, "Euthanasia – l'eu-tan-a-sie."

Oh. Got it. I could argue that.

FEELING HISTORY

At the American School of Paris, Sheena has a favorite teacher named Mr. Friday who teaches history like none other. She just finished a unit on communism during which time she received a pencil and eight pieces of notepaper, like all her other social equals. Any other materials were confiscated, and at the end of each class, all notes were randomly exchanged—her copious, tidy notes for the scattered jots and tittles of a neighbor—all to keep the comrades' playing field level. The test and essay grades were averaged, with everyone in the class receiving the same mark.

As Mr. Friday believes that history is nothing unless you can feel it, he had imposed a communist system for that epoch. The class had feelings all right, right up to their "rebellion" in which they insisted he reinstall the capitalist system even though it meant that the girl with the broken arm would fall behind.

As they moved on to study the roaring twenties, Sheena spent $10,000 "buying" stocks for homework one night. Google® didn't do very well and Apple® bombed, but Starbucks® performed nicely.

This same teacher had another class decorate their room with elaborate art projects: faux stained-glass windows and tapestries, a medieval feast, banners, and reproductions of the period's enormous portraits. They effectively created an exquisite French castle ambiance of 1780's royalty. While these students were on a field trip to an authentic medieval palace, Mr. Friday arranged for the "peasant" class to come in and destroy everything the "aristocratic" students had created. The French Revolution unit had begun. On the royal students' return, they thoroughly felt the rage of the aristocrats during the eighteenth century, and Mr. Friday felt the rage of their parents during the twenty-first.

Strikes, French Style

Sheena was immersed in a school musical theatre production for months. The Métro didn't disgorge her until seven each dark evening. Saturdays and holidays were hijacked by the play's obsessed director—at her school, moderation is anathema. When the play finished, Sheena felt restless. No volleyball, no play; only student council, an overbooked social calendar, and a crushing load of homework. We encouraged her to learn to live with margins and "still waters" in her life. She told us, "You're nuts."

The "still waters" arrived the day of the National Strike. The French high school (next to the American School of Paris) held a parking lot full of demonstrators and riot police, so the American School of Paris decided not to take any chances and closed down for a day. It was almost as good as a snow day. As demonstrations and student riots continued in other parts of the city, Sheena's greatest anxiety occurred later that week when the school bus she was riding with some friends got bogged down in a mob of rowdy, chanting protesters setting off firecrackers and harassing motorists. The students worried, wondering if the top-heavy bus would be tipped. It took an extra, tense hour to get home that day.

We don't have CNN, so we're not sure what Americans saw of Paris in the news; it was probably more dramatic than what actually took place. Yet it was disconcerting when Ron noticed charred debris and the remains of a bonfire in the university courtyard next to our language school. Students had taken control of the building and had hung a large banner with a red "R" added to the word "evolution" displayed on it.

On our way home, my observant husband pointed out a large plume of black smoke, visible from the vantage point of Trocadéro; it was blooming rather close to the hotel where our friends from Oregon were staying. Later that night, we couldn't drive them home since police had barricaded the area—car-burning parties had made another strong comeback. Other than that, this manifestation (demonstration) was fairly low-grade on the excitement scale; it was definitely less thrilling than snow, though both foul up traffic and cause us to drive at speeds my grandma would endorse.

Still, we didn't stay home, since union officials announced that only one out of every two Métros would be running. I couldn't tell the difference. Meanwhile, the communist party was cheerfully barbecuing sausages at Place d'Italie and serving demonstrators breakfast. Today, as Ron read the *International Herald Tribune* over French roast coffee and a baguette, he said rather softly, "This thing might get ugly yet." I'd rather have snow.

THE GREAT EXCHANGE

Justin's friend Mark stayed with us over spring break and the boys did more Paris in seven days than we've done in the past nineteen months. They had a few adventures I plan to continue avoiding, such as taking the stairs of the Eiffel Tower as opposed to the elevator.

I had seen a billboard advertising train fares to London for 55 euros, roundtrip. Justin and Mark were definitely up for spontaneity and took the Métro over to Gare du Nord to purchase tickets for an eight A.M. Tuesday departure, returning at six A.M. the following day. Being young, they had no plans or money for an overnight hotel; just a day and night in an exciting European city with a language in which they could function.

After purchasing their prize, they left the ticket agent to pack another Paris adventure into their pockets. Late that afternoon, as they took a moment to breathe, Mark examined his ticket and realized they'd been sold tickets that left Paris at eight P.M. The train would deposit them in London at eleven P.M. and leave at six A.M., seven hours later. They made the trip back to the train station, stood in line another forty minutes, calmly argued for thirty-five more with a clerk and two managers, took turns playing good cop/bad cop, and didn't leave until the tickets were exchanged for the correct return time of eight A.M. They seemed to have mastered the art of French negotiation. I could use their help.

MEXICAN FINGER FOOD

In spite of the extraordinary amount of adults I see on the Métro with their fingers in their mouth, chewing their nails down to painful stubs, this is a land where fried chicken and even pizza are eaten with a fork and knife. During mealtimes, fingers and mouths do not make contact. So when I invited Mesdames D. and R. to come for a Mexican dinner with their husbands, they became quite animated, clapping their hands together in delighted anticipation, exclaiming, "Oh-la-la, we get to eat with our fingers."

Justin spent the big day chopping in the kitchen. Well, not all the chopping was in the kitchen—while we were at language school, Justin took my only decent knife, the veggies, and a cutting board into the salon and diced all the tomatoes into minute pieces in the amount of time it took to watch the movie *Enemy at the Gates*.

Justin and Sheena really didn't want to put silverware on the table, but I insisted. You shouldn't push people too far out of their comfort zones. One of our friends just couldn't bring himself to eat the fajitas with his fingers. He had distinct, non-touching piles of fresh, apartment-made salsa; sautéed peppers and onions; crème fraîche (an upper-class cousin to sour cream); and stir-fried chicken that he carefully ate with his knife and fork. Justin's cuisine was an "'uge success" and our friends were completely impressed with his culinary skills. I can think of no better way to win a Frenchman's heart.

JESUS AND OUR STORIES

When our senior pastor's ninety-one-year-old dad died, he and his wife flew to Florida for the funeral. In this unanticipated absence, Ron stepped in to fill the Sunday speaking gap. He decided to teach on the Samaritan woman, someone with a story she was reticent to reveal—yet Jesus knew all of her story and was interested in every page.

Ron began, "All of us have a story, and the title for each of our stories, including Billy Graham's and Mother Teresa's, could well be, 'My Thirsty Life.'"

As Ron changed a few covers on the pile of books he had brought, he continued. "Often, we try to change the covers to our stories; we also have parts we'd rather not tell." He grasped a large black marker and inked out parts of one book. "Many of us want to keep some pages so secret we pretend they're not even part of our story." He tore out a few pages and then ripped out whole sections until the book fell apart.

Ron gently explained, "When we try to remove pieces of our story, our lives eventually fall apart. However, Jesus knows and accepts our entire story, just as He did the Samaritan woman's. Only His acceptance can quench the thirst of our lives."

Ron's sermon set off a ripple effect; a few of our pillar-type people have called and taken him out for lunch, wanting Ron to know all of their stories. They're so glad they've found a church where they don't need to hide pieces of their lives, and where Jesus makes beauty out of ashes. In exchange, Ron shares his story and we continue to cultivate a hybrid community of sinner-saints.

Yesterday as I had a Perrier® with Madame D., she asked me if this was normal in a church, to be so honest with each other. I told her this was the design Jesus intended. She pushed me again with the same question: "Is this normal, for people to be so honest about their whole lives inside the church?"

I sighed. "No, probably not, but it's a dream Ron and I share. It's the only way we can be truly changed by God's power."

May: Street Scenes

GRANDMAS IN FISHNETS

I sneak another sip from Ron's coffee cup since I only permit myself one per day. Sheena says I'm in denial, but I prefer to think of it as a romantic moment. We linger together, sipping his coffee at the little bar in our cozy kitchen, watching the French world parade by below us. From our perch, we see grown men in pinstripe suits on scooters, using their pointy dress-shoes to propel their zigzag flight between pedestrians on the sidewalks. Even funnier are the sophisticated women in their skirts and stilettos wearing oversized crash helmets as they roar down the street on their screaming motorcycles. Somehow it's less shocking when their bikes are pink.

I've noticed fishnet stockings on older women. Oh, sure, the young women are sporting them too, but it's much more entertaining to see them on grandmas with deeply pleated faces. I've even seen a few specimens who appear to be in their eighties sporting the sexy hose. I'm not talking about a fine net here. This hosiery could be used to catch dolphins.

Ron spots today's prize: an elderly lady in a vivid orange wool coat complete with black fishnet hose and green Converse® high-tops.

THE WAY OF THE CROSS

Genesis had been transformed into a quiet, holy refuge on Good Friday. That cold, gray day, we were whispered a greeting when we walked through the double doors into a candlelit reception area. A French or English booklet was offered to guide us, while a soft recording of chanting monks ushered us into another dimension. A hush fell over people as they sat to prepare themselves for a journey through eight historic moments along Christ's way to the cross.

When we were ready, Sheena and I moved to a garden setting titled "Loneliness." The guide reminded us what Jesus had endured and asked us to consider what parallel we may be called to experience. The path led to a bowl of water where we were invited to wash our hands and contemplate Christ's condemnation—how had we washed our hands of Him or of others?

The path led downstairs to six more interactive stations. There were swords and a whip to touch, painful sounds to hear, a mirror in which to look while considering for whom Christ died, a small cross of mercy to accept, and a large cross into which to pound our own nail of bankruptcy. Near the end, a portrait of Jesus holding a lamb with His deeply scarred hands hung on the stone wall.

Grown men wept. One French fashion designer declared, "I never understood the cross or the suffering of Jesus like this before. I felt like He was holding me in His arms." People were profoundly moved.

How often do we Protestants take time to reflect on Jesus' suffering? We seem to prefer the scene of the empty tomb.

Madame D. came. She couldn't speak at first. After taking a walk, she told Ron, "I was staggered and overwhelmed by what Jesus did for me. It was such accepted suffering." This was the day she was able to cross a line and embrace Jesus as the resurrected Lord.

My dear friend, Madame D., loves Jesus.

With Madame D.

Hazard Lights

We spy a garbage truck struggling to make the hairpin turn off our street. Someone has parked in the crosswalk, forcing the over-sized truck to seesaw back and forth to negotiate the impossible turn into the anorexic street. Little men swathed in fluorescent green suits swarm from side to side like mad conductors waving their arms. The guilty car in the crosswalk has hazard lights flashing. You can stop anywhere for a few minutes and be forgiven if your hazard lights are blinking. We've done it ourselves.

In spite of seeing car after car being towed from the bakery's delivery zone across from Genesis, Ron parked our car there and turned on the hazard lights while cleaning up after Good Friday's Way of the Cross. The flashing hazard lights bought him two hours, but at that point Ron had to run to beg mercy from the parking attendant in her sophisticated navy blue hat and suit. She gave him ten more minutes to finish the loading job. In ten minutes, we wedged Sheena sideways into the backseat of our uncomfortably pregnant hatchback and watched the tow truck arrive. We grinned as we slipped away in the drizzling rain. Gotta love those hazard lights.

An Unexpected Love Note

I had preceded Good Friday by abstaining from shopping for the six weeks of Lent. In past years, I had attempted to give up desserts. As I'd never actually been successful with that endeavor, I thought this new one held promising potential. How hard could it be?

The first four weeks went by without undue suffering, but it was the final fourteen days of Lent that brought my dark side to the surface. Suggestive store windows winked at me everywhere I walked; my thwarted desires birthed a blue bitterness. I complained that this was going to be the state of affairs for the rest of my life and took out my disappointment on my family.

Lent served its purpose. I came face to face with my darkness and experienced how deeply I need Jesus. Ironically, that was not the end of the story.

About two weeks after Lent, someone came to Paris and took Sheena and me shopping. She didn't know of my Lenten abstinence; we didn't know of her intentions. Her gift was overwhelming, humbling. I'm not at all suggesting this as a formula to "tame" God. Rather, it was a gift-wrapped, unexpected love note from God saying, "No matter how badly you behave, I will still be enough for your every need."

The Experiment

Not long after Easter, Justin moved to Canada. Tears were close to the surface for many days, my cheeks stained with mascara more often than not. Our neighbors and friends gave a lavish going-away dinner party for Justin; they even gave him beautiful gifts. It was a wistful evening as they reveled in how much our kids enjoyed their cats and new kittens.

There is something about the way my neighbor cooks that makes me wish for the four stomachs of a cow. She's pretty amazing. The dinner led to a walk arm in arm down our boulevard a few days later; it was the perfect moment for Madame R. and me to share more freely the pain and fears of our lives. I encouraged her again to try an experiment: "Ask God to meet you at your deepest need for thirty days and see what happens."

It was the first time she said she would try and added thoughtfully, "I suppose He knows I'm pretty preoccupied."

I responded. "He does know, but if you don't tell Him yourself, you are like the dear friends you love who won't share their pain with you. God is waiting to hear from you, too."

SHEENA GOES TO STARBUCKS®

Sheena decided to do some reading at Starbucks® before attending church. She set her phone alarm to make sure she would leave on time, avoiding the irritated-parent syndrome and setting it on the table where she would be certain to hear it.

A man who was circulating the room with flyers approached her, wanting to sell her a car. He was obnoxiously persistent. Sheena became irate, finally brushing him off.

As he walked away, Sheena looked to check the time. Where had she left her cell phone? Huh? She thought she'd left it on the table, but it wasn't there. In her purse? No? Oh, her pocket. No. Hmmm. Wait a minute! The creepy flyer guy had taken her phone while distracting her with a large brochure in front of her face.

She jumped to her feet, ran to catch up with him before he left the shop, grabbed him by the arm, and without hesitation, demanded, "Give me my phone back."

"I don't have your phone."

"Give me my phone back, NOW."

"What phone? I don't have your phone."

Sheena began to squeeze his arm and dig in her nails. Attracting the attention of coffee drinkers around the room, she used a voice she may have learned from her mother. "I want my phone back, and I want it back now." She dug her nails in as hard as she could, tightening her grip.

"Is this what you're looking for?" The man pulled her phone out of his pocket.

Sheena snatched it out of his hand and stalked back to her table as the man mimicked and waggled behind her, "Give me my phone, give me my phone."

Our victorious redhead didn't care. She had won back her phone, knowing Mom and Dad would be proud.

L'Été—
Summer 2006

June: The Jazz Soirée

W E ENTERED AN ancient building and began a steep descent to the basement via triangular, curving stone steps. A mild scent of musty mildew drifted up into our noses. After carefully navigating the plunging spiral, we entered a large, dungeon-like cavern and learned that we hadn't arrived yet—there was another whole set of treacherous, corkscrew, stone stairs.

By now there wasn't just a delicate scent of mold, we were embalmed in it. "Watch your heads," someone shouted. The ancient stairwell was obviously built by pygmies.

At the bottom we finally arrived to an underground world of musicians. The look was a French twist of "shabby chic." There were worn Persian rugs on the stone floor; the stone walls curved into a high, arched ceiling. This was where we would rehearse for our jazz soirée.

We met Francesco's friend Roland, who played bass, and proceeded to have an exhilarating rehearsal even though the drummer arrived thirty minutes late. The French-Cambodian bassist was delighted to be playing with real Anglophone singers for his very first time—pure jazz is sung in English, after all. When Ron began to belt out his "12-Step Blues," Francesco began to grin. After the pant-splitting finish, Francesco asked Ron, "Hey, how come you don't sing like that at church?" Ron just smiled.

After three hours of intense work, we set a time for our next rehearsal, but were disappointed to learn that the drummer would not be available again until just prior to the soirée on Saturday. We climbed our way to the surface and the quasi-fresh air of ground-level Paris. Our heads were drained not only by the musical demands but also by the necessity of communicating all our ideas in French. Occasionally, a few of the Italian words any serious musician knows would pop up, words such as *forte, ritard,* and *crescendo.* Whenever one of those words surfaced, the guys' heads would shoot up from their music as they threw us a shocked, impressed look that said, "Hey, your French isn't that good, but your Italian is great."

Five days passed and now began the evening of the jazz soirée, accompanied by a number of unexpected complications. I was spinning a silky serenade of "What a Wonderful World" when the first surprise package made its unwelcome appearance. The mic went out, and my voice abruptly disappeared. I could no longer be heard over the piano, guitar, and bass, let alone the drums. I improvised with a piano solo for a verse, thinking that would give Petre enough time to figure out how to turn my mic back on, but the problem was much more serious than I first imagined. The amp driving the speakers had rolled over and died. That's fairly critical. Ron told people to go on upstairs and enjoy the delicacies Carrol had prepared while he and Petre circumvented the technical difficulty. In ten pressured minutes they had sweated out a quick, makeshift solution—probably with duct tape or WD-40.

We were back underway with the last four songs of our first set. With the unexpected pause to address technical problems, the hired drummer was adamant he had already played two entire sets and proceeded to pack up his drums. This was the same drummer who was late to our first rehearsal and absent at our second. What a development; what a jerk. My other thoughts I'm more reluctant to commit to paper.

Francesco helped Jerk carry out his drum kit. He must have figured it was the right thing to do when someone lets you down. What a prince, so unlike me. As the second set resumed with guitar, contrabass, piano, and vocals, minus the percussion, I found myself ricocheting from wondering if God had implemented an improvement to bemoaning the catastrophic loss of drums.

As we drove home, Ron and I commiserated, recounting the ways the evening didn't go as we had imagined. Besides the death of the amp and the loss of the drummer, we also discovered a few acoustical kinks to work out in a room made entirely of stone. From time to time a low, muddy feedback had accumulated. Driving home on another grand Paris night, we hardly noticed its beauty.

As we got up the following morning, we struggled again with our perfectionism. We took small bites out of each other. The bites got larger. We realized that with the mixture of our fatigue and our high, unmet expectations, we might need to wait to talk about this until we'd had a little more sleep, or one of us would be devoured by lunchtime.

God's definition of success is so different than mine; I think He may have accomplished exactly what He had in mind. A woman who regularly attends our English conversation class came to the jazz soirée with her boyfriend. At the end, she enthusiastically kissed me and repeated, "Soup-AIR! Soup-AIR!" (the French pronunciation of "superb"). She'd never been so congenial.

Our tall Dutchman who's completing a Ph.D. in geophysics brought a colleague who loved the evening. I had noticed him grinning and closing his eyes as he swayed to the rhythm. The lady who regularly sells Ron crepes and paninis at the corner café brought two of her friends.

Not only did our neighbors below us come, but they also brought the Angels, who live above us, and our loyal friend, Madame D. Monsieur Angel told me that when Madame R. invited him to come along, he thought, *Oh, sure, they're doing jazz. Yeah, right.* He rolled his eyes expressively as he spoke. "But this, this was magnifique." He kissed my cheeks yet again.

There were other guests; I could see the curiosity in their eyes, wondering who we were and what was this "thing." It was good to serve all of them an evening of warmth and engaging music, and a moment to build friendships. I reminded myself that it's not about being impressive musicians; it's about loving people and giving God the space to show up. It happens, more than I realize.

The following Tuesday, Madame and Monsieur R. gave an impressive French dinner for our family and my brother and his daughter who were visiting from Canada. It was a full table; Monsieur and Madame Angel were there as well. I was seated next to Monsieur Angel, and it didn't take long for him to lean over and ask me in a low, confidential voice, "What's the full name of your church?"

"Trinity International Church."

He nodded his head, looking me closely in the eyes, and said softly, "I was so impressed with the people from your church. They're very warm and kind. It's good. I would like to visit. When will Ron become the pastor?"

"In September."

He drew back a little. "I am Catholic you know."

"We worship the same Jesus," I assured him.

He leaned in much closer and said confidentially, "I have God in my heart, you know."

I whispered back, "Well, then, you probably do want to come to church, don't you?"

"Yes, yes, I do."

I sensed God telling me again that He would do what He wanted to do outside of my agenda. Yet another blow to my perfectionism! When will I ever learn?

July: English in France

CONVERSATION CLASS

One of the ways we build bridges is by offering English conversation classes at Genesis. This day, the regular facilitator was away and I was helping a beginner. After the initial bonjour and normal pleasantries, I spoke very slowly and distinctly, "Do you do some different things during the summer?"

She hesitated and thought for a while. "Yes."

I prompted her with, "What are those different activities?"

She sat quietly, then finally said, "Uhhh."

I tried rephrasing the question. "What things do you do during the summer?"

She made some of those distinctly French lip-popping sounds, then "Uhhh."

I tried rewording the question. "What do you like to do during the summer?"

The light dawned in her eyes. "Oh, garrrden."

All right, we were onto something now; I could work with this. I continued. "OK. I like gardening too. What kind of a garden is it?"

She stared at the table. "Uhhh."

Perhaps she didn't know the word *kind*.

"What type of a garden is it?" Silence…still no prize. "Do you understand the question?"

"Yez."

I prompted her with a clue. "Is it a flower or a vegetable garden?"

Her eyes stayed focused on the table. "Yez."

Oh, dear, still fifty-five minutes left. "Is it a vegetable garden?"

"Yez."

"Oh, what kinds of vegetables do you grow?"

"I don't grrrow zee vegetable. I grrrow zee tomato."

I stared at her watch, the tiny little hands moving incrementally toward the finish. Oh, God, help me. Another fifty-four and a half minutes to go.

WEATHERING THE WEATHER

Our apartment block's central heat is always turned off on the fifteenth of May. I'd forgotten this tradition and for a few days wandered from window to window trying to find one accidentally left open.

There are only four rooms to check. Everything was closed unless you count the breeze that comes in from around the poorly fitted windows. We were so cold; even Ron was shivery. Sheena and I wrapped ourselves in quilts—this at the end of May.

Summer crashed in without warning. The surest sign of its arrival was the new odor of over-ripe humans in the Métro. Talk about forbidden fruit! However, the sunshine was irresistible. Like most Europeans, I couldn't bear the thought of the dryer heating up our tiny apartment any further. I dug out the clothes hanger we'd inherited from the previous occupant and hung my wash out to bake on our sunny balcony. I felt very French doing so in my high heels and red lipstick.

Sheena sat in the newly arrived, irresistible sunshine over her lunch hour, letting the rays soak into her T-shirted back. Sounds innocent, however it resulted in a severe allergic reaction to some medication she was taking. It was the week of the high school prom; it also became the week of Sheena's nightmare. She barely slept thirty minutes in forty-eight hours due to her pain. Her entire front and back were itching to the degree that it doubled her over in excruciating agony. Throughout the night she jumped into a cool shower every fifteen minutes in search of relief, occasionally moaning, "What if I can't go to prom?" I rubbed and rubbed her tortured back until I lost feeling in my anxious hands. After a night of no sleep, and an unchanged situation the next day, I called Ron at Genesis to come home and take us to the hospital.

Why didn't I drive her there myself? Aside from getting chronically lost in the diagonal streets radiating off the many circular roundabouts and fearing the aggressive, disorderly traffic oblivious to sporadic lane markers, I cannot wiggle our car out of its stingy little parking space. I use the word "space" loosely. So it was Ron to the rescue.

As our hero worked his way home from Genesis he ran into a "perturbation" (strike) on our Métro line. People were piling up on the platform for trains normally arriving every three minutes. After waiting thirty minutes for his perturbed train, Ron called to say, "I'm not sure if I can elbow my way through the body mash, but I'll do my best."

Perhaps Ron's negotiation of the heavy masses was the first miracle. Our champion made it home on the Métro in ninety minutes, but made up for it with his driving (he still dreams of driving on the German Autobahn). After rushing us to the closest hospital, ten minutes down our street, he dropped us off and began the hunt for parking.

As I hurried Sheena through the emergency entrance door, my heart fell; I thought we'd walked back into Russia. I couldn't tell if the cramped, chair-less room was a reception area or a storage closet. The only clue declaring I was in the right place was a little sign on a desk announcing, "Closed."

On our right we were confronted with a jaundiced woman, the color of over-ripe bananas, lying on a stretcher with tubes exiting from her every cavity. On our left was a paramedic wearing the tightest pants I had ever seen on a male body. I wondered how he was able to walk, let alone run to an emergency. Nurses looked through us as though we were invisible. It all seemed so incompetent, even scary. I really wanted to be able to function in the French world, but this...I didn't think I could do it. I looked at Sheena and whispered, "Want to go to the American Hospital? It'll take another thirty minutes."

Without hesitation she nodded. Away we flew, Sheena giving her dad directions for the best route between spasms of pain while I looked on and wondered how I had a daughter who knew her way around Paris so well.

The lady in the emergency reception area at the American Hospital was so kind I almost cried. Her English was beautiful. The rest was normal, by North American standards. Sheena was "shot from behind" and given prescriptions for two different antihistamines. By late evening, our exhausted daughter finally fell into thirteen hours of deep sleep. The next day there was only a mild itch. She missed school but still made it to the prom that beautiful May evening—we did have our priorities.

PROM

There was something Sheena didn't know while she was sick at home. Her prom date had returned from a foreign study trip to Croatia where he'd fallen in love with a fellow student. His new girlfriend of three days was pressuring him to drop Sheena and take her to prom instead. He was too much of a gentleman to comply, even though his new passion was without an escort.

During the highly anticipated Friday evening at the luxurious Marriott Champs Élysées, Sheena's date did his best to divide his attention between the two beauties seated at different tables. After Luke left his friends and Sheena for a third time to loiter loyally by his newly beloved's side, Sheena's friends teased, "Hey, Sheena, how awkward is this on a scale of one to ten?"

"Oh, about thirty," Sheena replied dryly.

"Hey, Sheena," another good friend added, "how about going to prom with me next year? I'll probably have a girlfriend, but I think we can work it out."

MOVING

Fred and Carrol, our senior pastor and his wife, were relocating to the U.S. after eight years in Paris. The whole moving experience is quite different here. The more flights of stairs there are to one's apartment, the higher the likelihood of the elevator being broken on moving day. As Fred and Carrol lived on the sixth floor, the chances of a dysfunctional lift were very strong. Sure enough, Carrol was trapped between floors in the claustrophobic, wrought iron cage the day before the move. Fortunately they had rented a conveyer-type lift mounted on a trailer in which a side-less platform moves up and down a long, extended arm, reaching up to the balcony. It's very fun to watch if it's not your furniture on it.

Loads began to descend to the rainy street as we waited for Ron to appear with the mystery rental truck. I say "mystery" because I was the one elected to make the arrangements. I was so proud of my accomplishment—it had been in French, on a fuzzy cell phone, without seeing hands or reading lips.

When it came to discussing the size of the truck, cubic meter words weren't triggering any synaptic connections in my brain, so I simply said, "Not the smallest truck, s'il vous plait, but the next one up." A flood of French followed of which I understood nothing. So I said, "Thank you very much." I was so pleased with myself. I exclaimed to Ron, "I got a truck!"

Ever practical, he asked me, "What size?"

"I don't know, but it's not their smallest."

Ron smiled at me. "Bravo." He understood.

Others, especially my French friends, were inordinately concerned. "You realize it could be a wee mini-truck, don't you?"

The morning of the move, there was nervous laughter as we waited and then sighs of relief as Ron turned the corner in the truck. As in fairytales, the size was just right.

Fête de la Musique

On June 21, the evening of Fête de la Musique (Festival of Music), bands play outdoors until the early hours of the morning all over Paris. It rained. After it rained, it poured. I couldn't believe it after all the days of hot, arid weather we'd just enjoyed. Neither could anyone else. There were very few umbrellas. We extended the outdoor awning of Genesis, our ministry center, as far as it would go, pulled in the sound equipment and hugged the wall as we played our music. The showers came and went throughout the evening; so did all kinds of people. I have vivid memories of one young man clutching his decanter of wine, dancing with great abandonment in front of us, and then losing his grip on the green bottle. The smell of fermented grapes filled the air; he looked heartbroken and stumbled away quickly.

He wasn't nearly as cute as our bass player, though, who danced with his eyes closed while he played. He's off to seminary in Chicago this August. I really don't like this goodbye thing we do so much of here.

This year we recognized the faces of our neighboring business owners. "Hey, will you be singing again this year?" they called throughout the day, looking pleased when we said yes. Our baker brought by a whole bag of pastries that disappeared before I even knew they had arrived. The owner of the restaurant, Tete d'Or, beamed at us from across the street while we sang.

After a great party evening, people hurried off to catch the last trains. By one A.M., Ron and I were finally ready to start loading our car. By two A.M., we were in the underground parking beneath our apartment. As we dragged our weary bodies out of the vehicle we remembered that the elevator was out of order. We would have to carry our keyboard and amplifier up seven flights of stairs. We groaned and stared at the open trunk for a number of moments before mustering the energy to pull out the gear.

At seven thirty A.M. we woke to the shrill sounds of a power grinder on metal. The elevator repairman was obviously going to be working outside our door for the day. It only made sense to get up and pack the 345 pounds of baggage we'd be dragging down the stairs at four A.M. the next day for our flight back to North America.

August: Back in the USA

VACATION

We spent a slow, lazy week of vacation at a friend's home on Devil's Lake near Lincoln City on the Oregon coast. It's not nearly as hot or unpleasant as the name may convey. Sheena and Ron buffed their biceps kayaking around the lake, exploring the inlets and ogling the impressive vacation homes undetectable from the road.

I didn't go. I don't like the water. My cousin drowned in a river when he was fourteen; I was there when my dad told my aunt the horrific news. As rivers are often connected to lakes, I don't like contact with either of them. Pools are better; they have well-defined edges and you can see the bottom if you clean them. All that to say—I avoid the water. It's enough that I get showered each morning!

So I stayed secure on dry land with my laptop and over a long, leisurely afternoon journaled my answer to the question that has surfaced repeatedly this summer: "How did you end up in Paris of all places?"[3]

American Impressions

While we were home from Paris in Oregon this summer, so many little things captured our wide-eyed attention—things like the bumper sticker "Who Would Jesus Bomb?" Salem's streets were wide and vacant, the sidewalks empty. Had the Rapture occurred and all residents of Oregon taken? Even Portland's downtown streets felt loosely filled and easily navigated. It seemed like such a quiet city with few diesel engines, high-pitched scooters, or blaring horns. Drivers were polite; no hands rudely gestured out of windows.

In restaurants, meals were completed from seating to payment in less than a brief hour; my fork hadn't completed its inaugural flight into my salad before the main dish arrived. If Ron had said grace any longer, we wouldn't have caught sight of the greens before they were whisked away and replaced with platters of pasta. Were we in a hurry? Waiters filled multiple boxes at the end of the meal, a meal designed to feed a small nation.

The grocery store was pristine; the shelves were neither stuffed nor scanty. No item was missing in action. The lines were zip-zip-quick and the malignant odor of cheese undetectable. What heaven.

Sheena begged, "Don't buy groceries without me!"

We went whether we needed to or not, just to look and sniff. We wandered the aisles like tourists on a high, a mega cart at our disposal, a car just outside the doors, and a spectacular aisle of infinite cereal choices. I jumped the first time a clerk asked if I needed help. That was unexpected; how did he know?

This was a land with different game rules. At the checkout, the cashier gave us a large, even, bleached-white smile.

"HI! HOW ARE WE DOING TODAY? DID YOU FIND EVERYTHING YOU'RE LOOKING FOR?"

We were unaccustomed to the chitchat, the volume. It felt a little invasive after the reserved silence of the French.

"SO WHAT ARE YOUR PLANS FOR THE WEEKEND?"

Wasn't this personal? I toyed with telling her I had a mastectomy scheduled for that afternoon, but questioned whether it would be in good taste.

"WHAT PRETTY PEPPERS. ARE YOU GOING TO USE ALL THREE COLORS IN ONE DISH?"

She wore a large nametag with bold letters declaring "Debbie." Once she'd handled my debit card, I became "Mrs. Fry-son." Names are personal in France and it's not polite to ask for this private information, let alone use it without asking. One waits until it is offered.

There are other differences: People don't smile at each other on the street and say, "Hi." However, it is basic good manners to say, "Hello" to the proprietor when you enter a store and "Goodbye" when you leave.

GAME RULES

Moving to France is a bit like switching from basketball to football. At times I think like an avid basketball player, let's call him Murphy, who has never played or watched a football game. After two weeks at football camp, an aggravated Murphy returns home to report, "Their stinkin' ball is deformed. It's pointy, it doesn't bounce right, and there isn't even a basket to stuff. Weirder still, those cheaters run with the ball, a clump of players take out the ball handler, and all the idiots pile on top of each other. The ignorant referee appears to reward them for this blatant misconduct. And the point system—it arbitrarily jumps by six, one, seven, who knows? And what's with the shoulder pads? They're so eighties."

We've caught Murphy venting in our Paris apartment from time to time. Often, I am Murphy, irate at how the game is being played in France. Now it's time to change from basketball to football once again.

After two months of reconnecting with great friends, being fed favorite foods, and gorging ourselves on all the conveniences and low prices of North America, a part of me doesn't want to go back to playing football in France. Tackling on a field doesn't seem so appealing compared to the posh, climate-controlled basketball courts of North America.

L'Automne—
Autumn 2006

September: Return to France

Flight Features

THE GIFT OF a summer break in our homeland passed all too quickly. Our threesome was hugging Justin too tightly, saying gut-wrenching goodbyes too long, and returning to Paris too soon. The ten-hour flight from Portland to Frankfurt seemed to extend into sixteen hours with the antics of an undone two-year-old spraying turmoil from the seat directly in front of us. The little guy displayed fantastic seat gymnastics previously untested in intercontinental flight. He made me miss Kenny.

Kenny was seated behind Sheena on the flight home to Portland in June. Unlike the flight, Kenny's discourse was non-stop; his twang penetrated. "The military is falling apart ever since they let women in—no offense, ma'am. We men need to scratch an' swear an' fight an'—no offense, ma'am—we can't do that with women around. They get all emotional. Causes problems—no offense ma'am. You see, ever since cavemen days, women are the breeders and men are the hunters—no offense, ma'am. I'm in the military, and killin' is what I do; everyday I just get out there and do my best."

I wanted to inform Kenny it wasn't possible to do his best every day, because if he was doing it every day, then by definition it was no longer his best, but his average. The flight attendant showed up to ask what he was drinking; a terse dispute developed: was it whiskey or Pepsi®? Another half-hour passed with Kenny enlightening our section of the plane; his beautiful French seatmate listened politely, hostage to his monologue. An older flight attendant finally stalked down the aisle in our direction; she operated a heavier, effective hand, particularly now as Kenny couldn't walk vertically. His personalized "Pepsi®" was seized and Kenny passed out for the rest of the flight.

Unlike Kenny on our June flight, there was little humor to find in the tormented toddler, who didn't pass out and had an amazing ability to scream with three tones simultaneously—shades of Janis Joplin. I looked at Sheena and couldn't help but contemplate our original flight to France two years earlier. Our own parenting skills were as ineffectual as the toddler's father. Sheena had melted silently, behind high walls, listening over and over to the melancholy CD a friend had compiled for her; she clutched the disc player Justin had lent her for the traumatic trip. Her despair was palpable. Sometimes there's nothing a parent can do. We stand by, silent handwringers, pleading with the heavens to…to what? Now, two years later, she relaxed with the iPod her big brother had purchased for her, eagerly anticipating the scent of fresh school supplies and an ecstatic reunion with Parisian friends.

We inhaled three and a half hours worth of smoke in Frankfurt's foggy airport, then continued on to Paris where the luggage carousel shut down after delivering half the baggage. It just quit. No explanations. Three of our nine bags slouched by our feet. We finally sat down and studied the big hand on our watches. The child with operatic potential finally slept in his stroller. This is France, where efficiency is not a predominant value. I remind myself it doesn't seem to be one of God's either. That still doesn't help my attitude.

Our Paris Home

While Ron unloaded 390 pounds of luggage onto the crowded sidewalk, I looked up at our sixth floor apartment and saw curtains blowing in open windows. Our neighbor had been in to make sure our flat was aired. A stunning bouquet of white roses waited for us, along with a meal, fresh fruit, and my favorite goat cheese in the fridge. A fresh baguette flaunted its crusty goodness on the breadboard. All the dead plants torched by the merciless summer heat had disappeared; the balcony was a mini greenbelt. Even the fridge was purged. It was a heart-warming, French-neighbor welcome.

In spite of twenty hours of travel, twenty-four hours without sleep, and a nine-hour time difference, Sheena rearranged furniture in her room and Ron washed windows. I, against all conventional wisdom, became one with my bed. I promised myself, "Tomorrow I'll plan the music for Sunday, tomorrow I'll make some calls to see if there are any musicians still attending our church, tomorrow I'll call my neighbor for coffee, and next weekend I'll have our French friends over for dinner. But right now, I just want to sleep. I wonder how Justin is doing…"

October: The Un-Martha

Not Martha Stewart

Fifteen years ago I came to a startling realization—I am not my mother. I gave myself immediate permission to quit trying to be a respectable cook. Therefore, it was rather foolish to invite our French friends for dinner the first week we were back in Paris, with the promise of new recipes I'd savored in North America. By Thursday I was overwhelmed trying to figure out which cut of pork might parallel tenderloin, whether prosciutto existed in France or where Boursin cheese might be found. I gave up on finding the correct cheese and concentrated on choosing a substitute Chèvre. There were only twenty-eight to choose from, so I closed my eyes, twirled my hand, and picked one.

I attempted Pavlova, a dessert requiring a meringue bottom. What was I thinking, making meringue for thoroughbred French connoisseurs, the inventors of baked egg-white creations? The whites wouldn't whip. I changed from the hand mixer to a newly inherited food processor. I took walks, watered the plants, did the supper dishes, and got ready for bed, leaving the processor humming in the background. Did they need three days to rise? I flung the flat mucus into the garbage. I tried a second batch, feeling proud I could at least separate the eggs. The feeling didn't last long. The egg whites lay prostrate, peak-less. OK, the base would be a little flatter than I'd hoped. Let's not be perfectionistic. I baked them, left them in the oven to dry overnight, and went to bed.

After two and a half hours of sleep, I laid awake in bed trying to convince myself if I stayed lying down, my body would eventually catch on to its normal nighttime work. But by three thirty A.M., I was up to stuff the pork tenderloin with goat cheese, wrap it in a coat of prosciutto, and brown it. For a nervous, non-cook type, pieces of me were somewhat relaxed. Dinner wasn't for another sixteen hours. There was plenty of time to have multiple disasters and still make course corrections. I made my grocery list with a Plan B for all the ingredients I might not be able to locate in Paris. I set the table while France slept.

I dragged through the day, hauling my loaded rollster behind me, resenting each store that didn't cough up the elusive cornstarch. Back home, I wrapped the chilled tenderloin in puff pastry and decorated it with pastry vines and leaves. It looked elegant; I wondered if it would be edible. Just when I thought I was finished with the two pages of detailed instructions from my American gourmet-chef friend, I caught sight of a third. What, a sauce too? And the recipe asked me to chop and sauté a gaggle of ingredients that were to be strained out later. Why not skip those things if you're going to throw them out anyway? I heaved a sigh and complied with the will of the recipe.

I attempted a nap later in the day, but I couldn't stop computing and re-computing how many ounces the 1.4 kilos of tenderloin might be. When my eyes grew tired of examining the ceiling, I got up and put the almonds in the oven to toast. Then I organized a search for another appliance that might have more success in whipping the cream than the egg whites; oops, almonds toast much quicker than I thought. By the time I smelled them, they had established a New Orleans connection—dessert was turning into "Blackened Cajun Surprise." I tried to whip the cream; the results were not impressive. One panic led to another. Perhaps my friend had emailed me the time required in her convection oven. I now realized I'd bought in kilograms what the recipe called for in ounces. Should I cook it longer? If the pig lounged a little longer in the oven, perhaps the pastry would burn. Why did I put myself into this critical culinary situation? I thought about calling my friend but had to finish making the individual Caprese salads. The cream still hadn't whipped, even after a spell in the freezer. What was I thinking? I may be forty-nine, but I wanted my mom.

Our guests arrived on the hour and conversation unfolded around the vegetable platter and banal ranch dip, something my French friends find exotic. After it had an extra ten anxious minutes in the oven, I removed the drop-dead gorgeous pork dressed in its sensuous golden coat, grateful these friends weren't Jewish. When I walked into the living room with the platter of artisan meat, our friends became hushed and reverent, repeatedly gasping, "Magnifique, fabulouse, fantastique." I felt like a rock star who suddenly realized she sang on key. Oh, wait, bad example. Rock stars don't care.

Our guests' reactions were so over-the-top that I decided we were approaching our relationship with the French all wrong. Send home the ambassadors and missionaries; Fed-Ex® in chefs—overnight them, in fact. They told me I was a true chef and I confessed it wasn't me; it was my friend Jocelyn of California. When her picture appeared in our summer photos, all of them nudged each other, whispering, "It's Joceleene, it's her. It's Joceleene!"

As our friends left in the wee morning hours, they chorused enthusiastically, "Bravo, felicitations, congratulations." It wasn't a perfect evening; they were not impressed with my blackened Cajun meringue and, far worse, Ron's careless confession during our wide-ranging conversation of shooting an innocent gopher during his boyhood. They were shocked. Appalled. He was prudent enough not to add there were countless conquests on his uncle's inundated prairie farm. From that point on my neighbor corrected Ron's every mispronunciation and grammatical error with narrowed eyes and strict tone. We've witnessed the French gently herd a cockroach out Genesis' door, so we shouldn't have been surprised.

I recounted the evening's gastronomic success and its mystifying effect to an American who has lived here for twelve years. I learned the amount of work one puts into a meal here communicates how much you love someone. Great. I hate cooking; it makes me nervous. I'm not good at rules, details, or science, and cooking is definitely in the chemistry realm. I live in France. That's just grand. Good thing God uses Balaam's ass, cracked pots, and the fools of this world to confound the wise. Perhaps He can use an un-Martha in food-obsessed Paris as well.

Preparing for Dinner Guests

THE MAN IN YELLOW BOXERS

It's Monday morning and I find myself dancing with a man wearing bright yellow boxers in my kitchen. Last night's church service was invigorating and traces of adrenalin linger in our blood. I realize Ron can't hit it out of the park every Sunday night, but last night was a solid run to second base. Ron described exchanging his summer T-shirt for a thermal parka to protect him from the sub-zero temperatures of his childhood's Canadian prairies, going on to say God's love can protect us from fear in the same way. I'm afraid he left the Africans behind, though; they were too traumatized by the inhuman weather conditions to make a positive connection between coats and God's love. Here's how the man in the yellow boxers hit it right out of the park:

Ron collected a pack of radios that filled our old sanctuary with a cacophony of sound. The receivers portrayed the voices surrounding us, radiating harassment. "Talk to the guy over there; you'll look smart....Make friends with her; you'll seem more attractive....That guy's cool; maybe you'll be cool if you hang around him....Don't admit your failure; people will think you're a loser." We can't hear God's still, small voice if we don't tune our receivers to Him. He sends us messages of security—we are precious and loved, even when we fail.

First thing Monday morning, a French-African woman emailed us about the debilitating voices she's heard in her head most of her life. Her powerful father divorced her mom when she was five. She lost her identity to a stepsister who had her same name and took over as Daddy's little girl. She now wants to hear God's reassuring voice rather than the demeaning voices of her past.

I just can't help dancing.

November: The Bakery

BRUGES AND BRUSSELS

We left the limestone grandeur of Paris for the variegated bricks of Belgium and spent the night in Bruges, an enchanting medieval town of canals and castles. Our awkward hotel appeared to be the site of a calamitous collision between Americana Country and Victorian decor. I had visions of Paul Bunyan chatting with Queen Victoria while his blue ox lapped tea from her china cup. Though a two star rating may buy you "clean," it doesn't often buy you ambiance.

Our umbrella was taxed by the storm stomping in off the North Atlantic, but we were determined to enjoy our day of breathing space. After hunching our shoulders against the horizontal rain all morning and touring the canals by boat while a fellow tourist's umbrella drained into my lap, the dry warmth of the car persuaded us to leave early for Brussels.

Ron expected to arrive well before Sheena's volleyball games began; our Saab® had other plans, taking us into the confusing ring of inner-city tunnels that dive deep underground, come up for air, then dive again. I felt close to Alice as, suddenly, we were burped out into Wonderland, where we slowly cruised by the grandeur of embassy row. It was definitely more impressive than our previous night's hotel. After purchasing multiple maps and reinventing the French language with a Chinese shopkeeper, Ron unearthed the hidden hamlet nestling the International School of Brussels. Sheena's face lit up when we blew in the door; it was the first time we were able to support her at an away game.

MEANWHILE, BACK IN PARIS

While we were cheering our daughter's team from Belgian bleachers, our retreat speaker and her husband arrived from Portland to our empty flat in Paris with only a difficult key and a helpful, non-English-speaking neighbor to rescue them. Our American friends tackled ambiguous French systems on their own to rent a car and make their way to Normandy. A week of exploring the historic beaches and tasting the villages' famous cheeses and cider before the retreat was generous compensation.

The people at Trinity were excited about the upcoming getaway. Ron had attached himself to the computer, designing and rearranging myriad details for a retreat whose parameters shifted more often than a rootless dune. Two weeks beforehand, nineteen people had signed up; by the Wednesday prior, fifty-one people were coming—almost half of our church. We needed to rent more hard-to-find vans; worse yet, we needed another driver, also hard to find. Ron asked me to break one of my dearest vows—the Never-Ever-Drive-In-France vow.

THE NORMANDY RETREAT

Friday afternoon found me desperately following Ron's bumper as closely as I dared. Getting lost in this grid-less city was reasonable grounds for an anxiety attack. A beat-up Citroen® rudely wedged itself between us in the glutted autoroute. The passenger kept turning around and looking backward; at each stall of the crawling traffic, the driver turned around too. They were under a spell cast by their backseat baby. Driving was secondary. Huge gaps blossomed between them and Ron's van. With each goo-goo face they made, another delivery truck merged into our lane, obliterating my guiding star from sight.

My rear wiper mysteriously whipped into action. I caught a fleeting glimpse of Ron on a distant exit ramp; it led to a circular no-man's land of lane-less cobblestones. Torrential traffic flooded into the grand circle from irrational angles and aggressively blocked my frantic plunge toward the van Ron so easily maneuvered through the confusion. A rebel orchestra of horns completed the sensory overload. Any sane, law-abiding, American driver would hyperventilate. I emerged with a dynamic prayer life.

Our speaker, Jane Wolf, and her husband not only arrived in Paris while we were in Belgium, they also arrived at the retreat center on the Normandy beach long before we did. After a cool greeting from the management, they were pointed to the parking lot where they ate dinner in their car, since our church group was not yet there.

Our underground meeting room felt more like a bunker than a pastoral retreat. The cold, linoleum floor was accessorized with orange plastic Kmart® chairs. The cement walls were windowless—no view of the English Channel; yet Jane held us in the palm of her hand. I'm not sure if anyone was even breathing, they were so thirsty for her words. Ron scheduled time to play on the Normandy beach, collect shells, and explore the charming French villages in the autumn sun. Our shepherd ended the retreat with communion. He built a cross out of the suitcases piled by the door, inviting us to come and lay down the exhausting baggage we carry through life. People knelt in the middle of the luggage cross, prayed, and dipped their torn bread into the cup as Ron or Jane whispered, "Jesus died so he could carry the weight of our sin."

We rushed away from Sunday dinner before the cheese course was served. It was a three-hour drive back to Paris, the service started at five P.M., and there was still equipment to set up and musicians to rehearse. I'd be driving into Paris's intestinal labyrinthine. Ron thoughtfully left me a parking space in front of the church where eleven pairs of male legs were visible through my passenger window. The spot was big enough for a Greyhound® bus, but our car had oddly elongated since Ron last parked it. I bumped into the car behind, then the car in front; but not to worry, that's what bumpers are for in Paris. I jerked backward, struggling with the clutch, got a bad angle, and pulled out again, forcing the traffic to stack up in the narrow street. Meanwhile the sets of legs were multiplying on the sidewalk. Before I had the chance to turn off the car, it choked and died. Jane told me to hold my head high—sometimes her advice is way off!

It was the first Sunday night I saw our people clap for a speaker. There were more people who wanted to connect with Jane and make appointments to see her. Later in the week she came to launch my first small group focusing on healing for damaged emotions. I wasn't holding my breath. I had assured our church everyone is damaged in one way or another, but who wants to admit they're damaged? I offered to take the smallest room at Genesis for our meeting.

Somehow eleven of us crowded into the stone, underground room on Wednesday night. When we got to the question, "What would you like the group to know about you?" I expected to hear answers like "I'm an engineer at Renault"® or "I'm not overly fond of frog legs." The first surprise came when a withdrawn, unsophisticated-looking woman started to speak. I thought perhaps she was a little slow, maybe a street person, someone who didn't really understand what was going on. Then she described her post-doctorate work in biochemistry at a famous research institute in Paris and her doctorate from a prestigious Ivy League school. I'm guessing she probably knew what was going on. A Dutch woman wanted us to know she'd been too busy to make time for God. A Croatian recounted a mean thing she did to her roommate and ended with, "I just wanted you to know I'm not one of those nice, godly people." A young Dane told us of his mission trip to Tunisia where he fell into an emotional abyss. An Asian admitted she was living with her boyfriend and didn't know if she could believe in God anymore. A Brazilian worried she wasn't going to heaven. A South Pacific islander confessed he had left his wife ten years ago, admitting he was no different than the dad who'd abandoned the young woman who cried earlier. The honesty was breathtaking.

Jane counseled many during the following week. She gave a seminar on boundaries; people soaked up her words of freedom. Ron asked her to teach on forgiveness Sunday night at church. It was powerful—she was swamped with people who wanted to share their hearts. Her words had a ring of authority because of the unmistakable authenticity birthing them. It wasn't just knowledge she'd learned from a book; her words came from a life lived in the trenches with God, a life marked by the pain of an alcoholic son she visited in jail. Jane is a beggar who found bread, now helping French beggars find the real bakery.

The following Wednesday at Genesis, Ron began a small group for men. Seven came. Even without the men, my group of women swelled to thirteen. People didn't want to leave at nine P.M.; they lingered by the door. Eventually we could leave, unlocking the door to our apartment at eleven P.M. with a sense of deep satisfaction.

Inevitably, all mountaintops are vacated; the next week it was all too easy to lose our way and our tempers in the gray fog of the valley. I guess we're living out being beggars and need more Bread.

L'Hiver—
Winter 2006–2007

December: Gospel Choir Perils

Slow Bus to Nantes

SUNDAY MORNING FOUND me on a bus, not on a high-speed train as expected, but a rented, crowded touring bus. It was a ponderous tub, packed with staff and teenagers who were generous with their French rap music. I was exhausted, tense, and unsure if I would make it back to Paris in time to lead worship at church that evening. Ron was counting on me. I landed in this situation by taking a walk two months before in the historic sixteenth arrondissement of Paris. The walk led me past two crumpled nuns who couldn't straighten their navy-clad backs or their heavily hosed, question mark legs. After passing a few more antique nuns I walked past a security guard onto the campus of a two-hundred-year-old Catholic foundation for orphans. I strode past the Basilica, where a vertebra of Mother Teresa was reverently ensconced, up to the offices of friends who work there. Antoine and Sophie started a gospel choir for the foundation's troubled and abandoned kids; now their choir travels around France, bringing reserved French audiences to their feet in a few fleeting minutes. Two months ago Antoine asked me if I would play for his choir.

Time revealed I would be taking over Antoine's spontaneous piano part while he played guitar.

A flush of panic sporadically flashed off and on me as I began to realize neither organized charts nor music would be provided. Listening to a CD would be my major resource; listening has never been my strong point. Desperation mounted within me as rehearsals with Antoine unfolded in a leisurely French-African style.

"Hey! How's it going? Let's take a coffee," he would say.

He talked by the coffee machine with at least three colleagues who happened by, serially. I practiced my French listening skills. We returned to his office. People dropped in. More French immersion for me. Students came by just to hang. We chatted. After an hour and a half, Antoine and I began to play, covering half the material. I dreamed of driven, task-oriented, Ron-style rehearsals. During our last practice, Antoine was so busy I never even touched the keys.

"Ça va, Lorelei? Everything OK?"

I was too proud to cry, "Heck, no!" My confidence lacked the American I-can-do-anything-I-want-to-do bluster. I'm predominantly Canadian. I felt like a numb teenager without the "right" jeans, headed for a new school, mid-year.

THE TRIP

Arriving at the train station Friday night, I couldn't remember most of the kids' names from my brief exposure during their music camp. No, no, wait a minute; I remembered the tall, cocky youth who has watched way too many rap artists.

"Hey, Sida," I greeted him enthusiastically.

He stared at me coldly, without response, while Antoine belted out belly laughs beside him. I had called him AIDS in French. Antoine assured me this wasn't my worst mistake; the day before I had asked in his crowded office if I should use "strings" on some songs—the English slang for a synthesizer violin sound.

"Streeng," he now explained, "is the word the French adapted for sexy underwear—uh, a thong."

His hearty laughter welled up all over and finally he just threw his head back and let it rip.

Between breaths he asked if I wanted to meet Smallpox and Bubonic.

This whole French immersion thing wasn't all it was hyped up to be.

The Saturday of the concert, I focused intensely, trying to pick up every detail not already scribbled on my pages of lyrics. I had five sheets with big, red STRINGS boldly written across the top. My dormant middle-schooler woke up to play guerilla warfare in my head. When would the real musicians find out I was a fake? I didn't think to bring a music stand, so I kept my stack of pages with lyrics, notations, arrows, and scattered chords on the end of my keyboard. They sat there from nine A.M. until eight thirty-five P.M., halfway through the first song of the concert. At eight thirty-five, my charts took flight, fluttering to the floor. The stage lights then went black just I was to start the next song, alone. This was not the look I was going for.

Toward the end of the concert, Antoine unexpectedly strapped on his guitar. I asked, "Am I playing piano on this song?"

He nodded.

Though I hadn't played the song before, I jumped into the fray with the extraordinary band Antoine had hired from Paris. At the hyper ending, the pros were vamping on a couple of chords indistinguishable over the drums, as the teen I had renamed "AIDS" began introducing these formidable music giants one by one. The percussionist unleashed a baby-I'm-begging-you-to-dance solo and I grinned; then the drummer beat out an intoxicating rhythm and I smiled again. The sax, trumpet, and trombone followed suit with equally impressive improvisations as I quit beaming. The solo was working its way down the band toward me.

"Are you kidding? You're going to make me play a solo I didn't know about, in front of all these people?" I cried out. "Anything, a trip to the dentist, a mammogram, just not this."

THE GERMAN EXAM

Ron had driven us to beautifully clean, flawlessly organized Germany; it would be much easier to live in this orderly country. Even the gas station bathrooms are a work of bleached beauty. We went to watch Sheena's final volleyball tournament—a somewhat painful experience this year, though not as painful as driving on the autobahn with Ron. How fast is 160 kilometers per hour anyway? Not fast enough—Mercedes® and BMWs® effortlessly zipped by us.

From the pristine gym's bleachers we traveled to an Italian restaurant where Ron completely charmed the owners with his beautiful German accent. He found their Italian-accented German more difficult to decode than the menus. We had no sooner deciphered the menu with the parents of one of Sheena's teammates when they said, "We want to know about your church and what makes it distinct. We both grew up die-hard Catholics, so maybe we should start with the difference between Catholics and Protestants."

I loved Ron's artful explanations, his winsome style of husking truth down to an essential core without creating myths out of our particular brand of corn. Aggie described how she had been deeply wounded by a brother who is a staunch, far rightwing, evangelical fundamentalist. Ron wove his way through the first minefields; then they got direct.

"Are you evangelicals?" one asked.

We nodded, reticent, knowing the accompanying reputation.

"You are?" Shock registered on their faces. Disappointment too. There was silence. "So you're going around proselytizing, telling people they're going to hell?"

I responded. "I tell my young women, 'If Jesus is truly in you, it shows, and people will ask questions.' We let people ask."

The subject jumped again with Aggie declaring, "If I got pregnant now, I'd want to have an abortion. Like you, I'm too old and, at this point, we couldn't afford it. Wouldn't you have one too?"

I hesitated. I thought about telling her I couldn't talk with my mouth full. Eventually, I quietly admitted, "I don't think I could do it. However, if I had a baby and you had an abortion, and for one second I thought I was better than you, God would be just as disappointed with me as He would be with you. My failure would not be less than yours in His eyes."

It was a conversation testing our expression of every belief we held dear, and some not so dear. They had been deeply hurt by evangelicals who don't understand who they themselves would be without Jesus.

At the end of the evening Aggie's husband said, "Well the five P.M. church time is really bad for us. We can't come this Sunday, or the next, but we'll come the Sunday after that and bring the girls. See you then."

SUNDAY EVENINGS

There is a lovely young woman from Sweden who is increasingly a part of our little congregation. She's a chemical engineer, blessed with brains and beauty. Ron noticed a different guy following her to church every Sunday evening. He teased, "You're so beautiful, they'll follow you anywhere."

Helga replied with her thick Swedish accent, "I know. I use it for God."

This last Sunday, Ron met a man who came to Paris to escape for one brief week all the painful circumstances associated with his wife's recent death. She had struggled with cancer for five tortured years and finally lost, leaving him with two young children. As he stepped outside his hotel he thought he heard worship music streaming down onto the street. He followed the sound and found us. He also found a measure of comfort in his spiritual family who mysteriously extends its arms around the world. It was Ron's arms holding him that night.

December: A European Christmas

LONDON IN OUR STOCKING

A couple attending our little church on Rue Madame generously offered us the use of their London flat during the Christmas break. I eagerly scoured the Internet, looking for cheap train fares, but holiday discounts had moved from endangered to extinct. A tantalizing offer to buy us tickets came from a group in our Oregon church. I swung between embarrassment and delight, unsure of a right response, so I gave them a chance to change their minds and waited to see what color the light would be. My favorite—deep green. We rushed to the Eurostar® office, hoping to find a better price in person.

"Would you like cancellation insurance with that?" the ticket agent asked.

"No, whatever for?"

We didn't have the extra cash anyway.

CHRISTMAS EVE

Before the London trip, there was still our Sunday Christmas Eve service to lead. We arrived early, as did our nervous soundman. It was his first time to fly solo. We were eager to quickly set up all our equipment and Christmas finery and rehearse beforehand. However, the French African church that rents the building before we do was still going strong. Preaching rose and fell behind closed doors; we leaned against the walls and waited. Singing began; we nervously consulted our watches and paced. Preaching rose again; Ron stuck his head in the door to catch the minister's eye. They all looked so fine—elegance in hats and heels—but showed little sign of concluding.

The early evening was a blur without space to breathe. I do remember a sense of intimacy and the radiance of many candles. Madame D., who arrived in iridescent velvet to read her part, translated Walter Wangerin's version of the Christmas story into lyrical French. Projected children's drawings and international art illustrated the story. Carols cradled by harp, guitar, and synthesized cello echoed the events. We lingered long, savoring our mélange of displaced expatriates. A Canadian couple threw out an open invitation for Christmas dinner. Twenty-one people and a con man showed up.

By eight thirty that same evening, we sat around our neighbor's festive table, being treated to a French feast. Madame R. was in first-class form. Elegant plates of foie gras and pink caviar were set before each guest. The goose liver pâté wasn't poisonous, but how to eat the pungent caviar? Sheena covertly conveyed SOS messages to me with huge, pleading eyes; I demonstrated unobtrusively behind the fresh bouquet how to combine one mammoth olive with one minuscule fish egg. We ate a plethora of olives. Succulent cold salmon marinated with ginger, cilantro, and lime, served with tiny cucumber and apple slices, followed. A beautifully roasted and stuffed chapon (a neutered rooster, more like a small steer with two legs, a beak, and an attitude) created a spectacle, prompting "oohs" and "aahs" as it made its way to the head of the table. It had an entourage of creamed pumpkin, baked chestnuts, and puréed celery root. We were too full to do justice to the cheese and dried fruit course or the chocolate roll finishing this fine feast. Porcelain plates of rich cookies were offered, but we were overfed, overstuffed, and overdue.

It was well past midnight when Sheena gave the sixteen kitties one last caress and kissed our French family goodbye. Our friends' heads turned to watch her close the door. With the sound of the click, four heads swiveled back to us. Joy was wiped away, a serious note struck.

"There's a high risk of terrorism on the Eurostar®," one said.

Surely they were joking. I made light of it but no smiles appeared.

"You should cancel your trip," another stated firmly.

We hadn't bought cancellation insurance.

THE DRAGON AND THE SHOE

On Christmas day I resisted images of a terrorist explosion under the cold Atlantic. Ron promised to find what news he could, but this was the prairie boy who drove through blizzards when prudent West Coast people stayed home.

Thoughts of terrorism vanished when Sheena realized the black ballerina flats she received for Christmas were not a matched set—one shoe was dark navy blue. Ron had already returned to the store three days earlier after I showed him the gift—one shoe was size 38, the other a 36. The day after Christmas, pressure returned with a rush; I needed to prepare for the Chœur Gospel concert.

"Please, Mom," Sheena begged, "exchange my shoe before you go. I can't do it; I know it'll be complicated. You know how they are. Please, please!"

I didn't have time for this; I needed to review my music. Why couldn't she do this herself? Sheena and I arrived at the shoe store and found a woman who had an air of authority. "Bonjour, Madame," I said. "I'd like to exchange this shoe for a black one so I have a matching pair. They aren't the same color."

The woman looked at the shoes. "They are the same color."

"Excuse me? No, they are not, Madame." I lifted the blue shoe from the box. "This one is blue."

"No, it is not."

"Yes, it is. It says so on the sticker. See? Blue, right there."

"They're the same."

"Why don't you come with me to the window? Perhaps you'll see it in the natural light." I walked to the window, held the shoes up to the light, looking over my shoulder to see if she saw it now. She wasn't there; she remained stolid behind her cash register in the back of the store.

I walked back feeling a little foolish but determined not to be intimidated. "Madame, I want a black, left, size 38 shoe."

"I don't have one."

"Well, then, I want my money back."

"I don't have that much cash."

"Why not? This is a regular business day and these are not expensive shoes. Are you not open for business?"

"I don't have enough cash."

"Then I want you to credit my Carte Bleu. That's how I bought them."

"We don't do that. It's not our system."

"Well, what are you going to do?"

"You can come back another day."

I knew the trick. "That's not going to work for me."

A young sales girl was passing by and the woman sarcastically sneered, "Apparently these shoes aren't the same color."

The young woman exclaimed, "Bah, oui, this one is dark blue."

The two women disappeared; they passed occasionally, no explanations given. We waited, our hope expiring as time ticked by. I felt increasing pressure to leave for the concert venue; this was taking too much time. At long last the identical twin was discovered, sleeping in the display window.

"It wasn't my fault, it was hers," the older woman accused sourly.

"That's not the point," I asserted intensely, my temperature high. "She was polite and helpful. You are a dragon; it's not necessary to be so unkind, so impolite." I thrust my righteous dagger in with an ungodly delight. I could feel the heat in my face. I may have expressed a few more times she was a dragon; I don't really want to remember.

Once outside, Sheena congratulated me. "You did really well, Mom, and all in French. I did think, though, you could have stopped once you got the shoe. I guess you won't be inviting her to church, eh?"

"Probably not."

I would like to take the helpful salesclerk a box of chocolates, but only if the dragon lady is around. Sheena says I need to let it go.

GOSPEL CONCERT NEAR MOULIN ROUGE

Ron and I exited the Métro at Montmartre, the neighborhood of Sacre Coeur, a famous cathedral, and Moulin Rouge, another renowned "cathedral"—for burlesque. The theatre must have been quite magnificent in its prime. Like an old woman without cosmetic surgery or Botox, her once breathtaking beauty had deteriorated. Her carpet was wrinkled and blotchy, her seats were sagging, and she needed major floor replacement surgery. The walls and ceiling retained their original frieze relief, tiers of ornate balconies rose up sharply, and the chandeliers were fit for a king. The stage was undersized, so the drummer and horn section played from distant, overhead box seats. They were difficult to hear; the energy from playing in close proximity was lost.

Many of the kids brought guests; the audience was rowdy, invigorating. Some teenage singers took unexpected liberties during the concert. A soloist with a swagger and a mic instructed the drummer to play a disco beat. It wasn't the next song, neither was it the way the arrangement started. With the drummer so far removed, our music machine sputtered uncertainly to life, caught unawares. The concert gathered energy regardless, peaking with the appearance of Passi, a well-known French hip-hop artist. We played rap in a throbbing auditorium with everyone singing along to a song they knew from the radio. My neighbors and Madame D. were impressed, my daughter less so.

Unexpectedly, the offstage soundman yelled at the director to shut it down. "Wrap it up. Now."

Was my French backfiring? The kids were confused too. They didn't understand why Antoine was telling them to take their bows. The concert beating with life and energy ended suddenly on an awkward note. It was too late to ponder the power of complaining neighbors who live in a theatre district. Plus, we were leaving early for England the next morning and hadn't packed yet.

What does one wear for an explosion in London? Gore-Tex® and flats seemed sensible.

January: Fine Friends

My Dear Friend, Madame D.

I sat across from Madame D. in a smoky French café, as we often do on Wednesdays, while steaming bowls of courgette and Chèvre soup evaporated spoon by spoon. We reminisced, recalling our first lunch together a year earlier at La Carette, across from the Tour Eiffel.

"I came full of cynicism, thinking you saw me as a lost lamb you needed to convert," she said.

"Yet within seconds of unfolding my serviette, you were lobbing loaded God questions," I responded.

"I did?" Madame D.'s eyebrows rose in unison, twin wipers frozen at the top of her windshield. "Bah, oui! That's right." Her dark brows refolded to the off position. "The Way of the Cross at Genesis on Good Friday was a turning point. The picture of Jesus holding the lamb in His arms capsized me; it was the moment I realized how much pain He suffered for me, for me. Then I got the job with the American CEO who goes to your church; my husband thought you had somehow orchestrated that event. You hadn't. At the moment Mr. Eve wrote to offer me a job, he was in Los Angeles and I was entrenched at your table with a migraine, despairing over my non-job situation. My husband suspected it was a miracle, but he kept his cynical silence. He's watching. What else can a brilliant economics professor do? He can't argue with how much I've changed; it delights him. Lightness has come into our lives; we laugh."

The waiter was a charming fellow who imprudently tried to remove my bowl before the last dregs were indelicately sopped up with crusty baguette. When he returned armed with a savory peach crumble, peace was renewed. With a three-course lunch tucked under our belts, Madame D. and I strolled arm in arm through the frail sunshine toward her office.

"You honored my hesitation; now I need to be patient with those I love," she said, drawing on her cigarette and blowing out the smoke. "I can wait."

A University Student

My day continued by hopping onto thoroughly modern Line 14, buried far below all the other Métro and train lines. I ignored the three elongated banks of escalators to the surface, hoping to fight a few French pounds, and still arrived early, though breathless, for my rendezvous with Yvette, a French university student. On Wednesday afternoons we're contemplating the gospel of Luke.

"Deed you noteece zee deefference between Zechariah and Mary's response to zee angel?" Yvette asked in her charming

Franco-English. "I wonder eef Zechariah doubted the angel because he had been een zee church for so long? He was disappointed weez God for many years. Mary was just a girl, yet even zoe she was afraid, she believed and submeeted."

I thought about how disappointments develop calluses on my heart; I've been in the church for decades.

"Lorelei, can I ask you a question zat has nozeeng to do weez Luke?"

"Of course, Yvette."

"What does One Teemozy 2:11–15 mean? Someone gave me a book to read zat's based on zat screepture."

Oh, brother. Why do some Christians tie weights around the necks of babies? I felt a fire start to smolder. "Well, Yvette, you can take many verses out of the Bible, stand them all alone and create a false theology. I could take a verse from the Psalms referring to 'dashing babies against the rocks' and create a theology of infanticide. It's always dangerous to lift just one portion of the Bible without seeing how it works together with the whole."

Quietly I fumed over who thought it was so important to burden a baby with this weight. It wasn't until the next morning that I realized how puffed up I had become—as though I had never strung weights zealously around necks. Images of bloated puffer-fish floated through my mind; it wasn't an attractive quality I could afford to feed.

AN ANAL FRIEND IS A BEAUTIFUL THING

We were beginning to feel a little desperate—not suicidal, just desperate. As pastor, Ron was watching the sheep, leading them to green pastures, finding water, trimming hooves, shearing wool, and doing all the organizational secretarial tasks as well. Saturdays often found him cultivating patience while guarding his place in line at Office Depot's® photocopier. Then a gift unfolded: gentle Jay Lee asked me what Ron needed. Her enthusiasm mounted as I told her our dream: someone to do the bulletin, create promotional materials, facilitate creative elements for the service, organize the batteries of volunteers we were beginning to assemble, create systems and databases, contact our newcomers...

She looked at me with shining brown eyes and said, "I love this kind of stuff, but you should probably know—I'm kind of anal."

"We love anal," I cried as I wrapped my arms around this slip of a woman (if Jay Lee and I were trains, I would be standard and she would be miniature scale; ten of her equal one of me). Jay Lee was a theatre producer in a former life and Ying, her husband, was one of Singapore's top commercial photographers. Ying's round, cherubic face is topped by a small island of white hair in a heavy, black sea. He's the guy who knows everyone by name, engaging whoever is closest with laughter and chatter.

"I'm not very Asian," he confided. "I talk too much."

They sold everything the year before, sensing God calling them to Paris. They acquired elusive work permits and then prayed for rent-paying opportunities in photography and film to open in Paris.

Jay Lee began to volunteer on Thursdays and Fridays. Ron was so excited he could hardly sleep the first week. Ideas multiplied like mice in her active mind; polite emails packed with proposals began to flow into our in-boxes. Labels appeared on the confusing light switches at Genesis; the workstation took on a new, streamlined appearance; all our Christmas events appeared in an artistic brochure. When I was sure Jay Lee's design work on the Christmas promo materials was finished, I wrote to say we wanted to go with more of an Elvis in Hawaii concept for Christmas that year. Palm trees, beaches, and sand were to be a new approach to the Return of the King theme. She believed it. This was going to be way too much fun.

At the end of two happy weeks, on a rainy Sunday morning just before Christmas, our phone rang. It was Ying. He simply stated, "Jay Lee's mother is in a coma due to bleeding on the brain. The doctors give her a fifty percent chance of living—and if she does, she will probably have some degree of brain damage." They booked the next flight to Singapore; Jay Lee was in a daze, packing through her tears.

Eight years ago, young Jay Lee had fought her own perilous battle with leukemia, a war that claimed three years of her life and her career in theatre. "How do I trust?" she cried. I told her of my bad times when I was unable to trust and all I could do was cry, "Oh, God, help." When I couldn't hang on, I told my friends and they trusted for me.

During our evening service we ached over the absence of Jay Lee and Ying and the pain engulfing them. We wondered if they would return to Paris, since business opportunities had not yet opened up as they had hoped.

It was a December night that felt doubly dark.

At church, Ron spoke about the second name given to Jesus in Isaiah 9: Mighty God. Together, we called on our Mighty God to heal Jay Lee's mom.

When Ron asked what the Mighty God had done in our lives personally, a brand new believer said, "He brought light into my darkness." A stoic, dignified gentleman stood and said, "He brought order into chaos."

May it be again. Come, Lord Jesus, come.

February: English in England, Italian in France

Mythical London

Sleep is a marvelous escape, so cost efficient, though less cooperative than chocolate. I slept deeply on the train all the way through the dark Chunnel and woke up just in time to see us shoot up from the ground's dark womb onto the vivid green earth of England. I felt sharply grateful for the profound gift of life and the absence of violence.

London was superb, or as the French say, "soupAIR!" People were friendly; they smiled and said, "Sorry!" when they made the inevitable body contact of urban mash and crash. Nothing in particular happened in London; we exchanged carbon dioxide for oxygen at a leisurely rate and euros for pounds at an alarming one. Except for the exorbitantly high prices (calculated compulsively by multiplying pounds by 2.16), it felt great.

The English grow grass in their city, and you're allowed to walk on it. The sidewalks aren't an obstacle course of dog deposit hurdles, making the walk around the parliament buildings a sweet, though less stimulating pleasure. After careful observation, we deduced the fall of London Bridge was a myth. We took out a second mortgage on our house to see *The Lion King* in London's bustling theater district. I sat by myself, exiled, watching six beautifully behaved children of progressive sizes with their parents. I couldn't decide if they'd simply handed their house keys over to the bank or if they owned one. Ron and Sheena sat together on the other side of the theater; last-minute ticket purchases had saved the family mutes from my incessant commentary.

The best part of England was the English. London gave us a reprieve from thinking in French and responding to a culture with game rules quite unlike our own. After four days, a piece of me didn't want to return to Paris; I wanted to go home, to be safe, and to talk at warp speed in my natural tongue.

After four lovely days, though, we returned to Paris for church on New Year's Eve. It was to be a simple service; most of our musicians were still in other parts of the planet. I played the black grand as Ron and I sang together. The candles flickered and glowed while Ron spoke about the Prince of Peace. It almost felt like family—and I remembered why I love Paris. It's the people in our church. They are enough.

Italian Food Report

What do you eat for New Year's Eve when an Italian man is cooking? I had a Pavlovian moment, salivary glands fully charged, anticipating authentic, fresh, Tuscan cuisine. Ron and I were hungry after taking the train from London to Paris, gathering ourselves for church, and leading the evening service. At eight thirty P.M., we dashed home to put on formal clothes and then back again to the shadow of Notre Dame. Ron circled and re-circled, searching for a wedge-able parking space and flirting with creative though costly options, while I played my veto card beside him. He finally opted for a crosswalk landing, snuggling the little Saab® close enough to kiss the bumper of the neighboring car.

Our Danish friend had dressed her table in heavy linens and garlands of pearls and crystals; the room blushed with candlelight. There were ladies in elbow-length gloves and bare shoulders; chiffon, velvet, and silk rustled around the room. We sat beside a Dutchman in a tuxedo and his Brazilian bride in an emerald evening gown. Ron wore his handsome marrying/burying suit; he looked quite tasty. I had panicked—the required floor-length gown wasn't in my budget.

"You look stunning," Helga whispered to me.

"Thanks. They're my pajama bottoms," I whispered back. I needn't have worried; the carefree Italians were a shocking contrast in their faded jeans and cotton shirts.

At about ten P.M., the meal began with Leonardo slopping what appeared to be Cream of Wheat® on each plate. It congealed as childhood images of cold porridge teased my gag reflex.

"Bon appétit!" they blessed each other as excited forks and knives dissected the yellow Play-Doh®.

"Wait!" Helga cried out. "We have to say grace." Several forks vacillated from mouth to plate to mouth, unsure what taboo was being pronounced.

"Grace?" There was genuine confusion.

"Ron, would you say grace for us please?" Fourteen forks were lowered and an unnatural silence hovered. Ron was brief.

The first round of polenta was with mushrooms. Leonardo circled the room a second time; more polenta in a pot, but with ripe Roquefort this time. This polenta made excellent sculpting material. The third round was polenta with Chèvre. I experimented with carving techniques on the telltale pile marring my plate.

What do you talk about with strangers from countries you haven't visited while molding entire continents from polenta? Why, grammar, of course. By eleven P.M. we learned how Dutch has three genders but the articles never change. Fascinating. I also learned the heavy polenta was only the entrée—as in "entrance" or appetizer. The main course was coming. Leonardo made an entrance, flourishing a platter of lentils crowned by an enormous, jiggling sausage and what appeared to be a raw pig fetus.

"I don't eat meat," I whispered to my hostess, "but I love lentils."

Leonardo had traveled to Italy to buy pigs' feet—the prized delicacy in the shivering, pink mass. The meal was saved by the third course of rocket greens, heavy with fragrant cherry tomatoes, fresh Parmesan shavings, and rich balsamic vinegar. By one A.M., a colossal, exotic fruit salad laced with puréed figs and nuts was paraded around the room. This wasn't the dessert, only the fourth or fifth course. An hour later, the smell of fresh chocolate fondant wafted from the kitchen oven. Unfortunately, the polenta had continued to swell uncomfortably in my stomach and, despite the forgiving elastic at the waist of my pseudo-silk pajama bottoms, only one tiny taste of Ron's magical dessert was possible. It was like none other. We were completely reassured of Italy's premier place at the peak of culinary art.

It was time to search for an exit, but not without the kissing ritual. Every cheek present in the room, even cheeks belonging to people we hadn't met, was sealed. We anticipated a quick trip home in the pre-dawn hours, but within minutes we were stalled in the impossible traffic exiting from the Eiffel Tower's massive party site. People stumbled across the street shouting, toasting, heedless of traffic lights or their precarious position. Once home, our bed was the most delicious thing I'd seen all evening.

Helga called the next day to give her friends' assessment of us. "They can't believe you guys are priests. Musicians, yes, but not priests. I told them it's because you are Protestant priests."

I still have a clear picture of the first time I saw Helga: she entered Genesis for my small group with her eyes guarded, arms crossed, her chin lifted defiantly. Life was painful; she was disillusioned. Over the past year she's found Jesus to be surprising; she's found hope again. Now her job may move her to Italy.

How do we survive this constant loss?

Le Printemps—
Spring 2007

March: Running the Numbers

WHY ALL THE NUMBERS?

A MONTH AGO I looked out over our tiny congregation and despaired. Were we shrinking, or was it one of France's eighty-five holiday weekends? The numbers weren't impressive. I hit my panic button with force—what if Ron and I caused this church to die? I chased a catastrophic trail of panic to a shameful end under a bridge, all while placidly perusing the faces focused on Ron.

We drove home through Paris's narrow streets, two lanes abruptly dissolving into one—a now-familiar pattern. As Ron maneuvered our way home, I generously shared my fears. A dense depression filled our black Saab's® confined cabin.

The next morning, the gloomy cloud lingered; I couldn't escape defining success in terms of numbers. With growing honesty, I admitted to reveling in belonging to a cutting-edge church in my previous life with the exhilaration of having more and more people attend. It fed an arrogant piece inside me.

Over the next few days I asked myself what was behind my attachment to numbers. Besides the trump card answer, "I just want more people to know Jesus," what other cards lay concealed at the bottom of my deck? A love of success and (gulp) recognition shuffled unwillingly to the top as I sat uncomfortably still. The love of "more, more, more" showed its ugly face. A mocking chorus of "may my kingdom come" played in my head.

I normally move straight to the whipping stage when my garbage surfaces. It's followed by a wallow in martyrdom, but my weary cycle was interrupted. I sensed my Great Father squeezing my shoulder, drawing my attention elsewhere, to a quiet undergrowth numbers fail to capture.

THE UNDERGROWTH

Cecile came to church throughout the summer. She had no personal interest in church or God; she came only to support her friend Debbie, who was desperately looking for help with her distressed marriage. Auntie, who truly fights pirates for a living, has an in-born radar that leads her to people whose ships are flirting with the rocks. It was she who prayed with Debbie regularly after church, gave wisdom, and graciously weathered an angry onslaught from Debbie's suspicious husband. When Debbie no longer could endure her marriage's condition, she fled France. Cecile was so impressed with tiny Auntie's response to the towering husband's tirade that she continued the Sunday pilgrimages, all on her own.

One cool, fall night, after Ron had spoken on God's unconditional love, Cecile asked Auntie if Jesus could possibly forgive all her sins. This young French woman then embraced Jesus, letting Him take her into His arms. The two women continued to meet after church to study, to discuss difficult issues and to pray for Debbie.

On Christmas Eve, Debbie reappeared at our service with her smiling husband in tow. She comes sporadically, and her husband looked astonished to find himself following his wife to church.

There are others. A Danish chemical engineer turned back toward Jesus this last year, her demeanor changing from cynicism to peace. An energy engineer is venturing out of his lonely hermit "cave" and loving church for the first time in his life. His marriage has dramatically changed.

Ron and I didn't realize a Colombian exotic fruit importer and his French girlfriend quietly had turned to follow Jesus this past year—just from coming to church and soaking it all in. Rather than an apple for the teacher, he brings pitaya for the pastor he has asked to baptize him.

There are the never-through-the-church-door friends who come to the English conversation classes over noon hours at Genesis. The room is relaxed, the chatter is animated, and when they play "Scrabbluh," the competition is intense but lighthearted (Scrabble® is a team sport in this country!). People ask cautious questions about other events they see posted at Genesis and some tentatively, nervously, suggest perhaps they'll come. They invite Trinity folk to their homes for dinner and ask intermittent questions about faith.

Todd faithfully organizes Open Mic (a make-your-own-music event) at Genesis; non-followers mix with followers and find each other surprisingly refreshing. This month an Egyptian doctor brought a retinue of medical colleagues (a good night for an accident) and a crowd from our drummer's jazz conservatory attended. The majority of those who came wouldn't dream of attending church.

Of course there's my dear friend Madame D.; I mustn't discount her monumental changes. Café Connections, our welcome brunch on the last Saturday of each month, carries on until three or four in the afternoon. People hang around and enjoy making connections. Of course, the exquisite French pastries, fresh baguettes, and rich espresso may have something to do with the popularity of this event.

A French girl meandered in off the street. As she and Ron talked, he learned she was on her way to take an English exam—the last hurdle before she was qualified to go to university in Portland, Oregon, our home area. She told Ron she'd never met any Protestants before but she'd read about them in books.

To top the "quiet undergrowth" list with a dollop of heavy Chantilly cream, I recall the tender miracle of Jay Lee returning to Paris just this week to tame our administrative beast. She felt set free to leave her mother who suffered three bleeds on the brain, lost six weeks of life in a coma, and of whom the doctors finally said there was nothing to be done. Now Jay Lee's mom is at home, lucid, walking and talking, though with difficulty.

BACK TO THE NUMBERS

In spite of all these developments, when daily life requires numbers—two tickets for the Métro, three mouths to feed, four days until rehearsal, fourteen days to payday, 2,400 dollars for rent—how do we embrace God's reverse economy, an economy where numbers are irrelevant and trust is the currency?

After I wrote about my numbers issue to some friends, we received a message on our answering machine: "I have someone I love dearly who has become very fat. Not all growth is good. Lorelei, let go of the numbers thing." There it was, word for word the same phrase I had written in my journal: "let go of the numbers thing." I heard it a third time when our prayer group called from Salem: "let go of the numbers thing." While the phone was pressed against my ear the story of David's census taking of Israel popped unannounced into my head.

The census story always puzzled me. I thought God sounded uptight, if not downright difficult, in this case. How much harm could be done by counting the people in a nation? It's normal, it's practical, and ever so basic. It's the first thing we teach our babies to do. "Here, honey, take a census of these Cheerios®—one, two, three…"

A provoking clarity arrived while I was on the phone: God doesn't want me, David, or anyone else to find security in numbers. He doesn't want pride or despair to breed due to numbers. God wants us to trust, to allow Him to grow His upside-down kingdom where contentment, downward mobility, and other non-competitive values reign. I might as well tattoo a big "L" on my forehead; this is exactly the kind of argument losers endorse.

Last Sunday, Antoine was leading worship and I had an evening without formal church involvements. I looked around and spotted Sarah sitting near the front. Sheena was sick at home so I didn't need to sit with her in our usual place on the side. Instead, I darted in beside my redheaded friend, second row from the front. It was a moving service; the sense of God's presence was powerful. Somewhere else, on another level, I felt this urge to look around. How many people were there? Shoot. I was sitting in the front and couldn't look without being obvious. I could look up and see my husband's face communicating earnestly, or I could look even farther up and sense Jesus laughing at me and saying, "This is a good spot for you! Let go of the numbers thing and trust Me."

April: Birch, Not Poplar

OPPOSITES REPEL

Ron and I are markedly different. He has his unique hand of cards and I have mine. He has a full set of shovels; I have none. I have a nice selection of clovers, he has very few.

Our personalities make it so he could say to me, "Oh, you're missing the Ace of Order card, Lorelei. Don't worry, I have it." And I could respond, "I see you need a Joker, Ron. I have three…what? They're not necessary?"

Unfortunately, the qualities that attract also repel. When Ron reads, he expects complete silence. I find it so friendly to share the best parts of what I'm reading with my best friend. I break his sacred silence to beg him to listen just one more time.

I figure out what I'm thinking by talking out loud and Ron doesn't know what he's thinking because I won't quit talking.

I accidentally end up in the middle of a garden, aerating the soil with my high heels, lured there by a magical path of irresistible flowers. Ron doesn't sniff the garden air before changing to work pants, work shoes, work shirt and work gloves. He points, not always in silence, at the clay mud on my ruined shoes.

Ron sponges the spots off my coat in the elevator; I don't notice these little friends who come to visit.

I love big, blurry art. Ron gravitates to small pieces with precise, fine detail; he specializes in detail. Normally detail isn't my strong suit, but when it comes to stories, he's a slacker and I'm a stickler.

He claimed, "We traveled through a forest of poplar to Tchaikovsky's home in Russia."

I was appalled. It wasn't poplar; it was birch—hundreds of miles of white tree trunks flashing by the Trans-Siberian train windows.

We have completely different working styles. I'm more of a scout who races ahead on a snorting, wild stallion, charging from hill to hill and back with extraordinary speed. Ron is a methodical, analytical—yet visionary—general managing an entire army of highly effective foot soldiers who move at the speed of…foot.

We work together constantly. Our lives have merged into one solitary revolution around a single planet—Trinity International Church. There's no place to escape each other in our tiny apartment, and the other option, Genesis, crackles with constant busyness and chatter. So Ron and I have been fighting—sniper fire, an occasional heat-guided missile, territorial skirmishes…

It gets worse. The job I have is worship leader at our church, and the guy who used to do it (Ron!) is still on staff. He watches me, makes critical observations, and points out the organizational tasks I'm dropping. I order, "Butt out if you want to keep sharing a bed with me."

Worse still, even though I've never done the job Ron's doing now—lead pastor—I have an uncanny ability to know what he should be doing and how he should go about doing it. I offer free analysis of his sermons. Occasionally it's more than an offer.

It was a rough week; we were engaged in a lockstep dance and neither of us could let go. I didn't want to spend time with God on Thursday morning; I suspected He'd call me to admit my faults, to say "I'm sorry," and to listen humbly to the pain I had caused. I wanted to be mean a little while longer. Unfortunately, if I avoided both God and Ron, I would be really lonely, and poor Sheena would be stuck with a major grouch-mother.

There's something clarifying about stopping, quieting the tempest inside my heart, reading the Psalms, and listening. It tenderizes my leathered heart. I enjoyed being alone at home; I spent time in my balcony garden, in heels, and watched the flowers grow. I experimented with admitting to myself I was wrong and found it eventually felt like relief. I called Ron at Genesis. When he heard my voice, I could tell he was yanking up the drawbridge and fortifying his castle remarkably fast for a methodically slow, general-type guy.

I said in my meekest tone, "I'm willing to quit being a witch."

"Oh," he was taken aback. "Well, I'm willing to quit being one too."

So I had to explain witch was a female term; he needed to find his own label. I had one in mind if he was stuck.

We decided to design a strategy, or one of us would be murdered by Christmas—not the cheeriest way to celebrate the season. Practical things developed, like scheduling days apart from each other and not talking about church on Mondays. The lines are so blurry; it's hard to decipher which is work and which is friendship. We want to reserve space for evenings out together. We need to go away into the countryside and remember what green looks like. There's humility to grow; I need to swallow my pride and admit I could benefit from a few organizational skills. I want to make my observations gently, without an edge, and to remember how much power I have to hurt Ron. We live so close; we step on each other's toes just by breathing too deeply.

So I didn't tell him about the birch trees; I just let it go.

LATER IN THE WEEK

Saturday night, some of our friends were playing jazz at a Madagascan restaurant north of Genesis. Ron and I saw an opportunity to refresh our romance and support our church musicians. As we walked up and down rue St. Denis looking for the elusive landmark alley cutting through a building, I had a sense of strolling through Paris' armpit. When I looked down dark side streets, I saw rows of leaning buildings, some tilted toward the street and some away, floor lines running in contrary directions. Paint was peeling. The usual Parisian ornamental iron was absent. It seemed I had crossed over into the surreal world of Les Misérables.

"What is it, what's giving me this creepy feeling?" I asked.

Ron began to point. "Well, there are the ladies of the night staking their territory; there, at the end of the block, is their pimp; here, we have sex shops."

I had only noticed the decrepit Oliver Twist ambiance. Men seem to pick up on these other things much sooner. The night-shift women weren't particularly attractive. They were overweight, heavily made up, and sporting black boots. *I wear black boots.* We wondered if these women could still make contact with the little girl inside them.

We walked and walked and walked. Then we trudged. Although we saw three fascinating side streets cutting through buildings with high stone archways, none of them was the right one. By ten P.M. we trudged back to our car sobered by the quarter's tragic women, disappointed to miss the jazz trio and dangerously hungry.

Sunday Arrived, Anyway

Sunday came, as it always does, even after a difficult week. In spite of our flaws, we again experienced a palpable sense of God's presence and the response of tender hearts at Trinity.

Antoine looked around the room after church and said, "Something has happened here. There's been a shift. What's going on?"

I couldn't help but notice a full room this Sunday and the Sunday before.

Ying's eyes were wide as he stated flatly, "We need to plan for growth." He had stumbled onto a Canadian photojournalist who was making a documentary in Paris; she mentioned becoming a follower of Jesus at our church recently. Ron met another new follower who landed at Trinity when she couldn't find an English international Buddhist center. And for the first time someone had crossed the bridge from our English conversation class at Genesis to church on Sunday.

Helga, our beautiful chemical engineer, brings a friend to church each week. Last night she brought Vincent and he was traumatized. Guitars? Drums? People singing too loud! A pack of us, including Helga's shocked friend, ate sushi together afterward—a pathetic excuse for big boys to play with sharp knives. Vincent plans on coming back.

When I turned around to start the service last night, there was my dear soul mate, Madame D., third row from the front, her smile stretching cheek to cheek. I arrived on empty at our little church and came away full. It seems the less there is of me, the more room there is for God.

MONDAY'S GIFT

Monday morning gifted us with a brilliant blue sky. Antoine took the bus instead of his normal, dark, Métro-mole route to work. Three minutes before his stop, a pretty blonde raced up the stairs of the Métro stop and dashed frantically for the bus. The driver waited, allowing the breathless young woman to find a seat in front of Antoine.

She kept turning around to stare at him and finally asked, "Do you play guitar at Trinity Church?"

He said he does.

"Did you play there last night?" she asked.

He replied yes again.

She told him how she lives near the church, heard the music, and followed it upstairs to our chapel. She and her husband loved it but worried about being Catholics. Antoine assured her of an open-arm welcome; we worship the same Jesus. This, in a city of eleven million—after the last week!

May: Holy and Not-So-Holy Week

COMMITMENTS

I committed myself to play for Antoine's gospel choir on Easter Monday without giving much thought to the season or my bothersome limitations. Antoine gave me the brass parts to play on a keyboard; I complained, but didn't say no. The music had three staves in two different keys. I can read two staves in one key. After scribbling some hurried notations, I trotted off to the only rehearsal as Holy Week began and stumbled into a full-grown disaster. I couldn't transpose two keys simultaneously at the band's maniac speed, nor could I decode the complex rhythms now obliterated by my illegible notes.

My deflated ego desperately inflated excuses: "The drummer is African," "The bassist is Brazilian," "The guitarist is an Islander," "I'm the only homogenized, pasteurized, sterilized white woman," "While they were dancing wild sambas in the heat I was memorizing Bach fugues in a cold Germanic valley protected from hippy Beatle beats." I was pathetic.

There was too much to do to indulge a well-developed pout. Holy Week demanded heavy commitments from all of us to be ready for our interactive exhibit, The Way of the Cross. In spare moments I transposed, rewrote, and drilled the brass music; Ron the Responsible didn't have spare moments. He sweated details with Todd and Jay Lee, from the Ikea®-palmed garden to the dark stone tomb where my only piano lay buried under meters of black fabric. During the weekend people spent hours in the reflective spaces at Genesis contemplating the agony Jesus endured out of love for us. Walls melted. Ron heard muffled weeping. Contemplating Christ's sufferings allows Him to enter our own pain.

Madame D. came. The heaviness of Christ's death was exacerbated by the raw grief of a friend of hers whose young brother-in-law had just died. Pierre had followed D.'s trail of crumbs toward the bakery and the Baker Himself, but now Madame D. wondered what the tragedy would do to his tender shoot of curiosity. Yet Pierre was captivated by her guidebook from The Way of the Cross. God Himself had endured unfair suffering. D.'s friend was intrigued, following her to the doors of Genesis, but he couldn't walk through.

A woman came back into Genesis after leaving. "There's such a contrast between out there and in here," she said. "I'm not ready; I need more of this peace."

When she finally left, she passed a beggar with a badly burned face. After her experience at The Way of the Cross, she couldn't just toss some change. She caught the Métro back and found the woman; a conversation followed, and then dinner. A beggar became a person who had lost both her family and her face in the explosion of a butane tank.

By Sunday I could feel my energy melting like Easter chocolate forgotten in spring sunshine; how would I make it through our five P.M. service after the week we'd poured ourselves into? I still had one more day of Holy Week: Monday's trip to Chartres with two musicians I hardly knew, my flimsy brass impersonations, and a day with the French-speaking choir.

Easter Monday

Monday morning arrived earlier than usual. I counted myself among the vertical dead. Ron remained horizontal in spite of his adamant, Peter-like vows on Sunday to follow me. He lay there snoring, completely comatose after the intoxicating high of Easter, oblivious to my dread.

Just as I feared, the bass player and I waited alone together for the chronically time-challenged drummer. How can an executioner of complex rhythms fail to grasp the simple rhythm of a clock? I felt the pressure to fabricate French conversation with an outrageously successful musical giant I found intimidating.

"Did you have a nice Easter?" It was Apollo who put out the welcome mat.

"Full, you know, church things." My French faltered in my blurry fatigue.

"Yes, it was Holy Week, wasn't it? I grew up Catholic but I've been a Buddhist for fifteen years. I find it more interesting than Catholicism, more positive and in the present. There's so much less suffering. Actually, all religions are the same at the base." Apollo carries a quiet peace; he's devoted to daily meditation and prayer.

In time, I offered, "For me, grace is the most important thing."

"What? How's that?" he looked completely puzzled.

"I fail a lot, and I could never do enough to earn God's pardon, so I depend on grace." I could see that zero of what I'd just said registered in him. I didn't worry about it—wasn't my job.

After thirty minutes of engaging Buddhism 101, the drummer arrived and the tête-à-tête dissolved. An hour later, the long fingers of the Chartres Cathedral spires were visible, tracing intricate art across the sky's virgin canvas. A fairytale village, with cars oddly superimposed, wound around the hill the edifice straddled.

I staggered to the coffee bar in the cathedral's shade, hoping caffeine would jump-start my catatonic music genes. I could hear rhythmic chanting in the distance; someone was wiring the choir for higher voltage.

A tall debonair man called, "Holy…"

Sixty voices yelled back, "GHOST."

"Holy…"

"GHOST."

"Jesus…"

"CHRIST."

"We're gonna have a Holy Ghost…"

"PARTY."

"Holy Ghost…"

"PARTY."

My jaw dropped; I stared, and then the shock heated up into rapid-fire judgment. Irreverent. Trivializing. I was lightning quick to label something uncomfortably different and to relish a rush of superiority. I wondered if I would ever become someone who believed in truth yet didn't judge. The gentle island of acceptance is hard to find between the continents of Condone and Condemn.

The sound check didn't go well for me—my entry was unclear. The drummer insisted I start after four bars. Apollo serenely stated six. Antoine smiled, "I'm the boss; it's three." Much debate followed without much illumination. Professionals don't do a second rehearsal; I was in over my head.

After waiting for sixty people to use the toilets, after walking down the lanes of Cinderellaville with the dawdling choir toward our picnic lunch, after a leisurely "peekneek" in what they call a garden and we would call an unkempt yard, I excused myself. I called Ron to see if he was vertical yet. He was enjoying the perfect day alone in the Luxembourg Garden under a cloudless sky and brilliant sun. My guy was reading behind a palace by a quiet reflecting pool with a whimsical fountain; it was a perfect place to meet with God and renew his soul. Ron assured me I would find therapeutic quiet time the next day.

The concert took place in a giant festival tent on a wooden stage that shook with the choir's jumping, dancing, and exuberant singing. It was my first time to play with security guards and a fence holding back spectators at the front. When it was over, I could feel waves of relief washing through me; I hadn't played perfectly but it was a good day to embrace average.

I couldn't get back to Paris fast enough; in spite of being an extrovert, I needed a break from people. We were near my stop when the drummer asked me if I was eager to go straight home.

I responded enthusiastically, "Absolutely, you bet!"

The two gorgeous guys, fifteen years my junior, burst out laughing. I sorted through the French phrases wondering what was so funny. He had asked if I was eager to go straight home with him. My French! Sometimes average would be a relief.

I Come to the Garden Alone

The day after Holy Week was finished, I anticipated sweet solitude in the beautiful Luxembourg Garden. Ron recommended the reflecting pond where he had spent an idyllic Sabbath the day before. I found paradise, a chair, my camera, and a man asking, "Would you like me to take your photo?" He looked like Curly from The Three Stooges; halfway back his polished head, hair sprung up in wild coils.

"No, thank you," I replied.

"Do I detect an accent?"

"Oui."

"Oh, so that's a dictionary you're studying?"

"No, it's a Bible."

"Really? You're religious?"

Although a serious conversation took off in which he echoed Apollo's "all religions are the same at the base," three voices squabbled in my head: Frank, my French tutor, cheering the free practicum; Sady the church lady, my collector of witnessing points; and my depleted introvert, Gerta, who just laid down and cried. Gerta prevailed.

I wandered around, soaking in the flowers flaunting their Easter bonnets, searching for a spot far from Curly. I was breathing in the solitude when another man fell into step beside me. He said something polite and an automatic answer popped from my mouth.

At dinner that night I reported these incidents and Sheena scolded me severely. "For Pete's sake, Mom, you know this. You never, never respond. You've gotta be rude." This stuff happens to her constantly. For me it's not normal, unless you count the Virgin Records incident. Though I told those men I was married, flashed The Ring and insisted dinner wouldn't work, they assured me it wasn't a problem—they were married too.

Dark 'n Handsome had noticed my accent, purring, "It's delightful." I was vain enough to secretly preen my feathers. He was persistent; normal turn-off words like "pastor" and "church" beaded off his religion-repellent back. I desperately looked for a polite departure and sat on a chair beside the path.

"Oh, we're stopping?" He sat beside me. "Dine with me."

"No, it won't work."

"Why not?"

"My husband would not be pleased."

"Well, that's too bad."

"No, it would be too bad if I didn't go home to have dinner with my family."

As I walked away, he called sadly, his mask slipping, "Will you say a little prayer for me?"

I nodded, turned away, and punched Ron's number vigorously on my cell. "You know the old hymn *I Come To The Garden Alone?* I'm certain it wasn't written in France."

L'Été—
Summer 2007

June: Drills to Trains

DRILLS

WE SEEM TO live in a small cavity located in a high-rise dental chair where we are forced to endure the incessant shriek of an obsessed drill. Nails on a chalkboard would be a relief. The apartment next door was demolished last summer and the industrial-sized construction noise has been pervasive ever since, the drill relentless. When the wanna-be dentists quit mixing cement, stop screwing on braces and surrender their drills for the night, Ron appears with his eternal vacuum. Even though generations have passed since his Mennonite roots were planted in German soil, he still retains their highly refined gene for dirt location and removal. Though a half-breed, I am a sorry mutant.

After Sheena returned home from a sports trip to Munich where her hostess vacuumed with daily vengeance, scrubbed her children raw, polished on, in and behind immaculate furniture and alphabetized her spices, Sheena confessed, "I get Dad now."

Perhaps the construction inspires her dad to new heights with his machine. When the construction crew finally bed their screaming machines for the night and my guy no longer can admire the crane operator from our balcony, out comes the vacuum. It's the only motorized thing he has to power up in our neutered apartment. Vacuuming is actually very manly, in a sophisticated city sort of way.

THE SHORT TOUR

For the most part we revel in city life. Simply driving through Paris on our way home from church is a pleasurable ritual; the streets are often quiet late Sunday night and the beauty has a way of seeping peace into our core. Every historic monument, each graceful bridge, and all the stately palaces and grand stone buildings are lit in a soft butter light too rich to drink in all at once.

When Ron's Kentucky cousins came to visit, we could hardly wait to show off our adopted hometown. We proudly began our evening excursion with the radiant Tour Eiffel. The filigreed iron lace is magnificent; at night the tower appears almost delicate despite its size. Ron boldly stopped our car in the far right lane of the busy boulevard, set the hazard lights flashing and waited while our guests ran to take pictures. After re-wedging two of us into the backseat of our inconvenient two-door, our experienced tour guide turned the key to continue our spin around town. Ron turned it repeatedly, but our Saab® had taken a sudden vow of silence.

On the great, bustling boulevard that lines the foot of France's world-renowned landmark, two women cruised noiselessly; only the sound of their husbands' panting breath and pounding feet polluted the atmosphere. I negotiated a stiff right turn and then another difficult uphill-right where a newborn parking space was birthed before our incredulous eyes. Our glistening men pushed the mute beast up and down, back and forth, trying to angle the unconscious behemoth into a tight space as the incline worked against them. Two French Arab men jumped in to help. Cousin Jim's Arabic flowed nicely to their shock and delight; Ron and I were stunned.

Monday morning found Ron agitating over multiple French dictionaries, collecting new mechanical vocabulary to rescue our stranded pet. There would be no sign language—indistinct phone work was unavoidable. Ron tried to pawn the dreadful chore off on me but I was adamant; this was a manly job. I left him there to go jiggle cereal boxes in the kitchen—my current definition of women's work.

THE TRAIN

With our Saab® sleeping at the garage we were forced to take an afternoon train to the suburbs where we were scheduled to celebrate the Cambodian-Thai New Year. We avoid the suburban trains; unlike the Métro, they are confusing. A car is significantly more time and cost efficient.

Ying and Jay Lee met us at the Charles de Gaulle Étoile station and from there the four of us conquered the train challenge to the suburbs, where an authentic Thai meal was meticulously prepared. Singaporeans, Cambodians, Filipinos, and Thais all evaluated the feast for authenticity. After the favorable benediction of "pretty close, pretty close," we lounged around, singing and telling jokes and stories just like Ron and I did as children at large family gatherings.

Ying, Jay Lee, Ron, and I were the last group to be ferried to the station, with plenty of time to catch the final train home. At eleven forty P.M. we waited on the platform whose monitor screen read "Paris." Though tired, we laughed and chatted all the way to… Cergy. Cergy? This town lies at the opposite end of the line from Paris. How had this happened? There was one last train going in the direction of Paris, leaving at twelve thirty-three A.M. The screen didn't actually list Paris, just all the little towns situated in the city's direction. It was our only option. As the four of us waited for the train, it started to get cold and I couldn't quit thinking about my cozy bed or calculating what time I could reasonably expect to fold for the night. I may have whined, intermittently. The late train arrived and we all hopped on with relief, relaxing in the warmth. The stations flashed by and we happily noted we were getting closer to Paris.

Two Slavic girls boarded our car and asked where we were going; we assured them the train was headed to Paris. They looked puzzled; they thought they had boarded a train for Cergy. The four of us laughed in a naughty, smirky way, and whispered to each other, "Silly tourists, they can't figure out the trains." We were confident we were finally headed to Paris, not in the opposite direction to the small town we'd left twenty minutes earlier.

The stations continued to flash by and as I sleepily looked out the window, it occurred to me I had seen the same incomprehensible name just a short while ago. I looked at the map above the doors. I looked again.

"Ron? I think we've somehow turned around and are headed back to where we started."

He looked at me as only a man can—a man who is excellent with directions and flirting with crankiness. He didn't need to say anything. We both know my sense of direction is nonexistent. But, I'm not illiterate. I watched carefully for the next sign.

"Ron, really, we've been here before; I don't understand how, but we're headed back to where we boarded."

I got The Look again. A rough translation would be, "You don't do directions. I do directions."

It's quite word efficient.

By now Ying was standing in front of the train door, his head tilted up toward the overhead map, reading and rereading. This couldn't be happening. We never felt the train turn; no loop showed on the map; the train didn't reverse. Ying and Jay Lee always faced forward so he could keep his Thai feast securely anchored.

Ying turned back toward Ron, his face grave. "Ron? It's true. Somehow the train turned around and we're headed back toward Cergy."

Ron began to pay attention to the station signs flashing by our window. The direction had inexplicably reversed. Perhaps a crack had opened between the third and fourth dimensions and we had slid in sideways.

Back at Cergy, with the next train not leaving until four forty-seven A.M., Ron tried calling a taxi even though it would cost a second mortgage; the dispatcher hung up when our remote location was revealed. Jay Lee and I started to shiver in our light spring clothes; a cruel breeze harassed the open station. We all craved beds and heat. It was after one A.M. when we began our surreal hunt for lodging. Taxis had vacated their post for the night and our footsteps echoed oddly between the tall cement buildings. The town was a bizarre remnant of the 1970s love affair with modern design; the Jetsons would have fit in well among the stacked tiers of round windows and oval balconies. I searched the sky for signs of incoming UFOs; my companions searched for a hotel sign.

Ten minutes of brisk walking through the cold night, guys' arms protectively wrapped around their shivering wives, awarded us the prize sight of the Premier Inn. Its sign was lit, the doors unlocked, the lobby heated. Slavic language, beer bottles, and a hearty party animated the not-so-premier lobby. Ron spotted the two European girls from the train; I looked the other direction, hoping they couldn't see me if I couldn't see them.

The cheery girls called loudly, "Hey! What are you doing here? You were headed to Paris!"

Ying mumbled something polite; I was too embarrassed to meet their eyes. Besides, manners are optional after midnight. I focused on the girl at the counter, who informed me the hotel was "complet"—as in no-room-in-the-inn complete. She graciously made call after call, trying to find us another option, but to no avail.

"Ask her if we can spend the night in the lobby," Ying and Jay Lee urged me.

After all the phone calls Counter Girl had made and all the French I had now exhausted, I refused. Jay Lee and Ying found the young woman's English to be excellent; they bravely asked if our quartet could camp on the inn's chairs. The stiff seats were unforgiving, the lobby boisterous; Jay Lee debated whether to ask the festive Slavs if we could sublet their beds.

If our car hadn't chosen to roll over and play dead and if the Cambodian-Thai New Year wasn't in April, we would not have taken the train that mystical night. We wouldn't have been sleep deprived, occasionally giggling like giddy middle-schoolers, snapping hideous photos of a strange scene, forced to party badly through the elasticized night. What a tragic loss we had dodged.

It was six thirty A.M. before our heavy heads made contact with the pillows on our bed. It was less than two hours before Ron's construction hero would climb the flimsy tower to the crane's eye hovering high above the earth and the drills next door would begin their daily scream.

July: The Antoine Story

AN UNUSUAL PATH

Sometimes a room can vibrate, almost hum, with an invisible electric charge. The night when Antoine brought fifteen members of his gospel choir to join our musicians was one such evening.

Antoine led the worship energetically, as he does once a month, and the vocalists sang with passion. There was black hair with sensational braided extensions, beautiful spiked burgundy hair, fresh naïve faces beside older less-innocent ones, and one pregnant teenager. For a number of them, it was their first time to attend a church service. Their hearts were touched; they hadn't expected the warmth.

Ron's talk fanned their curiosity. They struggled for words afterward to explain how they felt, gathering around us in shy clumps. Antoine and Sophie had searched for a church where it would be safe to bring their "kids" and colleagues from the gospel choir. They found us. When they looked for a new apartment last fall, they determined to find something close to Trinity. An unusual path led them to our unobvious church.

ISLAND BOY

He is a gregarious, tireless man who collects people around him like some grandmas collect spoons. Music runs out of his pores like sweat off a fat runner. His first instrument was an accordion, taught by a squat Italian teacher who coached Antoine to take first place in the music festivals of southern France.

His life didn't begin in Europe; the young, carefree Antoine spent his first ten years barefoot, running on the beaches and through the palm trees of a tropical paradise. His father was a tyrannical, quasi king to whom the neighborhood gave fervent, though nervous devotion—until the day the kingdom's cornerstone abandoned his followers and family to immigrate to Switzerland. Antoine's utopia collapsed; he was left behind with his sister and their myriad aunts, uncles, and cousins. After a year, Switzerland's door remained firmly closed to the two children, so their parents sent them to grow up with a kind aunt in France.

Without understanding why, Antoine was severed from his tropical vine and grafted onto an alpine fir without either mom or dad. Music became his comfort; accordion, then guitar and later, piano, articulated his painful rage. Music was a slender thread holding him together.

Grown-Up Realities

The adult Antoine met God and poured his fervor into building a church from fifteen to three hundred in hard-core France within a few short years. He became a high-profile pastor, the rising star in his denomination, married to the daughter of its president. Three beautiful children had completed his French family when the season of success was sharply amputated; Antoine chose to sleep with a married woman from his worship team. He confessed his failure to his wife and within the month lost her, their children, and his career, home, car and a stellar reputation. Miserable and shunned, the young father found a cramped room at a Red Cross hostel in the Paris suburbs; bar gigs supplied a questionable lifeline as the musician ricocheted down a dark hole.

Our friend eventually found meaningful work with a Catholic foundation caring for abandoned and abused minors. The bitter wounds of childhood abandonment were not unfamiliar to Antoine; he offered compassion, not from a pedestal, but out of his own losses. His music began to provide inspiration for the youth he nurtured. Over time, a choir sprouted and flourished with the

103

administration's encouragement. After some years, the foundation's director invited Antoine to establish and administrate gospel choirs for all 160 institutes around France.

"You can't possibly want me; you don't know who I really am." Antoine was painfully honest. "I'm a failed pastor, divorced, someone who cheated on his wife and abandoned his own children."

The director pushed him to dream again.

DREAMING

One night a vivid dream chased Antoine's sleep away. He was playing the piano and noticed his suit had a gaping hole in the knee; even in his dream he knew what the ruined pants symbolized.

A pastor appeared, exclaiming, "You've lost your ring! Where is your ring?"

The forceful minister told Antoine he had a message for him. The dream was strong, indelible; it drove Antoine to move out of Sophie's apartment and search for a church the following week.

At the first church he attended, the tall musician was shocked to see a preacher who looked just like the one in his dream. He endured the service impatiently and waited anxiously for all the pastor's fans to disperse. He made his way to the front to nervously ask a man he'd never met before, "Excuse me, Pastor, do you have a message for me?" Antoine smiled hopefully.

"What?" The reverend's tone was brusque. "Didn't you listen? I already gave the message."

Though embarrassed, Antoine was convinced there was a unique word especially for him. He persisted, "Please, don't you have a special message just for me?"

Rev. Duval gave a narrow, steely-eyed stare, communicating his zero-tolerance-for-fools policy. "As I said, I already gave the message."

It was a letdown. Disappointed, Antoine turned to leave. The dream seemed too provocative to only be indigestion. As he and Sophie strode toward the exit, a stranger called out after him, "May I speak with you? Come outside."

Antoine looked at Sophie who didn't understand what this man she loved was up to. She squeezed his hand reassuringly as they stood in the parking lot, not knowing what to expect.

"When you came into church I felt impressed you are a servant of God," the man said.

"Uhhh. Oh. Hmmm."

"The Lord put it on my heart to invite you to come to my country and to pray for you."

"And which country would this be?" Antoine's curiosity was cautiously aroused.

"I am from Brazzaville, Congo."

Sophie's mind began shouting, "Mayday! Mayday!"

"You should come; I believe God has something in store for your future," the African pastor said. He was convincing and winsome.

Antoine emptied his bank account and booked a trip to Africa. When the airliner's door closed at the Paris airport, he panicked. What had he done?

For two weeks Antoine lived under the tutelage of the slight African pastor who listens for God's voice, a man who has planted more than one hundred churches on his hungry continent. Pastor Moussa mentored the lost shepherd. He loved him well and taught him about God's curious specialization in murderers, betrayers, prostitutes, deceivers, adulterers, schemers—humans. They prayed and fasted together. The slender man with honey-brown skin and kind eyes whom we would meet years later at Genesis, told Antoine the story of the Prodigal Son and how that father put his own ring onto the hand of his son.

On returning to France, Antoine received an unexpected raise from the Catholic foundation. They eventually sent him back to Brazzaville at their expense, three more times. When the season was right, Antoine apologized to his first wife. Ten years after leaving pastoral ministry, he drove to his old French town to make painful amends with his former church's leadership.

This ragged story was laid before us during one long Thursday dinner last fall. Sophie sat quietly by Antoine's side, her gentle spirit as luminescent as the candles burning low on the table. Four courses passed by, our small salon became dark as evening fell; it was full of the mysterious fragrance that rises from exposing the unbeautiful parts of our souls. Now that we knew his unedited history, the vulnerable man asked if we wanted to change our minds about using him in the church.

Real-life Grace

Ron often teaches about ongoing grace, not one-time, good-thing-you-did-that-before-you-became-a-Christian grace. We understand God uses broken, sinful people since they aren't ever the real heroes of the story anyway—Jesus is. Ron and I didn't even have to look at each other across the dirty plates smeared with Bolognese sauce and baguette crumbs to know what the other was thinking. We claim to have Good News. How good is the news if only the pristine are God's trophies? That's just regular news. Both of us were convinced: embracing Antoine was embracing the heart of Jesus' message.

Ron and I often find it quite moving when Antoine leads worship at church. Sometimes the music is reflective; other times it rocks as his enormous white grin lights the entire chapel. We smile too, remembering our own shortfalls and encounters with grace. Occasionally Antoine will muse, "I just can't believe I get to lead worship again; I never dreamed...I don't deserve this."

"None of us is deserving," we remind him. "Some of us are simply less aware."

It was one of those Sunday evenings after Antoine led worship that Auntie and I hung around the almost deserted chapel. It was late. We were swapping stories when this woman I deeply respect asked me how much of Antoine's story I knew.

Auntie continued, "Did you know I recognized him the first day he walked in here with Sophie? I haven't said anything, but it was Antoine's ex-father-in-law who took my father's place after he died in Vietnam. It was his ex-father-in-law who gave me permission to marry, who walked me down the aisle at my wedding here in

France. His ex-father-in-law became my father. I attended Antoine's first wedding."

From the start, Auntie encouraged me to include Antoine, in spite of her love for the family he had bruised. I remember her prodding me. "He plays the piano very well, Lorelei; you should include him."

Such grace, given with an open hand. I hope I will be able to open my hands to bless with grace when the bruises are personal to me. God help me.

August: Holidays for a Non-Camper

MONT ST. MICHEL

Though it can be quite a bargain, I've never been fond of camping. It's an adventure for children, but hard labor for moms—hence the term "prison camp." How to holiday when one has Champagne tastes and a tap-water budget?

With Ron behind the wheel of our mostly trusty Saab®, four hours swept us from soggy Paris to a Normandy flood plain bathed in warm sunshine. The salt-flats were uninterrupted by hill, rise, or wrinkle—except for a startling spaceship parked prominently out on the sand. "Galactica" is officially called Mont St. Michel, an abbey and medieval village perched on an island rock. Surrounded by the Atlantic sea when the tide is high, it has drawn devout pilgrims to risk dying in quicksand as they've crossed the salt marshes over the centuries. Ron recommended the causeway.

Lodging rates were less than half those of Mont St. Michel's inns at an interesting, cash-only farmhouse on the mainland. From our attic room with its sloped ceiling, we gazed at grazing cows and bleating sheep silhouetted against the starship glowing offshore in the fading light.

Daylight revealed a tangle of steep and winding alleyways untouched by motored wheel. The tourist-trash boutiques were easily circumvented by climbing the ramparts that circled the village's stone cottages and shops. All tracks rose toward the abbey with countless high, non-regulation steps. Tourists filled every doorway and bench, stopping to pant along the way. The resident nuns and monks appeared gaunt, their gowns slack against their spare frames. Teetering on top of the world was the abbey with its inviting slate terrace; the salt flats sprawled far below. This was the ideal place to bask with sunlight on my back while I wrote. Ron wandered the village walls capturing art photos. By six P.M., the last of the herd of tour buses lumbered away; the island was quiet except for the cathedral bell's call to prayer. The a cappella music of ten, clear voices as pure—and as virginal—as the Vienna Boys Choir's sliced the air into slivers of rich harmony. It was celestial; heaven was close enough to touch. We read, pausing to wander in gardens marked by the French obsession with geometrically shaped boxwood.

As I gazed into the warm eyes of a nun, a scene from my second-grade classroom came to mind. I saw a knobby-kneed brunette shocking a petite, blue-eyed blonde. "You're going to hell," I condemned. The gentle blonde was Catholic. She cried all day. Though I was disciplined, I was unmoved. I "knew" only evangelicals like me were going to heaven. We were different, not cloistered, not manipulating people with guilt or abusing political power.

There was a persistent nudging of my heart while a thought slowly took shape. *If I see a flaw in another institution or individual, the clarity is given so my eyes can be opened to my own comparable sin.*

Our retreat ended too soon; it was time to meander home along the back roads Ron loves to explore.

Pre-Fête Prep

Trinity aspired to have a band cooking up some tasty music on the sidewalk in front of Genesis on the first day of summer. It was all legal; anyone and everyone can expose their gift of music during the Fête de la Musique. Unfortunately, my best efforts to produce a memorable event met with frustration. Musicians were abnormally elusive; three were available, five were not; some responded quickly, some slowly, others not at all. One drummer was touring in Germany; the other working the night shift. I called Antoine and asked him to find a drummer. We waited for an answer. Nothing.

Antoine contacted yet another drummer. "I haven't actually heard him play," he hedged, "but I'm certain he's good."

Uh-oh. Meantime, unproductive weeks slipped by; I was running out of time.

While I stressed over music logistics, another dilemma erupted. Ron and I faced a delicate, thorny situation at church—we weren't handling it perfectly. After yet another email or meeting, I would pass a wretched night giving it all to God, taking it back, giving it to God, taking it back... The arguments recycling in my head were exasperating; they wouldn't take place anyway. I forgot about contemplating my own comparable sin because I was too preoccupied with trying to appear perfect.

Antoine called. The dark-horse drummer wanted to play but he was currently in England. Unknowns continued to dangle. Would the drummer be available to rehearse before our deadline? What if he was useless? Perhaps no drummer was preferable to a bad drummer.

I couldn't let it go. At rehearsal the night before our untimely vacation was to begin, Ron and I finally added the missing percussion piece. The drummer was delightful.

ANTIBES

Time for holidays; I left behind sleepless nights and reveled in the love of good friends who had booked a hotel with a beautiful pool overlooking the sea. The website promised beach access. Sure enough, we had permission to open the gate across the road and walk onto the private beach—a cement pad poised on craggy rocks above crashing waves. Apparently beach didn't mean sand.

A travel show had intrigued us with the legendary castle of Eze, a village unmolested by the centuries, overlooking the Mediterranean from dizzying heights. Off we went with great anticipation. At the very top, past the enchanting village that rivaled the best of

Walt Disney's imagination, a few broken castle walls were all that remained. Legendary was quite literal.

Reality can't compete with fantasy. Our friends' young daughter was devastated. A garden of rare cactus plants among ruins was a foul substitute for castle walls. This would not have happened in Disneyland.

La Fête de la Musique

The high-speed train whipped us back to Paris for the music festival. The partying started early, so swimming the turbulent subway sea was precarious. Though music swamped the swarming streets, it wasn't old world romance; there was a conspicuous absence of quixotic accordion from the Marais to Châtelet. Instead, heavy metal rockers, Jimi Hendrix wannabes, and grunge bands competed for airspace.

We were quite a contrast. Our Romanian soundman mastered the complex outdoor challenge. Our band sizzled; the music was irresistible. Shock came first and then ecstasy. I felt rather proud until the past month's frustrations and God's intervention pinched my memory. A large, enthusiastic crowd gathered and stayed. A James Brown look-alike gyrated vigorously in the crowd, his shimmies in his unbuttoned, gold lamé shirt inspiring laughter around him. Our church folk sang, clapped, danced, and mixed with the crowd. French faces seemed mystified by captivating religious music and by church people who looked normal.

One couple was really getting into the music until they abruptly caught the content. They stopped and gaped at each other; the man then put back his head and screamed. He hauled his woman to the front where the pair defiantly danced away down the sidewalk. Most people were more subtle as they casually walked by, trying to connect the puzzling dots.

The neighborhood baker came with his twins, enthusiastically lifting his thumbs and leaving a bag of prize-winning pastries for us. Long after midnight as Ron washed the floor, the restaurant owner from across the street stuck his head inside Genesis' door.

"Every year you get better; this year was the best," he said.

Making music with friends I love bred deep satisfaction, all evening long. The Healer had gently massaged the cramp in my heart. Pain and peace flowed side by side. The following week, my journaling from Mont St. Michel again haunted me: *If I see a flaw in another institution or individual, the clarity is given so my eyes can be opened to my own comparable sin.*

Relief flooded in as I realized again I could never be perfect. Of course I would sin; so would others around me. The door of truth opened; gentle grace only waited for an invitation to enter.

Fête de la Musique

L'Automne—
Autumn 2007

September: Parades

AN ITALIAN PARADE

WE ACCEPTED HELGA'S tantalizing invitation to visit her in Italy and packed our bags for the flight on a brand-new discount airline. However, which part was discounted?

After eighty minutes in a seamless sky, we dropped into a land of leftover Fabio models with flowing manes and fluorescent pants competing for attention. The last time I saw trousers this loud, I was waiting for Dad to finish his golf game. The Italians were obsessed with designer sunglasses large enough to double as salad plates; perhaps the shades provided protection from the bright orange, red, and yellow pants. Voluptuous women sashayed past on sexy stilettos with skinny straps and big, bright baubles. Everyone was colorful; the uniform black of Paris was very absent. The loud, high-octane chatter was shocking after the omnipresent silence of France.

Helga coolly negotiated the maze of frightening autoroutes to Ravenna, where we eagerly anticipated exploring the beaches. Oilrigs hyphenated the sea's horizon and industry clung to the coastline. Neither that nor the littered sand and muddy water fazed the bronze Italians or pink Germans who blanketed the beach in variegated stripes of flesh tones. The women's self-confidence was fascinating; bitsy bikinis were standard wear for pretzel sticks, pears, and watermelons alike. No one cared; I was jealous of their freedom. In spite of the irony, lemon gelato at a roadside stand succeeded with its temptation. After all, it's what God meant to make when He created citrus fruit and Guernsey cows.

Ron and I passed four lazy days sipping morning espressos, lunching on pizza and indulging in afternoon cappuccinos in the town plaza. We were captivated by the endless parade of Italians bicycling through the village square. Skinny grandpas rode in suit jackets, ties flapping, pursued by thick grandmas vigorously pumping their bikes. Muscle-bound males with flowing hair chased females floating by in billowing chiffon skirts. Parents taxied babies honking rubber duckies and hugging handlebars while dangling over both front and back wheels. Children pedaled circles around stalled grandparents caught in conversation. Everyone was on two wheels, pedaling a greased chain while dressed for high tea with Armani.

The most spectacular sight unfolded the night five hundred people gathered in the plaza—for a whip recital. When darkness finally bloomed, spotlights speared the stage. Italian polkas played as each competitor snapped and flourished a whip in rhythm. I scrutinized the students for eye patches and interesting facial scars while Ron whispered jokes about Jack the Whipper. By the time boys grew big enough to raise acne, their whipping was serious art. There's something slightly hysterical about thrashing a weapon and calling it music.

A French Parade

It was our son, back in the U.S., who convinced his dad to go see France's armed forces converging on the center of Paris for the annual Bastille Day parade. "Dad, they're driving through your roundabout? You have to go; you must see this. Really, four thirty A.M. isn't that early." Justin was adjusting to France's parade philosophy and he didn't even live here.

My night-owl husband dragged himself out of bed in the predawn hours to wait for the military hardware to roll through our neighborhood. He was in place by four forty-five A.M. Thirty minutes later, he wished he had brought a book and a flashlight. After an hour, Ron found a ledge on which to doze. Finally, camouflaged jeeps appeared to block early-bird traffic; the army rated a rare, non-stop ride to the Arc de Triomphe, just like Napoleon, the Nazis, and, later, the Allies of WWII. When we turned on the TV in the late morning to watch the military parade through the historic arch and down the Champs Élysées, Ron exclaimed, "Hey! I saw that tank, but those artillery shells weren't mounted yet. That guy's shirt with all the medals, it was on a hanger when they came by our place."

There was a marked absence of smiling clowns, highly decorated floats and entertainers with whitened smiles. Instead, highly decorated generals and other unsmiling military brass passed by politicians with cemented smiles as Air Force helicopters thick as Moses' locusts flew overhead. I had flashbacks of Vietnam, though I was never there.

No Purse Parade

After locking the door at Genesis, we crossed the street to grab lunch at a neighboring cafe. On the hot summer day, salads were ordered—no meat in mine, double the meat in Ron's. We sat by the wide-open, floor-length windows, checked to make sure our bags were secure under the table, and got involved in conversation. It didn't take long to finish our greens and a carafe of lukewarm tap water. It was only seconds after the owner's wife came by to say, "Ca va?" that Ron groaned, "My satchel is gone."

Ron stubbornly insisted on patrolling the area, certain he would find the cocky culprit flagrantly parading his stolen bag. But to his immense disappointment there was no purse parade.

We headed to the police station, a ten-minute walk away. We were buzzed into a cramped bureau where Ron explained he was robbed and wanted to file a police report.

"Could I have some identification, please?" he was asked.

"As I just said, I was robbed," Ron replied.

"You can't file without identification. Besides, you should call your bank first."

We almost sprinted back to Genesis and called the bank.

"We can't block your account until you have a police report," Ron was told.

"But the police told us to call you first," he replied.

"We cannot block your account without a report."

Back we went to the small police station with the same officer.

"I was robbed; please let me file a police report," Ron pleaded. "The bank won't block my account without it."

"ID please," the officer replied.

"I was robbed, remember?" Ron was a little irritated. "I don't have ID anymore."

"You can't file a police report without identification."

Ron sighed.

I jumped in, "I have ID. Those are my accounts too. Let me file."

"Those accounts are yours?"

"Yes. We're married so they're in my name too."

"Your name is on the stolen cards?"

"No, my husband's name is on the cards, but both our names are on the accounts."

"No, Madame, it doesn't work like that."

We caught the Métro home. Ron went through his files searching for papers the police might require: electric bills, phone bills, phone contract, statements for credit cards, last year's visa documents, his passport...

As Ron turned my key to lock our dubious door on our way out, he asked wearily, "Can you think of anything else?"

"Dental records?"

He didn't think I was funny.

We walked briskly to our neighborhood commissariat and waited in another line. Ron specified each stolen valuable while the policeman scrutinized corresponding documentation.

The officer shook his head. "There's no number for your cell phone. You can't file a police report."

"Yes, yes, yes! Look at all these numbers." Ron spread out a desperate array of documents.

I was impressed; the policeman was not.

"You can't file without the correct documentation for your phone," the officer said.

We dragged our feet home. This was now a scavenger hunt with the clues in coded French. After more digging, Ron exhumed the mysterious number. "Can you think of any other papers I need?" he asked.

"TB test results, baptismal certificate, favorite recipe…"

There wasn't even a hint of a smile.

We looked hopefully for an uncooperative bus and then turned to walk to the station, again. We watched with numb resignation as the policeman inspected Ron's file. After four trips to the police station, Ron finally filed a report, though too late to contact the bank or cell phone company.

Over the next days I watched Ron sift through files, produce yet more papers and handle the prolific reporting requirements with his young French. If I were on my own, there wouldn't be papers to find. I felt ashamed of this appalling lack until I remembered Mafia godfathers were convicted due to their paper trails. Perhaps I was better suited to advising organized crime.

A stolen satchel meant stolen keys, which meant our door locks needed replacing. After numerous tedious trips, Ron arrived home with various parts to replace our deadbolt.

"You're replacing our lock? You, yourself?" I questioned.

"I can do this."

"The way you repaired the toilet? It runs all the time now."

"It runs intermittently."

"Okay, it runs intermittently all the time."

"Granted. Anyway, this will save buckets of money."

"And you say you love me? We live in an urban jungle where robbery is the greatest crime; our neighbors have five locks on their door and we'll have… have you ever installed a lock?"

The challenges continue. We can reclaim our check blanks for a ten-euro fee at the police station. The law requires a professional to change the lock on our mailbox, but it's August, the month Paris is abandoned and many businesses close. Our landlady flushes the letters out of our mailbox with a special wooden spoon she reserves for these occasions. We're sharing my debit card because getting a replacement isn't possible in August. This means I get marooned in the interminable grocery line with no means to buy supper, something I realize only as the cashier finally peeks into view.

On good days, it's funny.

October: Flawed

PASTOR ON DRUGS

It started on a Saturday night when Ron's problem tooth explored enemy territory in the pain field. His dentist was gone for the month. We headed to the pharmacy.

"Take two of these every four hours," the pharmacist said. She handed him a box of ibuprofen.

"I've already tried this; it did nothing," Ron replied.

She got another box. Her French was rapid. "Take two codeine plus two ibuprofen every four hours. Don't let the pain peak; keep a constant level of medication."

He missed the part about a maximum of six pills each per day.

Within twenty minutes of taking the pill combination, Ron felt immense relief. He took another dose four hours later and carefully set out four pills for the middle of the night. Sometime in the darkness, Ron got up to take his nighttime allotment and couldn't find the tablets he'd laid on our turquoise sink. He didn't remember taking them earlier. Confused, he took another dose and went back to bed. By Sunday morning, Ron was feeling fabulous and, shortly after, rotten. A cold sweat filmed his body. He got out of bed; I heard a soft bang and then nothing.

"Ron?" There was no answer. "Ron? Are you OK?"

He was slouched on the floor. I crouched down beside him. "Ron?" There still wasn't any answer; his eyes were open, glassy.

Five slow minutes passed until Ron croaked, "How long have I been here?" His head hung low. "I think I'm going to be sick." I ran for the bucket.

Ron was a frightening white; he was still involuntarily self-pumping his stomach when I left for rehearsal at eleven A.M. I didn't know if I would be minus a bass player for the Sunday evening service or if I would be preaching.

His flushed pink cheeks were the prettiest things I had seen all day when he strolled casually into the chapel at four in the afternoon and picked up his bass.

That same week, a distressed Sheena came to our bedroom early one morning saying, "Dad, can you take me to Emergency? I have that allergic reaction thing going again…"

COMPUTER CLASH

Ron decided to study at home after lunch. The clash started with the one computer we both needed to use.

"It seems to me you're getting the computer quite a bit." My tone was almost pleasant.

"I think you're mistaken; it's actually you who has used it the most."

"Are you angry?"

"No, not at all."

"You look angry."

He looked around at the clothing drying around our apartment. "I feel like I'm living in a Laundromat."

"Where do you expect me to hang our wet laundry—in the spare room or the laundry room?"

Neither room exists.

It was a cranky afternoon with precarious crossfire—this, on the day we were to dine with a Russian couple who made it clear Jesus was a crock full of soft pickles. We drove silently past elegant apartments with elaborate wrought-iron balconies, red geraniums dripping down from their railings. A fragile truce was in place, but we were battle-fatigued. I didn't want to wear my plastic happy face.

The conversation moved toward marriage difficulties and we began to tell our stories: what worked, what didn't, our discoveries, our disasters, and the afternoon's petty quarrel. The Russian couple began to share their pain, disillusions and adjustments. Walls tumbled down. Somehow, God wove together a surprising, intimate evening even though we supplied Him with snarled thread.

The Meeting Before Prayer

That same week, as we left our apartment underground parking for a prayer meeting, a car was blocking the only exit at street level. We honked repeatedly; the empty, locked car remained immobile. We waited, helpless. Even with the exhilaration of repeated horn honking, by the end of twelve minutes we were both seething. We had holy duties to attend to.

"Oh, désolée, Monsieur." A woman approached, proper in her blouse, skirt, and sensible shoes.

Désolée, my foot! She didn't look sorry. Her grocery shopping had been accomplished with a first class, front-door parking space—at our expense.

"Madame, is this a parking space?" Ron asked.

"Uh, no." A little giggle escaped.

"This is an exit from a garage. We have waited and waited." Ron's French flowed marvelously.

"I was feeling a little sick today," she said.

"My eye, Madame! It seems you have not been well brought up." He slapped the hood of her car to make his point.

"Do not use the informal 'you' with me; address me with the proper, formal 'you,' "the lady huffed indignantly.

"Evidently the informal, less polite 'you' is just right for you." The grammatical insult felt terrific. We drove away, suddenly not so proud of the anger surge, wondering how we would pray.

GRUMPY

At the end of that same week, Ron tenderly admitted his faults to me. I needed to make my own confessions, but there seemed to be cold porridge stuck in my throat. It was communion Sunday. Ron set up a portrait of Christ's expression of love on the cross; cushions were placed in front of the church; people knelt to take the broken bread dipped in the communion cup.

I recalled how God's grace makes it safe to be found wrong. How quickly I forget and try to prove myself right.

That week also marked the beginning of the season the oven was used for heating—the door left open to battle September's spasms of premature cold. My Russian wool socks provided scant comfort. Knowing that the heat wouldn't be turned on in our Paris apartment until October 15 made me grumpy.

The toilet developed multiple life-threatening symptoms, making Ron grumpy. Outside of baptisms, he's not too good at working with water.

Ron visited new varieties of dental specialists, all of them expensive. Our grumpiness grew.

Then came the lump.

THE LUMP

At first I couldn't believe it; I checked repeatedly to see if my imagination was over-reacting. Nope, I was gaining a lump, cost free, in an area many women pay small fortunes to augment. Fear flooded my limbs and sped up my heart. Sleep was elusive. Memories of two sisters walking arm in arm past Genesis replayed: one young woman had heavy hair and the other was shiny bald. Would I have hair at Christmas? Could Justin come to join Sheena and Ron for my last months? Cremation or burial? There were ten days to endure before I could see a doctor who didn't speak English in a hospital where gowns and American modesty are silly, where cold-hearted men operate woman-eating machinery and female employees merely answer the phone.

Medical places and procedures make my knees buckle. On hospital visits I usually hold the patient's hand while sitting on their bed with my head between my knees. I dreaded my fear, so I asked four dear friends to pray. Providence arranged for North American visitors to arrive at just the right time.

My regular responsibilities were finished in a flurry of productivity before I ran to meet our guests arriving by train. With them in tow, I flagged down taxis already filled with tourists; I explained the Métro's secrets; we toured the rugby-crazed city by bike, tracking Ron's bare head as he wormed his bicycle through insane traffic. He blithely assumed we would follow. We dined at an exquisite French café and breakfasted in the style we love. I was completely preoccupied with the present and surprised by the happy heart that surfaced, plunged, and surfaced again.

Helga called unexpectedly and providentially from Italy. "Lorelei! The machines are fascinating. Have you ever asked the doctor how they work?"

"Helga, I am not having a conversation with a man while I look like a native on the French Riviera."

"He's a scientist. Do you know how many women he sees in a day? It's not the same."

"This is comfort?"

"Don't worry—big lumps are nothing to fear."

"I also have a small one; which tumor should I worry about?"

"Oh, this is normal for your body then. It's your age."

I carefully hoarded her reassurance and love. I tried to think of my lump as a natural implant program. I told Ron he should find a quiet, subservient woman the second time around—one who would bring him slippers, cook real meals every day, work in the nursery, and meekly say, "Yes, dear."

He was reassuring. "I'm not interested; I could have found her the first time around, but I chose you." He gently added, "I love you very much...most of the time." I held those words tightly.

Ron held my hand all the way to the doctor's office and waited with his arm around me in a hall filled with chattering pregnant women. My French evaporated; my brain detached. It didn't take

French to grasp my doctor's expression when the lump was located. Her eyes popped wide open. "Oh! C'est gros, très gros!" She left the exam room immediately to walk to her office and schedule an appointment in radiology.

It was a man who met me there; he declined to let Ron come with me and also declined my further requests for modesty. I consoled myself by mentally scheduling a series of prostate exams for him. "Would you prefer to speak in Eengleesh?" he asked me kindly. It was an immense comfort. Within minutes he shook his head; it was only a "keest"—a cyst was great news. The reassuring English was finished; French resumed.

This season of stress has exposed our flaws and frailty all too clearly. What a flawed, frail couple we are—so full of weakness. Perhaps this is so there will be no doubt. When something good happens here in Paris, when Ron and I love each other through each season, when our children still love us, everyone will know and say, "Look what God has done."

November: Visiting the Prefecture

Our Visit

Ron and I were required to visit our district prefecture this month. It's an odd, cement building that would have a beautiful view of the Seine River if all the windows weren't painted over in solid white. We were not looking forward to a solid hour of waiting in a grubby government building with carpets worn through to the cement beneath, no view, no daylight, a surplus of bodies and a shortage of chairs.

At nine thirty A.M. we received the number 589, bypassed the tiny elevator to run up some narrow stairs, and rushed across the mezzanine to see which digital number was on display. A large 514 could be seen above people's heads, so Ron was sure we could risk walking back to the corner brasserie for a leisurely espresso. I didn't need persuasion. When we returned thirty minutes later, the number had crawled to 530. Our North American expectations were showing.

Ron took the Métro home to pursue pressing work; I promised to call when our number got close. Time crawled. I perused my French novel. I played spy, trying to decode French conversations with thick, non-Western accents. I called Ron for higher entertainment; he was busy and said not to call again. I renamed the photos on my cell phone. I postponed our lunch appointment. I pretended not to watch a passionate foreigner completely lose it with the powerful bureaucrat behind the heavy glass. I was a foreigner too.

Ron returned at noon with only eight more numbers to go; by twelve thirty we had cancelled our lunch appointment. Then to our dismay, the red digital sign declaring 581 was suddenly turned off. A few people unobtrusively edged closer to the two open windows. It appeared there were some fresh folks being helped who didn't have numbers. We casually slipped in closer; I'd already waited three hours and wasn't about to wait three more.

"Watch. When people figure out their numbers aren't being honored anymore, the crowd is going to get upset." Ron's voice was low in my ear.

Some grim-looking faces left their chairs and started to form a line. Others sidled up alongside the front, not making eye contact, elbows out, furtively vying for better positions. When someone else was served without a number, the crowd popped.

"Hey! Do it officially!"

"Bah oui, my number's next! Serve me!"

People started to wave their numbers in front of the windows and any semblance of a line dissolved. The two sulky bureaucrats shook their hands and yelled, "We're not doing that anymore."

The throng pressed in closer to the windows, raising their voices, waving their numbers and demanding their wait time be honored. Ron shook his white, one-inch square flag numbered 589, calling for justice with the rest.

"Do it officially," they continued to yell.

"Call out the numbers so it's fair."

The officials ignored our pleas; they kept their heads down and dismissed us with their hands.

"I've been waiting two hours." The young woman beside me was mad.

I looked at her and proudly declared, "I've been here for three hours and thirty minutes." I was a winner without a prize.

The minutes slipped by very quickly now that the melee was underway. As Ron wondered if we were about to see a riot, the crankiest official took a few steps back and flipped the switch back on for the number system. People settled down; a policeman arrived.

Madame Grumpy complained, "These people are pushing up at the window and they need to get back, they're too close. They're too close!" She neglected to mention the numbering system had been turned off without any attempt to honor the precious numbers collected in the early morning hours. The tall policeman herded us into a narrow, windowless hallway, telling us to put our backs against the walls. Our half of the crowd obeyed, even as a couple with beautiful British accents complained of being treated like cattle. The rest remained where they were, silently watching the herding process. Just then, our number showed its desirable face on the red digital sign.

We didn't actually get to renew our visas; this was just the process to make our annual renewal appointment.

Bogdan's Visits

Our trip to the prefecture was merely an annoyance tossed together with a little entertainment; sometimes these visits have the power to deliver heartbreaking disappointment. For our friend Bogdan, the prefecture proved difficult; officials stalled, his work papers were delayed, and finally they were altogether denied. As a Romanian from the newest member of the European Union, he understood he had a right to a low-level work visa. Yet, his hopes of decent employment and a better life in France were crumbling. Even though monthly wages back in Romania were only around a hundred euros and rent alone double that, he decided to give up on a new life in Paris and return to his homeland with his wife and toddler son. However, this plan was blocked as well. Maria, his chic wife with swingy black hair and deep brown eyes was going blind. By now the eyesight in one eye was almost completely gone and the other was rapidly deteriorating. In their homeland, new glasses would be her only possible treatment; in Paris, doctors had already placed Maria on the urgent list for a cornea transplant. The family couldn't leave; the frustrated father was trapped.

One Sunday evening, toward the end of our church service, Ron called the couple with the adorable son we all cluck and coo over to the front. They self-consciously shared their difficult journey and Ron asked for people who cared about them to gather around and pray. Half the church got up to surround them. Our people became passionate about praying for them.

Later in the week, Ron got a call from an intensely animated Bogdan who had just visited the prefecture. As he stood in the crowd filling those halls on a daily basis, an official had walked through the flood of people en route to his office. He stopped, pointed at Bogdan, and said, "You! Come with me." In the office, the bureaucrat asked our friend what he wanted. The official left to get the appropriate file. After examining it, he asked, "Have you appealed this?"

"Appealed? I was told that isn't possible."

"Well, there's no reason for your work papers to be denied. You just need to appeal. Wait a minute. If I do this here, and this here...uh-huh...hmmm...sign this...initial here...and here...and here...OK, this is looking good. Initial here too. You only need a more recent letter from the boss who's going to hire you and you're all set to get your work papers."

Bogdan was stunned, exhilarated. What an answer to prayer! He called Ron to tell him the exciting news and we called others to pass on the amazing word.

The slender Romanian was flattened when he learned his prospective employer refused to write a new letter to the prefecture. Disheartened, Bogdan returned to the official—who surprisingly decided to use the old letter the prospective boss had sent earlier.

The young father now had work papers for the job he landed six months ago. Everyone was ecstatic. What a God-moment!

The young man with intense blue eyes went back to the person who was eager to employ him some months earlier, only to learn he had hired someone else in the meantime. The job was no longer available, the employer now disinterested. Since Bogdan's work papers were only good for that specific job, the slow process would restart with each fresh opportunity he unearthed.

God's fingerprints seemed so evident when Bogdan was plucked out of the crowd at the prefecture, but now, nothing—just more disappointment. The little family dangled precariously from a slim, almost frayed-through strand. We wondered what God was doing. How long would these friends have to live with unanswered questions? Many of us cried out despairing, pleading prayers. Maria contracted an eye infection. Even though she was number one on the donor list, no transplant would be possible until her eye healed. The infected eye wouldn't stop weeping; a rivulet of tears ran constantly down her cheek.

A Visit in the Park

The demands of parenting an active two-year-old continue to press whether life is heartbreaking or not. As Maria searched for an English-speaking playmate for her toddler son, she found a possibility through an association for English-speaking foreigners. The mothers soon arranged a rendezvous on a sunny fall afternoon in the Jardin du Luxembourg, a Parisian park of statues, formal flower gardens, fountains, and fenced play structures where the English-speaking moms and sons became quick friends. On the meandering trail of conversation, Maria mentioned going to church. Her new acquaintance told of wandering around and around this area the previous Sunday, looking for a church that was supposed to be in the vicinity.

"Really? My church is just outside the gates of this garden, on Rue Madame," Maria responded. "It's called Trinity International Church."

"That's the church I was looking for." A little shock registered in the new friend's voice.

Arrangements were made to meet the following Sunday, and Maria's new friend came with her to Trinity. The two women introduced their husbands and they dined together as couples. The new friend's husband inquired about Bogdan's employment and the fruitless journey was recounted. Bogdan explained dismally the futility of searching for another job; it would be the same story of waiting for work papers from the prefecture while the job disappeared to someone else.

The Prefecture Revisits Bogdan

The power of the prefecture showed up again in Bogdan's life. Unexpected mail arrived and inside the envelope lay precious, prized work papers good for ten years, for any job. Their arrival coincided with the husband of Maria's new friend offering our Romanian a promising job; Bogdan hopes to start work this week. Maria has now received word from her doctor; her first cornea transplant is scheduled for December 13. None of us can find adequate words to convey God's mysterious goodness.

As a foreigner in a place I don't always understand, my powerlessness confronts me regularly. Perhaps it's a disconcerting, poorly received gift to live where I constantly bump into my need of God. It keeps me in touch with reality.

L'Hiver—
Winter 2007–2008

December: Getting Together

WITH DEAR FRIENDS

A MAJOR TRANSPORTATION strike had crippled traffic, making Ron's erratic progress toward the airport most frustrating. With minutes to spare, he caught his flight to Berlin, leaving me behind to orchestrate retreat details. I stayed glued to the laptop from Ron's early morning exit long past the time Sheena stabbed the doorbell at seven P.M. Only two days were left to polish retreat plans, arrange Thursday's rehearsal, organize Sunday's service and be Sheena's study partner before we picked up Morris and Ruth at the airport. It had been ten years since we'd spent extended time together—I felt like a child anticipating Christmas morning.

Thursday, we squished our dear friends into our inconvenient two-door car's backseat and combed the St. Germain quartier looking for lodging with personality. Morris remembered a tiny inn with a lobby resembling a hobbit's home, hanging bouquets of dried flowers and herbs camouflaged the ceiling. The cash-only lodge was squeezed in among quaint, family-run boutiques in crooked buildings on a very narrow street. The price was right, if one could live with midnight hallway hikes to the toilet and a shuffle to the shower up some stairs and down another corridor. Morris and Ruth collapsed into their swaybacked bed as Ron and I moved on to Genesis for a music rehearsal.

What a pleasure to flaunt Paris to friends who saw us marry and watched our babies grow! It didn't matter which of our favorite cafés or castles we sampled. It was enough to share our passion with this couple that understood us, talking for hours on end as we huddled over café crème and thick hot chocolate at sidewalk cafés.

With Sister Churches

Every year our French denomination has a complicated, convention-like gathering. It revives girlhood memories of formal 1960's conferences in Vancouver's Queen Elizabeth Theatre, minus the organ. Ron spearheads the music for Journée Fraternelle, though coordinating music charts and lyrics for a French gathering is a stress test for any Anglophone. His painstaking diligence was rewarded at Saturday morning's practice by exuberant musicians from sister churches. After the rehearsal in Genesis' twelfth-century stone basement, the band migrated upstairs to the ground floor and stepped into the bustle of Trinity's monthly Café Connections. The pastry selection had already thinned badly as people came and went in unpredictable waves. Conversation and the rewashing of miniature coffee cups continued until mid-afternoon when Ron subtly turned off the lights. We finally evacuated friendly Genesis to introduce Morris and Ruth to authentic French onion soup at a historic tea salon around the corner.

Early on the Sunday morning of Journée Fraternelle—earlier than any self-respecting musician functions—our drummer left his warm bed downtown to catch a train to south Paris where he parks his car. He drove back to the city center to pack his cumbersome drums, then headed out to Paris' west suburbs. Ron collected gear from our fifth-floor apartment and its "cave," the storage room at the church, and Genesis' basement. I stood by, delicately, marveling how his skinny back survived, wishing we played harmonicas.

Traffic was good to us; the band set up efficiently. Unfortunately, the soundman, a mandatory requirement for renting the auditorium, was less good. Connecting each instrument to the house system proved to be a puzzling process for the "professional" soundman. Time ticked on. We stood by our instruments while the singers parked beside empty mic stands. The minutes crawled by. The sulky technician was not open to suggestions. I longed for coffee.

Our drummer disappeared, but we were unconcerned; a sound check was hardly imminent. Microphones worked and then were exchanged for others that didn't. We remained on standby, mute, waiting on pudgy Napoleon at the soundboard.

Our young drummer reappeared, carrying a tiny plastic cup of espresso now pressed into my eager hands. His eyes were troubled.

"Here—I found coffee at a gas station. It's not bad."

I felt like a well-loved queen.

He continued with his charming French accent. "I asked some of the organizers working upstairs if they knew where I might find coffee. They said, 'You don't have time for coffee; besides, it's Jesus who raises the dead.'" He paused. "You know, I have more trouble with Christians than non-church people."

"I'm so sorry," I said as I looked at his small, hurt face and thought about the heroic effort he expended to participate. I thought of his family connections to Islam. I was irritated, but what could I say? My own culpability itched in the background.

The service began late, without a full sound check. Mics quit functioning. By the end, only the tenor's harmonies rang out strong and clear. Our saxophonist's mic was dead from start to finish. I wasn't pleased. Afterward, there was equipment to repack and return to Trinity—set-up for our evening gathering loomed. This was going to be a two-cup espresso day, maybe three.

WITH OUR PARIS FAMILY

A full week of meetings with our colleagues followed in Le Mans. We rushed home Friday evening to address last-minute retreat details. Saturday morning found us outside the church we rent. By seven A.M. Sarah, our intern, and Marcos, my lunch chef, were already on the sidewalk waiting with overflowing handcarts. We were anxious to get started but…the doors were locked. We made small talk in the drizzle, wondering when the great, wooden doors framed by iron gates would open. While Ron repeatedly pressed all the available buzzers without response, Marcos told us of arriving the day before with a heavy load of groceries. He was informed Trinity hadn't booked the church.

"You've got to be kidding!" Marcos had exclaimed, "There's going to be sixty-five really disappointed people lined up at this door tomorrow. Check again."

"No, no, no. There's nothing on the books; your church has not reserved the room."

"Look again. I know the room was reserved by Ron."

After some time and dispute, the concierge's face cleared. "Oh, wait. This book is 2006, let me check 2007. Here you are; go ahead."

Marcos shook his head. "This locked door is no surprise; my whole week's gone like this."

Our quartet stood outside the giant green doors until a buzz sounded arbitrarily at seven thirty-six A.M. We had entry. Tables swirled around the dining hall, angling for visibility around the pillars. Sarah artfully arranged tablecloths she discovered in bohemian northeast Paris. Myriad candles and white twinkle lights, fresh flowers and vases with rocks appeared—people were startled by the enchanting transformation. It set the stage for good surprises all day long. The excitement continued to build as more people came. The band moved in and Sarah cheerfully draped the drums with more mini-lights, the breakfast team brought the promising scent of coffee, the media group erected a techie paradise, and my adrenalin kicked in. After breakfasting on perfect croissants, we dived into energetic worship and paved the way for Morris and Ruth to begin.

As the day progressed, new connections were forged, souls were stretched, and some found peace with Jesus. A new understanding of working grace was forged for many of us. We feasted on the joy of simply being together. The day was everything I hoped. I woke up Sunday morning knowing there was another service to pull together with an overworked band—yet savoring a rich sense of contentment. People were eager to return, to have Morris ambush them with grace one last time.

WITH SHEENA IN VIENNA

The following week we flew to Vienna to support Sheena in her final volleyball tournament. I had found tickets for sixty-five euros. Ron had booked a cheap hotel hoping it wasn't in the red-light district. We arrived in a storm, just beating the delays plaguing air traffic later in the day. The wind turned our umbrellas inside out, right side out, and inside out again, repeatedly. The cold, pelting rain came in sideways and our sightseeing extended to the black undersides of our umbrellas. Our noses competed with the rain for saturation points. Ron's dogged determination to experience Vienna was satisfied by exploring the cozy apartments of Mozart and Freud, and indulging in schnitzel with sauerkraut.

Being the mom of an athlete is agony. I don't experience this kind of tension doing a concert for three thousand; then too, bystanders don't usually shout out running critiques during a music performance. By the end of three days of competition and criticism, I was drained. Sheena was the captain of an undefeated team; not one set was lost. Our hard-working redhead was elected to the all-star team. Now it was time to return to everyday reality; the cheap return fare required getting up at three thirty A.M. on Sunday. After waiting in a freezing Austrian shelter for a train that arrived forty minutes later than Ron's German had grasped, we were zipped efficiently to the Vienna airport.

I thought at five twenty A.M. the airport halls would echo with emptiness; instead, we joined an overflow crowd standing in neat, immobile lines. Flights were delayed; there was a distinct lack of seating. The constipation continued until eight forty-five A.M. All computers were down; eventually, tickets, boarding passes, and passenger lists were laboriously handwritten. Ron suggested this was the moment we paid for our discount tickets.

We made it to Paris in time to go directly to a rehearsal for the evening service. The team straggled in, the demands of the previous intense weekends on a small pool of musicians showing. With the three thirty A.M. rising, I had difficulty jumpstarting my engine. How would church go?

When the church's leaded glass windows are silent in the dark winter night, the candles glow warmly and the room feels safe. Our Trinity family shared pieces of their journeys, recounting challenges and encouragements, answers to prayer, and the effects of the retreat. My soul began to fill just from being with my community. In spite of our fatigue, an intimate moment was framed within the chapel walls.

The next week, a debilitating transport strike hit France hard; the unions were serious about taking on the government. There were no Métros, no trains, no buses. It was as disruptive as heavy snow in Florida, creating world-class traffic jams that added excruciating, nail-biting hours to one's commute. People walked hours to work, taxis made record profits, and our drummer's employer housed his employees at a nearby hotel. Bikes took an unprecedented surge in popularity in spite of the robust cold and rain. Ron and I had the nerve to enjoy the strike; it ensured a refreshing rain of sweet solitude. It's important to be alone—for a while—but getting together with people we love refills our tanks. It keeps us moving in the right direction, regardless of strikes.

January: A Foot Outside the Church

SOUND

Like everything else in Paris, the campus of the Catholic orphan foundation is old, not American-old, where time is measured in brief decades, but European-old, where time is bundled by the century. Roads grumble under the weight of time, broken patches breed puddles, steps dip, paint peels, and no one seems to see.

My German friends tried to buy tickets for the concert we came for, but none were available until seven P.M., the time the concert would begin. They wandered among the outdoor Christmas booths and sparkling trees while I continued my search for Ron. The campus boasts a cathedral recently housing a vertebra of Mother Teresa during a two-week festival. Despite the disturbing medical imagery this conjured, the chapel's beauty stole into my soul, quieting its chatter. The soaring edifice felt silent; spiral windows were lit, announcing the glory of someone, or Someone.

Ron worked in this grand stone cavern all afternoon, setting up mics, cables, speakers, and endless cords while solving complicated feedback problems for Antoine's gospel choir event. I saw Ron loving the contact with people outside our church. He reveled in the concreteness of his technical task, the ability to resolve a situation and have it stay fixed. There were children and youth choirs to serve, plus a lyric soprano from the celebrated Paris Opera. She splashed the evening with contrasting color.

The famous opera singer went through quite a metamorphosis between rehearsal and performance. Faded jeans were replaced by a rich red dress that was exquisite, iridescent, and occasionally plunging, depending on where her silk shawl slid. She stood erect with perfect posture, one hand resting lightly on the yawning grand piano. Sound charged out from an unnaturally wide-open mouth displaying both finesse and eyebrow-raising height. Although I was completely impressed with her skill and fame, an urge rose to imitate her (as children, my sister and I had mastered opera mockery, our Sunday afternoon's entertainment). Unlike my rousing childhood performances, there were neither fits of giggling nor chiding from the audience; the opera diva's performance was framed in perfection.

Then the children entered. They wandered to their places, stray lambs with sheep dogs, lost as soon as guiding hands reached for another shoulder. The littlest ones were distracted by dust-mites they reached for in the shafts of brilliant light. A few made "rubber" arms while the smiling soprano sang Christmas songs with them, their clean T-shirts slouched beside her sweeping evening gown. Her prowess lifted their raw, innocent exuberance.

The teens arrived, adding mega energy to the children's choir. The music began to pump. On the sidelines, Sophie stood quietly rocking a teen mom's baby. My eyes absorbed the happy contradictions of note-perfect opera alongside improvised gospel, stone echoing cordless mics and youthful freedom bounding alongside disciplined control. I spotted Trinity family among the audience, like proud parents, enthusiastically supporting Antoine's and Sophie's work with the abandoned children. It was all good, so good—especially the handsome soundman.

WEDDINGS

Ron gets another occasional foot outside the church by performing weddings for English-speakers who dream of marrying in Paris. He has performed ceremonies in the garden under Notre Dame's shadow, on a bridge over a shy pond by the Eiffel Tower, in elegant French salons, and at one famous, legendary hotel. I went to that one—couldn't miss the professional harpist, the intriguing guests, or the gourmet feast of finely tuned courses finished with a pyramid of caramelized cream puffs.

Ron enjoys his quiet talks with couples and the chance to be Jesus' hands and feet to them. During his interview with the last bride and groom, the conversation took an interesting twist.

"You had a civil ceremony where?" he asked.

"In Michigan, just last week. Our friends don't know we've come to Paris; we wanted an intimate, private service here," the bride said.

"Have you come to Paris before?"

"I have, he hasn't. I think it's so romantic, the perfect place to get married."

"How long have you been together?"

"About six years."

From the shallows of small talk, Ron steered the ship toward deeper waters. "And what made you decide you wanted a religious wedding?"

"It's going to be religious?"

"Well, I am a pastor. It is what I do."

FOOT IN MOUTH

No, no, wait; this wasn't the funniest conversation Ron had lately. Our neighbors invited us to come to their home for another fabulous French dinner. Ron asked if there was anything we could bring—well, that was his intent.

He actually politely asked in French, "Is there anything we could wear?"

Our polite neighbor said, "Nothing, just bring Sheena."

PHOTOS

Ron loses himself when he takes his camera for a walk; he forgets all about the church-weight he carries on his shoulders as he focuses on framing one little piece of the world that will then stand still forever. I thought it would be delightful to spend an evening driving with Ron around the cluster of old-world villages that form Paris, capturing Christmas photos. I imagined the romance of twinkling lights, decorated trees, and well-swagged streets, laughing together and savoring one of those "I'm-so-in-love-with-you" evenings. What movie had I been watching? Normally when Ron takes his camera, Sheena reaches a point where she exclaims, "Do I need to take that thing away?" Both of us accidentally tap our impatient feet while Ron lags far behind, playing with his shutter box.

So my love and I were out on a clear night, brittle with cold, the streets over-parked with no place to even semi-legally leave the car. He began on our tree-lined boulevard where one line of white lights snakes up and down each treetop ten times, outlining five crooked fingers. My eye saw uplifted, arthritic hands marching down the street; Ron's eye saw something else. It fell to me to baby-sit the black Saab®, which Ron double-parked, leapfrogged onto a sidewalk, or stopped in a traffic lane. While he skipped away to deliberate on best angles for the shot, the hazard lights ticked, perforating holes in my brain.

I had forgotten how long it takes to adjust a camera—to stand in silent reflection, to readjust the camera, to cast about an eye, to wait until the traffic passes by, to meditate, perhaps to pray—before depressing the button, before depressing me.

I took a few shots of my own with my phone. It took me about four minutes in total; Ron needed two and a half hours. But then, his photos of the Champs Elysées aren't divided by a windshield strut or partially obliterated by side-view mirrors.

CHRISTMAS

Trinity gave the kind of normal, creative Christmas program that tenderizes tough hearts and celebrates Jesus, the original Christmas child. With only sixty-eight minutes to set up a sound system, rearrange pews, hang hasty decorations, run through morsels of music with scattered musicians and cue readers and a dancer, time was squeezed like fresh orange juice. I didn't feel so fresh.

A young Nigerian with a high, clear voice and inspired improvisations led a pulsating, irresistible "Go Tell It on the Mountain." He was as timid as a small, wild bird, until he gripped the mic and stepped in front of the audience. He opened his mouth and all heaven broke loose, lingering on into the night.

The following Sunday afternoon, a Christmas open house filled a festive Genesis with food, folk, and conversation. Good connections spread at other dinner parties that kept me chopping in the kitchen and freezing in lines at the outdoor market. It was more than worth the effort since it's over low-burning candles and clinking silverware that my dear international family abandons its reserve.

That reserve continued to melt in the notes we received. People with backgrounds of atheism, church abuse, perfectionism, New Age belief, the occult, and communism wrote:

"Thank you so much for helping me to let Jesus enter my life. I can tell you that the 12 Steps have helped me to look at myself in a different way. I am grateful for this. Thank you to be here in France with us."

"I've never been a part of a church where one could be so real."

"Since I started coming to your small group, I feel like I'm on vacation. Time has somehow expanded."

"I feel like a stone fell off my heart."

May Jesus lift the stones from all our hearts.

February: Bateau [bat-oh]: n, boat

DROWNING

Technically, the church building on Rue Madame isn't ours until four P.M. on Sundays. Since the French-African congregation that rents it before us often winds down by three-thirty, we often tiptoe then into the lobby. Drums, guitars, keyboards, amps, speakers, soundboard, Bibles, easels and signs—the whole kit and caboodle are loaded from a storage room on the first floor into the elevator and shipped to the second floor. Every week a sound system, projector, and computer are reinstalled. Tables are dragged out; a wide array of candles and strategic swaths of fabric help distract attention from the residual mess.

If there's a large enough team.

If people arrive on time.

If the French-African church gets out by three thirty.

If there aren't any technical difficulties.

There's just enough time to be ready by five. It only takes one of these fragile "ifs" to falter and trouble is crouched on our doorstep faster than you can say, "Lord Jesus, son of David, have MERCY."

Yves let me know early in the week, "I can make it to Thursday night's rehearsal but the service is questionable; I'm picking my wife up at the airport. If everything goes smoothly, I can make it to church by four P.M."

"No problem. We'll set up the drums for you; just come when you can."

An airport run can take from forty minutes to three hours; it is an untamed, unpredictable animal. Some songs would sag sadly without his dynamic rhythms, but we could flex. It would be OK.

Friday, I learned Antoine would be working on Sunday; he hoped to arrive between four thirty and five to plug in his guitars. No problem; he was so capable; it could work.

Sunday morning our dancer called in sick. It was disappointing; she would have portrayed the song "Empty Me" in an unforgettable way. I could let it go; no problem.

As I prepared plates of choice cheeses and deli meats, packed up pickles, nuts, and fresh baguettes and carefully cushioned favorite platters into my rollster for a leadership meeting after church, it dawned on me: My un-notified small group was responsible for the coffee hour and kitchen clean-up, also after church. I was caught between kitchen duty and disappointing Ron. Crankiness knocked sharply on my door and I let her in. Ron suggested a short nap before we took off for church. I complied with relief.

About half way to church, cruising down the quay alongside the Seine, Ron gasped, "I think I left my flash drive in the computer." He'd clocked a lot of time on his PowerPoint®—it was a great asset. I stretched to the back seat to grab his satchel and search with anxious hope; other essentials shuffled around my blind hand, but no flash drive. I dumped the bag out; still nothing.

"We have to turn around and go back," Ron insisted.

"No, no, no, I can't be late—there won't be a leader there, no one to unlock the storage room door and fire up 'the launch.' You have to take me all the way to church and then go back."

In good traffic, missing the weekly Paris rollerblade parade, traveling one-way takes thirty minutes. If he hit the parade, he would be stalled another twenty. At present, it would take him another fifteen minutes to get me to Rue Madame. It was three ten.

We argued, or had a spirited exchange of ideas. Ron urged me to get out immediately at the Eiffel Tower, near an inconvenient Métro stop. It wasn't one of his good ideas. I insisted he take me all the way to church, go home, and come back. Ron wasn't indispensable to the set-up. He knew his music; he could miss the preliminaries. By my calculations, he would be back at church by four thirty—with thirty minutes left to prepare.

At church, the team was loading the elevator when Earl sent a text message. He had just returned from England on the Eurostar® with his guests—guests who desperately needed diapers for their baby. As French store organization is profoundly puzzling for American minds, Earl needed to help them locate this specialty item. He wasn't sure what time he could arrive—would we set up the keyboard for him? Our Nigerian songbird headed down the stairs to find the keyboard and stand.

Three inexperienced vocalists were on the team, all unfamiliar with the set-up routine. Cables were mysteries; music stand assembly was a riddle only mechanical engineers could solve. The singers worried, "Will we go over the music?"

"I hope so."

Meanwhile, everyone heard it—the dreaded screech of feedback driving needles through our ears.

Two mic stands were missing. Ron couldn't sing and simultaneously play bass without one. I had time to search while the feedback continued to throw a fit. Down the stairs I scurried, hoping to find stands hiding in the storage room. Four broken pieces lay in a corner. The saxophonist offered to hold her mic for Ron during his solo.

Back upstairs, the rebel sound system screamed each time the calm soundman turned it on. Earl, Antoine, and Ron, the experienced band members who could have helped troubleshoot—they weren't there.

People were beginning to fill the square chapel. I saw guests arriving—guests with their first impressions—while speakers on their skinny portable stands threw another tantrum marked by shrill screams welcoming the brave.

It was the first Sunday in our little Paris church after our Christmas holiday in North America. It was a Sunday back-to-back with those just spent in large, impressive, grade-A churches. I saw our sputtering rowboat half sinking, the crew bailing water urgently, against the recent backdrop of a beautiful, sleek yacht, sailing smoothly to its port. I pushed the image firmly away; it wasn't helpful.

Moses came upstairs with a keyboard I'd never seen before; I wasn't sure we had cords for it. "Let's find another," I suggested as we ran the stairs again. Moses spotted the blue case for the needed keyboard near the ceiling, fifteen feet overhead. A ladder was found. Cords were not.

"Lord Jesus, son of David, have MERCY."

Our beloved drummer arrived, breathless, hair uncombed, focused. He settled into bringing order to his drum set. Earl sauntered in, the essence of cool calm. Nothing rattles him. I wouldn't mind so much if he weren't incredibly gifted as well. The first time I heard him play piano, I looked at Sheena and said, "Shoot, I'm jealous." Fortunately for me, Earl's genius is wrapped in unassuming generosity, making it easier to confess to the envious green troll sneaking around my heart. Earl put his head together with our tall soundman, both studying the uncooperative board. Antoine arrived, quickly setting up, tuning.

The heartless clock crept on, twenty minutes before five, with us still not ready to make music. The saxophonist came to tell me, "You know, no one has arrived to set up a laptop and run PowerPoint®. How will people sing without lyrics?"

As the sound system continued its protest, it was evident: a run-through would not happen.

"Lord, have MERCY!"

I tried to be careful not to leave dead bodies floating in my wake.

Ron walked in the door. His jaw tightened as his eyes took in our obvious dysfunction; normally music is going full tilt by this point, two-thirds of the songs reviewed. After a hundred minutes of intense city driving, our un-progress was not lighting up his face. Rather than preparing his music, tuning his bass or collecting his thoughts for the sermon, Ron turned to collaborate with the soundman.

Ten minutes before five, PowerPoint® Man flew in, unflustered and efficient. He was up and running by five—but failed to see the flash drive Ron had driven all the way back home to get and to then carefully place on the computer.

"Oh Lord, mercy, mercy, mercy..."

And yet, and yet...our leaky rowboat had an inexplicable fishing expedition that quirky evening. On the first song, one which would normally inspire the rocks to cry out, the vocals were so out of balance, I winced—very unprofessional. The rocks were crying, but not in a good way. Front-row, redheaded Sarah caught my agonizing eyes and laughed as she rolled her own. Ron made hand signals to the soundman. I hate that—only obnoxious gesturing musicians do that to their vulnerable soundmen—but I loved him for it that crazy night.

Jesus didn't seem to mind any part of our leaky boat; He didn't jump ship though our tippy vessel was taking in cold water on a wild sea. The evening had elements below my eager expectations and below previous exhilarating experiences in well-equipped, well-staffed, well-oiled auditoriums.

As Ron and I wound our way home late Sunday night through quiet Paris streets, we couldn't resist the tempting critiques. In the nick of time, we remembered how fatigue doesn't allow us to see the good and give it the weight it deserves.

"Let's not talk about anything that went wrong tonight, OK?" Ron said. "Let's wait until Tuesday...or next year. For whatever bizarre reason, in spite of everything, there was a wonderful spirit tonight."

"People really entered in."

"So crazy. Unexplainable."

We went home, warmed, contented. This is our boat, the bateau we madly love.

I recall reading about Jesus sailing in another boat on another stormy sea. As He reassured the men with him, He wanted to reassure me: "Peace, Lorelei. Be still."

I was busy, desperately bailing water. All I could hear over the crashing waves was my own voice: "Do you care if we drown?"

Forgot to listen. Again.

Leading Worship at Trinity

Le Printemps— Spring 2008

March: A Reliable Forecast

THE DEAL ON DIRT

NEXT DOOR, DISAPPOINTING cement walls rose noisily over the winter months, progressively blocking our salon's windows. The view of the street is long gone; the sky has mostly disappeared. I miss the fluorescent sushi sign of the Japanese restaurant below and the warm sprinkle of lights stretching into the distance. If a view was to be blocked, we would prefer it be the one from our kitchen window, where naked neighbors occasionally flaunt their toned bodies.

Ron improved our salon's view by cleaning out the winter debris from my overabundant collection of planters on the balcony. Sacks of over-drained dirt were hand-carried through our apartment, into the elevator, and to bins seven floors below. I volunteered to go to Bricorama and buy fresh soil. Ron simply instructed, "Fill the cart, hon."

The best deal on dirt was a 40L bag + 10L gratuit. I put one in the cart and thought, *That's not heavy; there's room for more.* I slid another off the stack and slithered it into my caddy's mouth.

The second bag refused to go all the way in, flopping like a dead body hanging half out. I tried to move the cart and realized I'd just made a bad call—it was too heavy to maneuver. I wrapped my arms around the bag and gave it my best Olympic lift. It didn't budge. It lay there, comatose, stinking like a whole herd of cattle crap, and now I did too. I was not pleased to be the sack's Siamese twin, its bulky head becoming one with my hands as they gripped the cart handle. I started down the boulevard, rolling 100L of foul dirt and then realized there wasn't any way I could make it up and down the Métro steps—I didn't have enough muscle to push it up a lip in the sidewalk. The cart was so heavy we wove an unsteady S down side-roads. Though I desperately tried to avoid the dog ka-ka, I could turn around and see the drunken S we drew on the cracked cement.

I panted all the way home, cursing my wool coat, intermittently phoning Ron for help. He was contented, preoccupied in our elevated backyard, patio doors closed. The cart bumped behind my legs. I pushed it unsteadily in front of me. I stopped to gasp for oxygen. Energetic children ran through a plaza like wild yo-yos moving to and from curious parents who stared as I staggered by.

I dragged on, the sole Parisian not wisely carrying child-sized servings of dirt for a few modest geraniums. I shrugged it off; anything was possible in the radiant sunshine after a month of dreary rain. January's forecasts had been depressingly accurate.

A Reliable Forecast

January 9 was the gray morning when Jay Lee softly explained over a stiff decaf laced with steamed milk and one sugar how she and Ying couldn't continue living in Paris in light of their financial reality. After two years, business hadn't developed and debt was mounting. They were giving God until January 31 to pay off their debt; if He didn't, they would move back to Singapore. I understood. I opened my hands to let them go, sadness drifting in like a bleak fog.

My Poster Twin in the Paris Métro

Within a week, Ying reported three old Singapore accounts had made overdue payments and new work was coming in. It all added up to thirty percent of the required total. Graphic design work, something new for them in Paris, also began to emerge. Wet January days drizzled by and nothing more developed. Nothing. Continued clouds and cold rain were the only reliable forecast.

MEDICAL EXPLORATIONS

During the same gray month Jay Lee appeared to be leaving, Ron's tooth and hole-in-the-jaw problem required two-hour surgery and Sheena severely sprained her ankle. She was pinned to her bed with intense pain, immobile, unable to sleep. A visit to the hospital was unavoidable. After repeated, futile efforts to find a route not marked "Emergency Vehicles Only" and reversing back down plugged lanes, we asked for directions from the guard at the hospital entrance...again.

"It's marked!" he snapped, waving an arm in the direction of the maze plugged with illegally parked vehicles.

Ron snuck the Saab® down the "Emergency Vehicles Only" road; we were having an emergency and we were in a vehicle. He boldly parked alongside doctors' vehicles. The sprain cost us a cheery fifty euros and five not-so-cheery hours in Boulogne's hospital emergency ward where the yellowing paint peeled and faded notices curled off the walls. Ambulances bled an almost non-stop river of patients—except during lunch. No lines were evident. A "closed" sign sat on the abandoned counter. We caught on eventually to the unspoken contest: discrete but aggressive patients were admitted first, though ambulance-riders leapfrogged over everyone.

As Sheena waited out a third hour with her elephant ankle swelling to new proportions, a young woman arrived by ambulance, flat on a gurney, one shoe removed, a dainty foot exposed. She won immediate admission behind the curtain. Within the hour, she was examined, x-rayed and returned to the holding pen. We watched a starched lab-coat inform the lady her skinny foot wasn't broken. She leaned down, put on her pointed high-heel, and marched limp-less out the doors. We continued to wait.

When Sheena was finally taken to an exam room, she spotted a used, bloody gauze lying on the floor; the orderly furtively rolled her wheelchair directly overtop it. Our competent doctor was a brilliant ray of reassuring sunshine. A lime green mini-dress peeked out from her lab coat; her funky athletic boots were ready for medical marathons. Sheena quickly learned to declare she didn't speak French in beautiful French; it allowed one parent by her side at all times, even in the forbidden x-ray room. After diagnosing a severe sprain, the doctor prescribed an air-cast and medication in the morphine family.

None of us thought to be vigilant about taking the pills on a full stomach. So on the day of our long-awaited prefecture appointment, the appointment we waited three and a half hours to make four months earlier, Sheena was overwhelmed by her body's rebellion against a tiny capsule on an empty stomach. We missed our date to renew our visas and hurried back to the prefecture the following day, praying for grace. The cost? A five-hour wait plus a lecture that included a demand for a note from the doctor. I was a child again…with wrinkles.

BACK TO THE FORECAST

In the downward spiral of Ron's surgery, Sheena's sprain, and French bureaucracy, we met Jay Lee and Ying for lunch on January 30. I was heavy-hearted. My hands were no longer open.

I tried a little marketing for God. "Don't you think, considering all the grace God's given you, you could give a little grace back to God, and extend His deadline?"

Jay Lee was quiet for a moment. She gave it serious consideration. I held my breath, hoping. Then she swept her shiny sheath of hair from side to side. "No. I said January 31. If we're supposed to stay here, God can do this."

I pouted and took a poke at God. "My God isn't big enough to supply the remaining seventy percent by tomorrow."

The proprietor was charmed by Ying's enthusiasm for her café's cuisine. This is the Singaporean who once savored each bite of his crème brûlée, shutting out conversation with closed eyes, declaring, "This brûlée is better than crack." The café owner was delighted by Ying's Asian-accented French and beaming face.

Everyone loves this couple. Jay Lee and Ying are a reliable river of grace in our church. They're the spine of administration, graphics, and technical support; they are quietly passionate about prayer. Ron and I felt the weight of a great loss as we left the café.

Outside, our umbrellas were useless against the heavy wind whipping the rain sideways. We ran for the Métro.

At ten o'clock on January 31, our telephone rang. "Buon giorno!" Only Ying greets me in Italian. "A film proposal from Singapore just arrived; it will more than cover the remaining seventy percent." He laughed. "I guess we're staying!"

And I said my God wasn't big enough. It bothers me that I said it out loud. It makes it too challenging to pretend I am like those who firmly stated, "I knew this was what God would do all along." I'm bothered that I'm bothered.

A bouquet of brilliant blue days followed; friendly flowers waved from our greening balcony. Sheena braved the stairs—the elevator was stuck between floors. Our old Saab® earned a prize packet of stamped documents, having passed the arduous Contrôle Technique inspection. Ron showed me the island behind Notre Dame whose inviting charm and stone buildings wrapped us in quiet romance as we wandered its back streets late one night. Jazz piano drew us deeper into the island like a pied piper enchanting children. Those euphoric weeks were interrupted by an email from Singapore, where Jay Lee and Ying had several photo shoots during February.

"Ying and I heard through the grapevine that the big film client also asked for quotations from some of our peers. That is quite worrying."

What? This wasn't a done deal? The sensational last-minute miracle was actually…not?

Jay Lee ended courageously. "We'll see. I think if God has brought us this far, He should be able to bring us further."

I now had a second chance to walk in faith, no matter how ragged and uneven. So I asked God if He would lend me His—after all, fathers love to rescue their children when it's truly for their good. Didn't Ron chauffeur Sheena to school through the Paris rush hour because the Métro stairs were insurmountable with her sprain?

Some days passed before Jay Lee replied to my panicked note. "Ying and I were surprised too that there were other people quoting for the job. We walked home troubled by the fact that our quotation had expired and no news was heard. So we decided to wait. Today, at dinnertime, Ying got a text on his phone for us to resend our quotation. The job is confirmed!"

Ying says he's a cynic—he'll believe it when the verbal yes becomes a hard-copy signature.

He wrote from a bench in front of a McDonald's® where wireless and sweat flow for free. "In January, my faith, or what I thought was faith, died. In its place, a new seed was planted. I am not sure what it is, but it's something different. It says that God loves us, regardless. Through these two years, many things have changed in my life. My need for fame—it's completely gone. I don't need it to complete me anymore."

Now there's a forecast I can trust. Every day of this unpredictable life, God's love will shine—uninterrupted. It's a love big enough to complete us, strong enough to carry each wounded lamb, bright enough to light our darkness.

April: Perspective

DINNER ON THE STREET

It felt like a party; the room vibrated with teasing and chatter. Freshly baked baguettes were sectioned and slit, waiting for cheese implants from pregnant Ruth who sliced pounds of it while hunkered over a low coffee table. There were no latex gloves or stainless steel counters, just skinny patio tables wobbling on thin legs. Crews hovered, constructing traditional ham and cheese sandwiches stuffed with spicy Dijon, crisp butter lettuce, and ruby red tomatoes. Eager hands filled bags with yogurt and plastic spoons. Soft fruit and a dessert landed alongside the sandwiches. Our intern, the brain behind the festivities, reminded us to take our time, to linger and visit out on the streets. I secretly longed for the drop-and-run method; Jesus only mentioned giving a cup of water, not my whole night.

Our team headed over to Place St. Michel where we met Hugo and Natalie holding court between two bank machines near the famous fountain. My partner, Chehung, squatted comfortably beside them and asked about their health while pouring hot, sweet tea with perfect balance. I silently calculated how many lunches we had left to distribute—it was bitterly cold and my feet were beginning to bond with the concrete. I pulled my scarf tighter and hugged my long wool coat close. It was a bad night to be out on the streets. Chehung gave a pair of gloves to Natalie, who lifted her striped hands to the sky with child-like delight. She and Hugo were happy for the lunches that looked so generous at Genesis, yet now seemed so meager.

More street people materialized. One young man, unsteady on his feet, put his hand on my back and leaned in close. My eyes sought out Chehung, my small protector, who weighs substantially less than me.

"Madame," the weaving man's breath was heavy with the scent of sweet liquor, "you have beautiful eyes." He immediately looked less threatening.

I continued moving around, handing out meals and starting to converse a little too benevolently. Wait. Were those angels chanting? Nope. Only me singing my own praises.

God forgive me for becoming lost in my own "goodness."

FRANKLIN ROOSEVELT STATION

The hunt continued for homeless people on the streets and plazas and under bridges. In the bitter cold they had left the streets for the relative warmth of the train tunnels. I saved my last two lunches for a woman at the Franklin Roosevelt station. She works a late night "shift" on the underground platform, asking passengers to spare some change. Over the years her kisses have become wetter and have moved from the cheek district, by my ear, nearer toward the mouth region. I resist wiping them off while she's looking. I spotted her halfway down the platform, staring into the distance, her thick glasses unnaturally magnifying her eyes, her gray hair pulled back neatly in her standard ponytail.

Her eyes brightened as she saw me approach; the kisses were soggy, farther from my ear than I preferred.

"Bon soir, Madame, how are you?" I asked.

"Ça va, ça va, and how are you, ma chérie?"

"Très bien, merci. I came tonight wondering if you would like something to eat." I offered my last two sacks, hoping I wasn't offending her.

She was startled, silent for a moment. "Weekdays, there is a man who runs a snack counter and gives me leftovers. But on Saturdays and Sundays he is closed. I haven't eaten today."

It was nine thirty P.M. She hugged the lunches close to her chest. When she realized I wasn't grabbing the next train, she swept her arm toward the institutional platform chairs set in a military row as though she was inviting me into her living room. My companion had taught French in Morocco in a previous life. After her Moroccan husband died, she returned to France, out of sync with both worlds. Her daughters remain behind with the Arabian families into which they married. She rents a small bedroom and begs to supplement her spartan stipend.

A Métro rumbled in the distance and I made moves to leave. More kisses were squashed onto my still damp cheek by the delightful woman I had so carefully ignored when we first saw her four years ago. Back then she had shouted at us, incensed by our indifference. I had been anxious, impatient to escape on the next Métro. Now she was someone I cared about.

ON THE STREETS WITH RON

Two Saturday nights later, Ron and I were together, our team again in search of Hugo and Natalie at Place St. Michel. A lengthy conversation sprang up between two of our teammates and the charismatic Natalie, who excitedly explained she was in a rehab program and clean from heroin for two months.

Ron and I ran out of conversation with Hugo who felt the pressure to keep "working"—potential clients were leaving the cash machines while we chatted. Ron and I moved on.

"That old guy looks homeless." Ron pointed to a stooped man whose pant legs exposed his ankles. His once sophisticated coat now looked vintage Salvation Army. Was it coolness or poverty?

Should we offer him a lunch? We followed him nervously, well-meaning stalkers. We hesitated; he could be offended by our incriminating offer. Our courage turned-tail and ran. As we turned back, Ron spotted a young man nervously sticking out his hand, embarrassed as he asked for money. He appeared, hmmm, hand-some; could he really be needy? We watched. He looked defeated and lost on the narrow cobblestone alley fronting several cafés.

"Good evening, Monsieur. Would you like a lunch?" Ron asked.

At first glance, everything looked so normal. Nice cord pants, a handsome sports coat. Even the homeless dress carefully here. Coming closer revealed the clothing's frayed age, the tattletale holes and an unfortunate odor.

The young man's gentle spirit caught me by surprise. He clasped our lunch in both arms, too polite to eat it while we were still there. The unshaven Frenchman told us he had come from Strasbourg to Paris in search of work. His profession was rigging—working the catwalks high above the stage of sophisticated productions, setting lights and cables. He'd first found work in Paris at a restaurant a year ago. The owner often paid in promises and, after six months, the restaurant disappeared, along with the owner and the wages owed the young man. Unable to break into the tight rigging com-munity, here he was, hungry and on the street. One glance at his hips ascertained they no longer filled his pants.

"Here, please take another lunch. It will still be good tomorrow," I said.

He was quietly grateful. We gave him a card for our church and invited him to come. There's always warmth, hot coffee, and a snack afterward, if nothing else.

LUNCH AT THE LANDMARK

Two days later, I traveled with my Brazilian friend to an imposing stone edifice capped by a soaring landmark steeple. It was the famous church Rockefeller gifted to Parisian expats. My friend and I climbed four flights of winding marble stairs to an enormous apartment with fifteen-foot ceilings and leaded glass windows overlooking the Seine. The graceful bridges looked more romantic from the perspective of the luxurious manse than from the improvised tents beneath them. I was there to read my

Baguette stories at a copious lunch flowing over more square yards than we could graze our way through in one ambitious afternoon. Wide, southern accents described where to find fabulous barbecue in Raleigh and peanut butter in Paris. With Giselle close by for security, it almost felt comfortable. It was easy to give more than a cup of water.

Giselle praised our modest church that meets in a borrowed building not blessed by Rockefeller. She invited people to come, and she gave directions, even while the prestigious pastor's wife hovered nearby.

Afterward, my friend and I walked briskly along the stormy quay, almost blown off the bridge by heavy winds. I couldn't help but laugh. "Giselle, I don't think they invited me to read my stories so I could woo people away from their church."

"That's OK, Lorelei; you do your job and I'll do mine."

"I was disappointed how normal it all was. No story material there."

"You thought it was normal? It was bee-zarre. I visited Amereeca without leaving Pareese." Her Brazilian-flowered English was as beautiful as her chic hat and boots. "And the lunch! Verrry strange. It was so, so meexed!"

"Ah, mixed. Yes, well, that would be the 'luck' part of potluck. Some meals are less lucky than others." We caught our Métro, and before parting, lightly touched one cheek to the other under the brim of Giselle's hat.

May: Ground Floor Grocery Stories

One Year Ago, March

Last March, the early days of the month sputtered by without the arrival of a paycheck. At first my sparse cupboard inspired floury flurries of robust creativity; but by the fifth, my ingenuity seized up, gasping for oil. I scanned the vacant cupboard, hoping to jumpstart my imagination, but no edible inspiration coughed to life—only science experiments involving vinegar and soda. I could no longer avoid visiting the ground floor grocery in my building to scavenge a few supplies, even though it meant resorting to an American Visa card—an option we're reticent to use.

"Madame," the cashier's French broke into my brooding, "your Visa card doesn't work."

"What? Of course it works. Try again; you probably just swiped it too fast." I watched him push it slowly through the narrow slot. Repeatedly.

"Ça ne marche pas," he asserted curtly. Those are unfriendly words when dinner is hanging on the line.

"Try this one." I fished out my American debit card. This card game wasn't over yet.

He slid it through, forward, backward, stopping to clean the magnetic strip vigorously, slowly, quickly. No rate of speed produced a cure; people bunched up close behind me, penetrating my personal bubble.

"The cards are American, Madame," he stated brusquely.

"They've worked here before," I insisted. I was desperate, bolder than normal.

The dour cashier called his supervisor and while we waited, the queue continued to swell, stretching back into the freezer section. I easily understood the whispered French moving down the line: "Her card won't pass." "Her card won't pass." My face burned as twenty pairs of eyes seared tiny, smoking holes into my profile and twenty pairs of ears cocked to catch every comment. The supervisor finally appeared, repeating the same, futile tricks the cashier had just performed. This was her best shot? She shook her head firmly. "No, Madame, these cards don't work here."

It didn't matter how often I had successfully played these cards in the past. Today was more of a board game kind of day, as in a Do-Not-Pass-Go, Do-Not-Collect-$100, Go-To-Jail kind of day. As I put the two American cards back in my wallet, the supervisor spied my French debit card.

"But Madame, why don't you use your Carte Bleue?" Her penciled eyebrows rose into her hairline, her eyes wide with surprise. "It's French—the kind that does work here!" She was incredulous; the solution was obviously in my hand all along.

"Eh, no, actually, ehhhh, it, eh…" my French skills melted under heat. "In fact, ehhh, normally, ehhh, it doesn't work—today."

I left the meager pile of groceries on the counter and walked out of the store, empty hands swinging by my side, forty eyes following me to the door.

I don't remember what we ate for dinner, nor do I remember how Sheena managed for lunch the next day. It's blissfully repressed. I do remember walking three tiresome blocks in the rain to the next closest grocery store for a week. I also remember our mission implementing a pay advance on the twentieth of each month after this incident. It was their best shot.

This March

Spring passed, summer flew by, winter blew in and out, and it was March again. I took the stairs to the ground floor to pick up a few items—strawberries, feta, pine nuts, and rocket greens. I was constructing my favorite green salad with a balsamic vinegar, olive oil, and Dijon mustard dressing for company. Being the middle of a Saturday afternoon, few people were in the store and only two lanes were open. One was for the privileged "rapide" customers—a club I have yet to be invited to—and the other a regular "non-rapide" line.

The cashier's seat in the "non-rapide" lane was vacant. She was at the end of the lane, helping an elderly woman with snow-white hair load groceries from the store's cart into her caddy. It was progressing slowly. I settled into the wait and watched them, enjoying the gentle kindness the graceful French-African woman was showing the grandma. As I watched, I noticed one of the old lady's legs was severely burned. The skin seemed to be badly deformed, almost as though it had melted and run down her leg in rivulets. Pictures of Hiroshima victims came to mind. Something wasn't quite right. Her thick brown hose were darker on the burned leg. Then I noticed that the "burn" had run onto her shoe.

The puzzle teased my eyes until clarity exploded: the elderly lady's waste management system had erupted in an untimely fashion and she was oblivious. I wondered why my nose hadn't identified the problem. As the woman began to slowly shuffle toward the door, the air shifted and I caught a whiff.

Oh, my. Oh! My! All was abnormally silent; cashiers froze as they stared into their cash drawers, unable to count change, avoiding eye contact. When the glass doors slid open and then shut, the normally mute employees burst into animated conversation. The chubby man who couldn't make my Visa® card work a year ago went berserk with a can of aerosol, emptying it with fervor, giving the problem his best shot.

MONTH-END

Within a few weeks, the end of March arrived, bringing its habitual, month-end financial pressure. I realize we are hardly unique in this tension. My stress is downsized as I remember Madame D who is unemployed, Ying and Jay Lee, whose miracle film project has fallen apart, and American friends who are being wiped out by the housing crisis. Regardless of how my peculiar difficulty ranked, it was March 28 and we had company coming for dinner. As I faced grocery shopping, it provoked raw concern for Madame D, Ying, and Jay Lee.

"Please, God, won't You give me a sign? Tell me You haven't abandoned us." I whispered whiney prayers as the elevator carried me to the ground floor where I hoped to uncover the makings of a dinner worthy of a thoroughbred Frenchman.

I first saw our guest at Antoine's gospel choir Christmas concert. Lucien sat ramrod straight on the piano bench, playing with flawless precision and tone as he accompanied the opera diva. Nice tuxedo. I was impressed; he was a professional musician, from the very top shelf of Paris' finest. After telling Lucien all about our church, Antoine and Sophie reported the pianist was intrigued with Trinity; he wanted to come. I thought he was being polite—who could say no directly to Sophie's sweet face? Yet there he was; Lucien was sitting in the audience when Antoine led worship in January. He came again a couple weeks later, and then he became a regular.

Lucien became part of our music team, reliable, and more than a little helpful. At the end of the Easter service, I heard this incredibly fantastic music going on behind me—rocky, wild, inspired, funky jazz. I turned around and there was Lucien, the refined classical pianist, pumping it out on the piano with the band flying energetically behind.

"I play for..." He named a successful rock band with many enthusiastic fans. He also plays jazz, Dixie, and swing at Euro Disney, arranges symphonic music for operettas, and gives solo classical concerts—what couldn't he do?

Now I was at my ground-floor grocery, remembering love is communicated to the French by the quality of the meal. We had thirty euros left until the next payday. I bagged my carefully chosen dinner items.

"Twenty Euros and three centimes, please."

I handed the cashier my last three ten-euro bills.

"Madame, do you not have any change at all?"

I checked again, but the wallet was stripped bare, denuded. "No, nothing—see? It's empty."

"Why don't you cagnotter?"

The word was new to me; I grabbed a guess out of the air and handed him my Carte Atac, the store's fidelity card. Voilá, a ten-euro bill was returned.

"Madame." The normally irritated man took the receipt from my hand with kindness and pointed to a number at the bottom. "This is the credit you have earned with your Carte Atac. It's the same as cash."

"It's the same as cash? Really?" my voice was higher than normal. So were my eyebrows.

"But of course."

"I can use it any time?"

"Any time."

"I don't have to pay some money or buy something special?"

"No, Madame. This is just like cash."

I looked at the number at the bottom of the receipt—eleven euros and twenty-five centimes. God did care! He supplied us with another eleven euros to carry us to the next payday. I couldn't wait for the elevator and instead ran up the six flights with my small sack of groceries. Ron heard me panting at the door and opened it before I could get out my keys.

"Ron, God just did something for us...," pant, pant, pant, "... we have another eleven euros to make it until we're paid again. He's going to take care of all of us, He really is."

The evening with Lucien was unforgettable. He arrived at nine P.M. with an extravagant bouquet and relaxed with us until one thirty A.M. The conversation spun in a tantalizing mix of French and English over a meal whose delights were "magically" multiplied. Of course, we had a lot of questions about his life as a Parisian musician and he had a lot of questions about The Way of the Cross, our interactive Good Friday exhibit. From the light-hearted to the spiritual to music—round and round the evening danced. Lucien wandered back often to muse about his strong experience at The Way of the Cross.

Our gentle friend is on a journey, and we get to stand on the sidelines, cheering him on. Such evenings are priceless.

I've been thinking about negotiating a deal with my grocer: one priceless evening in exchange for one month of groceries. Sounds generous to me. Even if I gave it my best shot, most people would call it a long shot.

L'Été—
Summer 2008

June: Stars—Michelin and Otherwise

LUCILLE AND OLIVIER stood waiting by the door as Ron and I pulled luggage from the Saab's® trunk. Though Olivier is old enough to be my father, he insisted on carrying my bag up the steep staircase to our suite where white lace curtains fluttered at the open windows and pooled on the floor. Crisp, white paint freshened the airy bedroom; an apricot loveseat invited us to curl up and read in the corner. Unlike the irritating screams from motor scooters thrust into high speed from low gear outside our Paris apartment, only the choir of birds, the chatter of a happy three-year-old, and an occasional sedate sedan in the distance drifted through. Our batteries immediately began recharging on arrival.

Appetizers were served in what had been a plumber's workshop for a century. Original stone walls and floors and an enormous table of heavy beams exuded history. Olivier waited on us as though rare royalty lounged on his sofas while I did a gauche, un-French thing—I asked my elegant host questions.

Olivier grew up in the Caribbean. He wasn't the carefree child of a sunny, palm-studded beach; his island recollections are dark. His father left early each morning to work in a bank and didn't return until late every night, under the influence—way under. His mother's remedy was Mass every morning, religiously followed by tarot card readings. Olivier recalls the house and foundation shaking without cause—other than the black magic his mom imbibed. Wanting to escape the everyday heaviness of his young life, Paris became his destination at the age twelve. At twenty-one, Olivier sailed The Liberty to New York City.

"My first American job was at the French Hospital as an arder… arder…"

"Orderly?" Ron guessed. "Someone who pushes people around on gurneys?"

"He's still pushing people around," Lucille teased.

"Do it again, Mummy." A little voice clamored for her attention.

"Orderly, yes," Olivier continued unperturbed, watching the busy child. "From there, I got a job at the United Nations, delivering their mail. I never had to pay taxes." A smile flitted across his gentle face. "In time, I discovered the working world of high-end French restaurants. I was really good at it. A waiter has to know how to be entirely invisible, and then appear just as your table needs something, without asking."

The child climbed Lucille's legs using her arms as rappelling hooks. Reaching her waist, he jumped down, calling, "Do it again, Mummy, do it again."

"Last time." She patiently smiled at his eager face, abandoning a tantalizing chocolate batter.

As our wandering conversation continued, Ron glanced at the pitcher of orange juice; Olivier rose to fill it wordlessly. The laughing child ran circles around the warm kitchen. "Watch me, Mummy, watch me!" He had big green eyes and blond curls that bounced off his head at all angles. His mom paused in her risotto and roasted vegetable preparations to congratulate him on his fine circles.

"One can make a lot of money working at high-end restaurants. That's how I bought my house, my cars. But I was a bad boy." Olivier hesitated, then confessed, "I chased skirts and drank too much booze. I was an alcoholic until I quit smoking."

Eventually, Olivier headed to Florida. At the time, there was only one high-end restaurant in Orlando with the coveted Michelin star.

My questions turned to Lucille, who graduated from high school at fifteen, setting her sights on a world-renowned culinary school. In New York, she noticed how much fun everyone else was having and, though raised in a Christian home, selected a vacation-from-God option. A married man and drugs were part of her holiday package. After graduation, she headed home to Orlando where there was only one high-end restaurant with the coveted Michelin star.

The young American chef and the debonair French captain met under that celebrated star. Captains weren't allowed in the kitchen—only lower-level waiters entered the back work area—but once Olivier discovered Lucille, the captain made excuses to loiter in the forbidden chefs' domain. Olivier found Lucy and God irresistible; his intuition sensed freedom from his relentless darkness and an authentic love lying cradled in their hearts.

So the elegant Frenchman asked Lucille, "May I buy you a cup of coffee?"

"I don't drink coffee. But…I do eat steak," was Lucy's blunt reply.

A French pastor, his wife, and their four children arrived at the bed and breakfast on our second evening. La Madame was correct, from her Versailles French to her impeccable manners; Le Pasteur was stern, from his stiff "good evening" to his imposing silence. We began Lucille's exquisite eating experience with garlic and dill-stuffed shrimp, accessorized with a ruby necklace of puréed pepper sauce. As I picked up the shrimp delicately between my fingers and took a polite bite, I locked eyes with the French Madame. Oh, horrors! I was holding a shrimp in my now-buttery hand, caught with half in my mouth and half between my fingers. One never, ever eats with primitive digits in France. Not even pizza. The severed body was whipped to my plate and silverware grabbed with Olympian speed; I guiltily ate the rest properly, leaving a disappointing chunk of meat behind.

Conversation started and stopped in awkward, uneven spurts for me; it was easy for Lucille who was relaxed and in her element. Olivier glided behind us silently, anticipating desires, doing his invisible routine admirably.

I found the minister intimidating—his God was serious. His children were delightful.

My newfound allies informed me they loved to read "star life."

"As in astronomy?" I queried.

"No, as in brrrah peet."

"Brrrah peet?" I was puzzled.

"You know, brrrah peet and parrree eel-toe."

I rethought their French, turning it over and around in my head. "Ahhh, Brad Pitt and Paris Hilton?" They crowed at my pronunciation, laughing as they tried to mimic my English.

The next morning, Ron and I hid in bed, waiting until the overhead footsteps on the fourth floor faded, car tires crunched on gravel, and the house was quiet. I hopped down the stairs, hoping story time would continue.

During Lucille's vacation from God, Olivier had his first Protestant church experience. She took him to the impressive church where she had grown up. He was shocked to see people carrying Bibles; he grew up before Vatican II, before Catholics were allowed to own a personal copy. Wayward Lucille bought him one he read from cover to cover, wondering what all the fuss was about.

"So what brought you back to God, Lucy?" I asked.

"The teacher always learns more than the student. Olivier asked questions; I searched for answers. He embraced the truth for himself and inspired my return."

"And then?"

It was Olivier who answered. "Lucille told me she wouldn't marry me without her father's permission. So I asked her dad. He said no. Just like that."

"Mom and Dad weren't overly enthusiastic about me marrying someone older than my father," Lucille said.

There was silence. Olivier asked if we wanted more juice or another French press. He rose, eager to serve, less eager to talk.

"And so?" I prompted.

"Months later, her father said to me out of the blue, 'OK, you can marry her.'"

Olivier and Lucille were the perfect couple to serve the ultra-rich; a world-class butler and chef in one superb parcel. They worked at a Connecticut estate where an independently wealthy man and his wife spent their weekends. Lucille received $1500 every weekend to prepare meals for two—twenty years ago. The grocery budget was increased for guests. Henry Kissinger was a regular from down the road. A helicopter and private plane stood ready for others.

"It wasn't good for me," Olivier mused quietly. "It's too easy to habituate one's tastes to the fine things of life."

After the isolated Connecticut countryside, they selected the orbit of another multi-millionaire. Neurotic obsessions, delineated on exacting sticky notes, wallpapered the multiple mansions Coleman and Maybelline built. The good life was not all good.

The spinning of stories stopped when the pastor's family returned. The daughter perched on her father's armchair, playing with his bouffant, pulling out strands of hair to stripe his forehead. He sat still, holding her hand; I glimpsed a tender heart crouched behind his stoic mask.

Breakfast the next morning was my last chance to catch the end of our hosts' story. The couple felt called to ministry, so Olivier bought a classic 1975 Honda® Gold Wing even though he had never ridden a motorcycle. They biked throughout the U.S., Canada, France, and Italy, their possessions in two saddlebags, their memorabilia in a van stowed on Lucille's parents' yard. For over a decade, they built, repaired, cooked, and served with refined Michelin skill, enabling pastors and missionaries to continue their work.

The pregnancy came as a landslide shock. Olivier already had grown children who had children of their own. The motorcycle would not accommodate life for three. An aging house in a

Burgundy village was miraculously purchased and renovated. Now their stars beckon from a bed and breakfast they designed for a unique ministry in France.

Their little boy jumped from one couch to another in the remodeled atelier (workshop), calling, "Papa, Papa, watch me!" He bounded unsteadily from one precarious cushion to the next, Olivier's eyes following his precious son.

My host mused softly, "I wasn't there for my first family. Like Paul, God gave me a second chance. Every day I watch my dear son and see the grace of God running barefoot through my home."

I asked another question. Olivier dropped his head into his hands, bowed almost to the table, and said, "Oh, no, not another question. Please. No more."

A month later, Ron and I returned with a van and a car packed with my Tuesday evening small group.

"Why did you choose this place for the retreat, Lorelei?" one of the group asked.

The question had been repeated often during the protracted trip in endless, weary, weekend traffic. But from the time we drove down the narrow alleys of Arcey-sur-Cure, alongside rock fences and stone houses colored with climbing roses in full bloom, from the minute my friends were shown their generous suites furnished with donated antiques and down-filled duvets, from the moment we sat down for dinner at ten-thirty P.M. and gasped over the extraordinary food Lucille fashioned with whimsical artistry and Olivier served with lovely dignity, the question never resurfaced.

My French friends taught me to eat shrimp with silverware finesse while the South Americans and Scandinavians barraged Olivier with the inevitable questions he attracts. Jay Lee listened with big eyes while Ying shot art photos of the food. The four-story home with rooms tucked into surprising corners provided an irresistible air of invitation as we digested truth from the misadventures of Moses. It was a weekend to tuck deep in my heart, where it will perfume my France memories forever.

Thank you, Olivier and Lucille. Thanks also to our Father who can transform all of us into stars shining in the darkness.

July: A Seed Collection

I.

An artist trundling along in a Paris train spied a passenger reading in English. "What's the name of your book?" he boldly interrupted. A discussion developed around the volume by John Piper.

"Where are you headed?" the artist eventually asked the visiting professor.

"Trinity International Church."

"Mind if I tag along?"

The artist encountered a room full of warm hearts singing passionately. He was touched by the service and by a pastor he saw taking a journey alongside his people. He stayed long after the physics professor from Pittsburgh left, waiting to talk with Ron.

"What do you do during the week?" he asked.

"I prepare next week's service, handle administration, meet with people who have spiritual questions…"

"So just the people from your church, I suppose."

"No, anyone who is searching spiritually."

"That would be me."

They met on the sixth floor of a store where banks of windows overlook an eclectic tangle of rooflines. In spite of the lofty view, the sandwich bar is inexpensive by Paris standards and one only has to buy a thimble of espresso to secure the table for an entire afternoon. The artist's story began as a spiritually hungry teenager falling into the tumultuous 1960s on the UC Berkeley campus, losing his faith.

He had questions.

Some seeds waken after decades of dormancy.

II.

I also trundled along in a train, talking on my phone. My French encouraged a stranger to break the usual code of silence.

"Your book is in English?" she asked.

"Oui."

"It's about one's interior?"

"Oui, oui."

"It's for children?"

"Non, non. It's for adults."

She was captivated by the ideas in *Changes That Heal*, so as I neared my stop, I offered her my copy, quickly inscribing my email address and apologizing for the heavy markings. She was surprised, pleased; I was exhilarated.

The next day an email arrived. "The book is about God. Please take it back."

We met, we kissed, and the offensive gift was placed back into my hands.

Some seeds are carried away by invisible winds.

III.

Giovanni found Ron practicing with the band in Genesis' basement. The quiet Colombian waited patiently for Ron to pack up his bass. The two climbed the stone stairs together, leaving us behind to continue rehearsing while they dined on fine French food next door.

The men seated themselves at a narrow table; the exuberant proprietor explained the fresh daily specials with flair. Once roast duck on a bed of puréed potatoes was ordered, Ron settled in to hear more of Giovanni's journey.

"After growing up in a close family of twelve, the loneliness during my first years in Europe was crushing. I walked into a Swiss church and asked to see the priest. He wasn't available. I bought a sandwich, sat on a park bench, and cried, 'God, my heart aches. If You are real, please give me a sign that I'm not alone.' Within a few minutes, a little bird came and sat beside me. I gave him a crumb; moments later there were a dozen gentle creatures nearby. The church secretary found me and insisted I take some money, realizing I could barely afford the simple baguette and cheese. I was touched by a profound sense of God's presence, but all was forgotten when I met a beautiful woman.

"Some years later, when all was ready to immigrate to Canada together, she told me to move out. I lost my love, the opportunity in Quebec, and my Parisian home. My studies were finished and I didn't have a job. In desperation, I prayed again. Work and an apartment materialized quickly, unnaturally. It had to be Him, so I began searching."

The meat was a warm memory, dessert a lingering taste, and now demi-cups of espresso steamed before them—Ron's a decaf with two extra shots of hot water. Between sips, Giovanni's saga continued.

"I was in a Paris neighborhood café when I heard the magic of a Colombian accent. Sebastian invited me over for tea. He didn't waste much time bringing up Jesus."

Sebastian was the untamable son who had distressed his mother. She had taken him to the Catholics, then the Mormons, and finally to the Jehovah's Witnesses, hoping someone could rescue his wild soul from destruction. A decade later, Sebastian was one of the first to initiate Trinity's turquoise wading pool. There was some difficulty immersing his lengthy, cross-legged frame under the baptismal waters. It was Sebastian who brought Giovanni to Trinity.

A month after they met, the tall Colombian asked the not-so-tall Colombian if it wasn't time to trust Jesus. Giovanni had responded, "Not yet. I have to work on my life some more first."

"And Sebastian said…?" Ron prompted.

"Even our pastor isn't perfect!"

Giovanni grinned while Ron threw back his head and laughed, cherishing the words.

"Sebastian said my life would never be good enough and that was the whole point. It's about the goodness of Jesus, not my own. You know, Ron, I searched for God in the cathedrals of Europe but

I didn't find Him there; I found Him in the warm hearts of people at Trinity."

So the wading pool with the bright blue lining was inflated once again, Sebastian taking care all Sunday afternoon to make the water warm.

Some seeds fall on fertile soil tended by loving hands.

With Sebastian, Ron and Giovanni

IV.

Lucien was deeply touched by The Way of the Cross exhibition at Genesis during the Easter season. He stayed long past closing time, saying nothing as he left, soberly kissing both my cheeks, then quietly disappearing into the night. A few weeks later, he and Ron tested the Moroccan café a few doors down from Genesis. Over couscous with raisins, the men discussed difficult spiritual questions. The French pianist told Ron he couldn't resolve how Christ's death on a cross could pay for his sins. Nonetheless, Lucien was already family to many of us.

I loved to watch Lucien close his eyes during rehearsals, breathing in the song lyrics, storing them in his soul. He soaked up the garlands of love our musicians showered on him—long dinners, concerts, late-night conversations over a glass of wine, singing side-by-side... Some Sunday evenings he played piano solos carefully chosen for the space they created to reflect on Ron's words and prayers; his tender soul created wonderful moments for all of us.

The Sunday night Giovanni recounted his "bird" experience, Lucien listened intently. After church, sitting in front of his computer, the musician listened to the worship music he downloaded after learning new songs at rehearsals. As an image of a cross appeared on the screen, barriers evaporated. He sensed God with him. Tears overcame him for two hours as he wept by his computer, overwhelmed by God's presence, knowing he would never be alone again.

A few nights before we left Paris, Lucien treated us to a sumptuous dinner on Île Saint-Louis. Our friend tipped his head and raised a shoulder as he softly explained, "I don't know how Jesus' dying on the cross works. It just does. My guilt, my constant anxiety, they're completely gone."

Some seeds fall on rocky soil, enduring heavy traffic, until a gentle hand replants them in a safe place.

V.

I met Helga for coffee at Odéon Café where we sat beside expansive patio windows, soaking in the rare sunshine. Important, hard conversation flowed. The waiter interrupted to make us move our coats off the neighboring chairs uncomfortably close to ours. The table was pulled out and a young woman cautiously inserted herself without tipping our water glasses. Our new neighbor studied her books intently. I discreetly checked to see if she was listening, but her head was buried. "She probably doesn't speak English," I reassured myself.

An hour later, I carefully wormed my way between tables to the sunshine outside, and then into the darkness of the Métro station. It had been a heavy "heart-to-heart" and Helga was pensive. I waved one more time after pushing through the turnstile.

The phone rang as I unlocked our door forty-five minutes later. Helga was energized. "Lorelei, I only had an hour before my next appointment, so I went back to the café. The girl beside me said she couldn't stop listening; her life circumstances are incredibly similar to mine. She thought we seemed open and asked who you were—she wants to know if she can meet with you."

I was taken aback. She *had* been listening! "If she comes to church tomorrow night, I'll talk to her afterward," I said.

The service had already started when Helga arrived. The chapel was full so she shoved aside a bundle of jackets on the front row, asking people to make room for her and "the eavesdropper," who looked uncomfortable, with arms crossed and a demeanor much like Helga's two years ago. After the service, we headed to the remote hinterlands of the balcony. I don't know what well-watered seed was planted, I only know God placed the Harvard student beside us in a crowded café where her ear couldn't resist the music of English.

Some seeds fall outside our view.

VI.

Our friends flew back from Asia finally able to admit to God they wanted to stay in Paris and pleased to have won the miracle film contract that would make it possible. So it was painful and confusing to receive news of the project's cancellation two weeks after their return. Was God powerful but disinterested in small lives? A dark period descended; then things got worse. Jay Lee's sister was believed to have Dengue fever. The menus they had produced for an upscale Chinese restaurant fell apart; the printer didn't care. Much worse, it was visa renewal time.

The official was crisp. "Since Sarkozy became president, the rules have changed. You must show an income of 1300 euros per month, per person."

Ying's face remained expressionless at the time, but later his dismay showed. "Twenty-six hundred euros every month! That's a lot of money, man! But she said we could include our Singapore income, so we should be OK."

Our prayers rose and their prospects fell. The specialist who managed their visa case broadcast further gloom. "The prefecture informed me your Singapore income isn't admissible. My Japanese client who averaged 1100 euros per month in France was rejected."

Our friends' French profit-line hovered at zero.

Later, over Jay Lee's delicate, hand-made sushi, the couple revealed how different their Parisian life was from their home culture. As we reclined comfortably on the floor around a low table, they shared their fear of losing their newfound freedom and grace if they returned to their old matrix. They didn't feel released from their call to Paris.

The couple entered the prefecture halls for their final rendezvous, knowing only God could open the door. The official was antagonistic.

"What are these papers?" He ripped out the staples angrily, flipping them over his shoulder.

"Our income statements from Singapore."

"Inadmissible." More staples flew over his shoulder. "These documents aren't originals. Unacceptable."

"In Singapore, we go online to print documents. Everything is computerized."

"The rest of the world may use Internet copies, but that's not how we do it in France." A few more staples took flight. "Your income is inadequate. The law requires a couple to make 2600 euros per month. What's this? This photo is not acceptable."

"Actually, it's the same photo I used last year," Ying stated matter-of-factly.

"Unacceptable. Your face is too large." He got up from his chair abruptly. "I will speak with my superior."

Jay Lee and Ying trudged to a photo booth where Ying cheered himself by repeatedly pushing the retry button. He laughed. "My face is too big to fit in their outline. I move back to get it all in, but my head hits the wall."

Jay Lee, ignoring our teasing, said, "When we returned, the official stated, 'Your income must improve this next year. Pick up your visas on July 11.'"

She laid her head on my shoulder and I put my arm around her. All four of us sat motionless, awed by God's miracle. Then hysterical laughter bubbled back as we imagined the frustrated photographer stabbing the retry button over and over in the photo booth.

Some seeds, well rooted in good soil, are harassed by thorns and drought.

August: The Tale End?

An American Event in Paris

Sheena finished school in a flurry of decidedly American events. Graduation plans filled mealtimes with dreams of grandeur and worry. Which shoes for which dress for which grand gala?

"I remember my outfit," Ron said as he leaned back in his chair at dinnertime, recalling his flowered shirt, white tie, and double-knit polyester blue blazer. I described my long hippy dress with floppy sleeves and pink butterfly print.

"You wore that...in public?" Our teenaged fashion consultant was horrified.

I continued, unperturbed. "As I swept down the stairs for grad, my brother was testing his new fishing rod. The line flew, my date arrived, and the hook unraveled my skirt and my confidence. Both were fragile."

My graduation memories are rather homemade, involving my mom bent over a sewing machine, a school gym, and a hockey arena; Sheena's are sophisticated events in fine, Parisian settings. Six hours of academic and sports award ceremonies on Thursday were followed by an elaborate prom with lavish pre-events the day before. Standstill traffic clotted major arteries; police officers, police vans, and military buses scabbed minor capillaries. Bridges were barricaded, the city twisted into a tight tourniquet. Why? It was George W. Bush. His last presidential fling in Paris also caused our graduation speaker to scurry away prematurely, not willing to forfeit a formal dinner with a head of state.

Saturday was the grand finale. We were accompanied by Sheena's brother and our French friends, Madame and Monsieur D. Though Monsieur D. teaches economics at the university level, they had never attended a graduation ceremony—French diplomas simply arrive in the mail. As we walked through a heavily wooded park, over a bridge spanning a hidden pond, the path rounded a corner and we emerged on a lawn crowned by a magnificent monument, fountains, and the music of a French horn quartet. The graduates milled around the edifice honoring WWI American aviators who served in the French air force. Madame D. gasped. I saw beauty, Ron saw musicians—she saw something else.

"Gowns. They're wearing gowns? They are wearing gowns. Jacques, regarde! GOWNS!" Her hand covered her mouth as she gaped in amazement. They absorbed every detail with wide-eyed attention, memorizing acronyms ranging from IB and AP to NHS and ASP. After the ceremony, all was recounted over a feast of French delicacies served in billowing white tents. The event became note-perfect when our friends spotted unmistakable glass bottles alongside the traditional French wines. It was Coca Cola, Jacque's favorite.

How could I leave these people for a year? My heart won't be whole on one continent again. So many memorable names we've left behind...

Anne Marie, Anna Marie, Anna Maria, Anne Maria
Marie, Marie, Marie
Marie Pierre, Marie Claude
Mari-a, Mari-ose, Mari-oh
Tea-Bow, Tea-Bow, Tea-Airy
Sharl and Magali
Veek-tor and Oo-go—not to be confused with Veek-tor Oo-go.
The names inspire a rush of tale-end memories.

MARIE SOPHIE

Marie Sophie and I sipped coffees in the sophisticated business district where two old-world buildings are linked by a glass atrium generously sprinkled with statues keeping watch over lush gardens. Umbrellas graced the tables; expensive heels swung from legs crossed nearby. We lingered after lunch, willing the noon-hour to last a little longer, sneaking peeks into rich conference rooms dressed by King Louis's decorator, stopping to pass through frequent security card and fingerprint checkpoints. I checked out the plush ladies room, getting lost on my return as all the doors matched the wooden walls.

My friend grew up in a church prescribing a strictly regimented route to God; doubts were disdained, questions forbidden. As an adult, she decided to fashion her own way to God, not wanting to abandon faith altogether. Marie Sophie had tried and left churches where there was much disapproval and little patience for someone who questioned Jesus as the only way to God. She took quiet note of marked differences between churches of the same orthodoxy, concluding they did some designing of their own as well.

Marie Sophie, while in my small group, often prefaced her comments with, "Well, I'm not a Christian, but…" She often grasped a concept before others, leading the uphill hike to honesty. After finishing off the group's study with bread, cheese, and chatter, we usually rode the Métro home together. Over the incessant clacking of the rails we leaned in toward each other to speak quietly.

"I admire your consistent discipline in listening for what I believe is God's voice," I said during one of those rides.

"What you call 'God,' I call my 'inner compass,'" my friend clarified.

At our small group's retreat, the tragedy of the Salem witch-burnings came up.

"I probably would have been burned," my lovely friend commented softly.

I've thought about her assertion often since then. It causes me to pray our dialogue will continue, to pray I will listen well, and to pray she will not be "burned" by the devout again.

GRACE

Sebastien found me after church and asked me to pray with someone. He led me to the back corner of the chapel where I met a lovely girl sheltered by the summer shadows. I learned later my wild hair melted her defenses, the curls reminding her of a professor who had loved her well. Her pain came tumbling out. Torment showed in her clear blue eyes. Tears flowed. I learned she was romantically involved with a young woman.

I listened and finally responded by explaining only God's love could fill the aching hole in her heart. I believe His love comes first, before anything else. I also believe some relationships are too close, putting a human in a center designed only for God. For Grace, it happened because she didn't know she was precious to God. Like many of us, she hadn't experienced His kind of love and acceptance—first-hand or through the hands of others. I offered to work through a book with her on building healthy relationships.

Over the following weeks, Grace eagerly ate up everything. She read. She wrote. She reviewed her old journals, finding the head waters of her river of pain. Multiple chapters of the book were digested at a time. I insisted she wasn't a worse sinner than anyone else. My greed was just as hurtful to God as her putting a woman in the center of her life. Replacing a woman with a man was not the answer either. We talked about how much time it was taking for God to deal with my desires for more. Brokenness takes time to mend.

Grace was tenderly supported by Sebastien and Angelle, our music ministry administrator. The church family quickly became mothers, brothers, and sisters to her. Angelle included her in the worship team. I loved to see Grace's earnest eyes as she sang, sometimes shining, sometimes brimming with tears, often closed. My last week in Paris, Grace was transfixed with the story of the Samaritan woman and Jesus' response to her. She understood the feeling of not being worthy. She couldn't even whisper the words, "I am precious to God."

Grace wrote me recently, saying, "My sense of unworthiness drove me to impress people. I think this is a problem that lies deeper than my relationship. And it explains why I put a human in the place of God...I did not know God yet."

When my friend learned Jesus wouldn't move into her life without being asked, she invited Him to be her center.

Grace's short internship in Paris was over all too quickly. A few weeks after I left France, my petite friend moved back to her homeland. When she was found sobbing one day, wanting to go to church but not able to bring herself to walk through the doors alone, Grace's girlfriend offered to go with her. So it was that Grace found a church where they sing the same songs she learned in Paris, a church where Jesus continues to sing His love songs over her.

Helga

Helga's roommate situation was desperate; she needed to get rid of one and find another. With the first daunting project swept out of the house she asked God for an immediate replacement.

"Lorelei, he's terrific. Turkish and totally different than the last wretch."

Helga sensed my reluctance to endorse her new flat-mate. I interrupted her articulate arguments. "Helga, you don't need to persuade me to agree. Trust me to disagree and to continue loving you the same."

The Turkish roommate was fascinated with Trinity; he came to services, small groups, and Ron's seminar on relationships with the opposite sex. He had many profound questions. Helga agreed to let him join us for dessert during our last dinner together. She had selected a café with a hobbit's warren of inviting stone rooms and wavy lead-glass windows where ivy fringed the portholes like heavy eyelashes.

Earlier, Helga and I had met for our last rendezvous before my leaving Paris. On my arrival, she pulled a pair of brilliant red patent-leather shoes out of her closet, asking, "Aren't they gorgeous? I found them at the sales."

Helga's glorious foot ornaments were normally 130 euros. She had found them for 20.

"Try them on," she urged me.

They were lovely. A perfect fit.

"You must have a pair," she said. "It'll be my farewell gift."

Off we wandered around Île Saint-Louis, behind Notre Dame Cathedral. We laid on the walls girdling the Seine River, taking snapshots, giggling, and sharing our girlish hearts. By the time we reached the shoe store it was eight P.M. The iron gate was locked as customers queued inside to make final purchases.

"It's too late, Helga."

She ignored me.

"Please let me in; I must buy a pair of shoes," she said through the gate.

The sales woman waved her hands dismissively.

"You don't understand. I won't try on anything. I know exactly what I want."

The annoyed clerk mouthed, "Non, Non, Non," wagging a forbidding finger.

"They're right there by the door."

The sales woman walked away.

"Come on, Helga." I tugged on her arm. "What would I do with red shoes?"

She shrugged me off like an irritating fly while calling to the customer closest to the locked door, "I have 20 euros." She waved the money hopefully. "Buy those shoes for me and I'll pay you when you leave."

The woman looked at Helga like she was on a day pass from the Institute of St. Idiot.

"This is an emergency. My friend is leaving the country tomorrow and she must have those shoes."

The customer turned her back.

"Helga, I don't need the shoes."

She didn't hear me.

"Madame! My friend is going to the United States tomorrow. It's now or never."

I wasn't leaving for another five days, but who listens to a fly? I was getting embarrassed. I moved onto the sidewalk where I could overhear the entertaining river of French without being associated with her.

"I can see the box from here. I don't need to try them on."

As I watched buses disgorge their heavy burden and swallow another, the pleading continued.

I had lost count of the buses when the gate suddenly slid open, allowing Helga to happily snatch up the box of shoes and stand behind the customer she had harassed earlier. As the evening moon rose, I walked the cobblestone road to our restaurant in shiny red heels, the one splash of color in my constant parade of black. Every detail of the dinner was just right, including my shoes and the Turkish gentleman who joined us for dessert.

With Helga

A Final Jewel

It was our last, poignant Sunday, singing, playing, and being near our Paris church family. We were reluctant to finish worshipping, spontaneously singing "How Great Is Our God" one last time—when "it" happened. A refined, elegant woman in a well-tailored lavender suit of fine linen unexpectedly moved to the front of the church. The ambassador's wife closed her eyes and, with a smile on her upturned face, wove a dance with all the liquid litheness of the grand cats from her country. Joy emanated from her pores and filled the room with its intoxicating perfume. I felt as though we had waited all our lives for this impromptu gift of love. Our energy rose; heaven descended. It was a final jewel crowning four fabulous years in France.

L'Automne— Autumn 2008

September: Mercy, Mercy

CHURCH DEFINED

A S THE MONTHS began to slip ever quickly toward our departure, I received heartwarming reports on the progress of the vintage 1920's house the Salem church was remodeling for us. Madame D. listened as I described the painting, fence building, furniture collecting, and people's concern over my color preferences.

During one of our regular Friday lunches, my dear friend said, "I told Jacques about the house and garden these Salem people are preparing for you. He says you must have a lot of good friends over there."

"Ron and I do have good friends there; however, most of these people have never met us. It's the church; they're being very kind to us."

One of our heartbreaks before leaving was finding out that Sheena would not be eligible for American government financial aid funds for college. As the American dollar fell and our Paris rent rose, it required more U.S. dollars to keep our apartment in France. On the FAFSA form, we appeared to be making more money than we actually were, so our daughter lost the grant for which our family would have qualified the year before.

In the last week before we left Paris, a note arrived with someone offering to replace a substantial amount of the FAFSA funds. I told my Madame D. the stunning news.

The following Friday lunch, she said, "I told Jacques about the grant Sheena was given last week. He said again you must have a lot of really good friends over there."

"It's crazy, Marie, we haven't even met these people. We don't know them personally. It's the church. I don't know how to explain it."

Who can explain someone doing acts of kindness for people they don't know, people who have never done anything for them and probably never will? Who can explain giving when there is no return? Perhaps this is the picture the word *church* is meant to conjure.

The Salem church worked overtime gutting and remodeling the little house on Church Street. In the process, soft spots in the floor were found, a sinking roof in need of new trusses showed up, and old wiring and windows required replacement. Even the yard was redone and a fence erected. Donated furniture was stripped, refinished, and recovered. Household items were offered with someone around to say, "We'll take that; but not that, that, or that!" Perennials were hand-raised from seed, a garden created complete with my favorite herbs.

The final touch was the stocking of cupboards. When I opened door after door the morning after our arrival, I started to cry, overwhelmed by such thoughtful generosity. Jacques was right—we do have a lot of really good friends. I just haven't met many of them yet. They are a picture of God's hands and feet on earth, a church showering grace where none is earned or deserved.

A Bag Situation

Here's the problem: You are leaving an entire continent for one year. You will need winter and summer clothing, files of vital documents, books, underwear, and mascara. One bag for necklaces and shoes. Buying what you forget or don't have room for is not an option. Running home is also non-optional. You may bring two suitcases, each not weighing more than forty-eight pounds.

My solution? Panic. Sheer panic can drive a scattered, haphazard woman who forgets to read her calendar and loses planners regularly to complete packing ten days in advance. Fear is a highly effective motivator, though it does slop over onto other people.

"Ron, aren't you going to start packing?" I asked.

"I have the 'Healthy Relationships with the Opposite Sex' seminar to prepare."

The lack of panic on Ron's part—his relaxedness about packing for a year—was starting to bug me. A week later, I pushed again. "Ron, have you even started?"

"I'm getting a worship seminar ready for the Hmong Church, south of Paris. Ben is coming with me to translate. It's going to be great."

"Uh-huh. You know we have to figure out a way to get the rest of Sheena's stuff home too, don't you? We don't actually have two whole suitcases apiece."

"You're trying to control, Lorelei."

"I'm having a hard time letting this go. Can you just tell me a day so I have something to count on?"

"I have time on Tuesday."

"Ron...We leave here Wednesday morning at six A.M. Tuesday night there's a church dinner."

"OK, I'll start Monday."

"Monday!?" I'm sure my eyes said it all.

Monday, Ron began methodically sorting through books and cleaning out drawers, initiating a painstaking, careful "take-leave-toss, take-leave-give away" process. Separate give-away piles multiplied, depending on where they would go. I couldn't watch; my controller was convulsing.

The night before leaving Paris, we attended a long, heartwarming dinner party with forty-five people from the church. The restaurant was charming, the food exquisite, our beloved people engaging. After giving Ying and Jay Lee a last ride home through the quiet city, hugging them fiercely, we dropped off Grace at the desolate Métro station near Genesis. Tears ran down my cheeks as she disappeared down the stairs.

Ron picked up a last few items at Genesis. We drove home quietly through glamorous streets we still find breathtaking. It was bittersweet.

Reality returned as we walked through our apartment door after midnight. Ron had six hours to finish packing. He asked me to fold his shirts. I said no—out of principle, of course. I went to bed while Ron continued. At five A.M. he hadn't slept, was cheerful...and was still packing. I had slept and was not cheerful. Steam escaped through my ear vents. A fifth bag had appeared during the brief night. I was certain we would pay dearly for it.

Ron calmly walked out the door at six A.M. for our uneventful ride to the airport. Our check-in person was a new, inexperienced Air Berlin employee who was being hounded and harassed by a supervisor more uptight than I. I dreaded hearing the price for the fifth bag and our surplus pounds. In spite of the overbearing supervisor, the new girl mistakenly charged us only twenty-five euros for the extra suitcase and ignored the excess weight of the others. We stood in another line at Air Berlin's payment counter where the official studied our paltry surcharge bill. She picked up the phone and talked to the agent we had just left.

"This isn't the correct fee..." Instructions were given to the new girl. The payment agent then smiled at us. "What a deal! This is our little secret, OK?"

In Dusseldorf, Germany, we stood in line once again. Eyebrows were raised and questions asked about the ridiculous fee; it was decided it was Paris's problem.

We arrived in green, green Vancouver, BC, with hardly a nick out of our bank account. I scolded God; if He was going to let Ron get away with this kind of behavior, it would only continue. I was conflicted by a confusing mix of relief and anger until I sensed God asking a question: "Do You want me to treat you with the same lack of mercy you're recommending for Ron?"

I dropped it. I'm very fond of God's mercy.

Family Vacation in Greece, Summer 2008

TRANSITION TO AN AMERICAN HOME

We're back in a land where we get the language. Even phrases like "pay through the nose," when you've just handed over cash, and "there you go," when you haven't gone anywhere at all, are understandable. I find my hands unclenched in a land where I am a citizen and there is no visa paperwork to be annually renewed. Imagine the relief. No requisite chest x-rays for foreigners conducted by people who play Frisbee on topless beaches with half-naked grandmas. We're home where everything should feel natural, yet...

We arrived at Christos at seven thirty P.M. and found the Italian café so closed the chairs were already upside-down on the tables. We meandered downtown for First Wednesday, a monthly event when galleries begin new exhibitions, businesses stay open late, and bands play on the sidewalks. The streets were vacant at eight P.M. No one was around, not even a janitor pushing a broom.

Friends are working by seven A.M., an hour I call the edge of night. Where is everyone? Where are the cars? Vehicles are parked so far apart, looking rather lonely. Frenchmen easily double the amount of parked cars on their street; they use the bumpers. Unfortunately, bumpers aren't really meant for bumping here.

It's a solitary fifteen-minute walk to my grocery store; I rarely encounter a body to sidestep. I find myself going every day. The cashier greets me with an astounded, "You're here again?"

I feel criminal walking on grass but cross the springy turf every chance I get. I feel wicked ordering lunch after two P.M. I feel rude eating with my fingers, and instead automatically eat pizza with a fork and knife. I feel guilty leaving a store without calling "thank you" or "goodbye" to the proprietor. The words slip out accidentally and people look at me oddly. So do my friends.

Worse yet, I have this urge to lean forward and kiss people's cheeks when we meet. That's going to get me in trouble yet. I feel naughty jumping into a car and burning gas to do my errands, but sometimes naughty feels very nice.

I feel lonely; I miss Madame D. To receive more of her emails, I simply threaten to wear her gift of citrus perfume during the winter. According to her, that simply is not done. Who else would instruct me on which perfume to squirt during which season, what cheese to serve at room temperature, and how to wait for the end of a meal to drink a miniscule demi-cup of superb black coffee? Who else would wait for me at a bus stop holding a red linen bag emblazoned with the famous Hediard name, hiding a box of award-winning French macaroons?

"I thought you'd need cheering today," she'd said as she handed me the bag, taking my arm to steer me toward my mammogram appointment.

Who else would take me to a French AA meeting where I met unsung heroes going against the flow of an entrenched wine culture? I think this loyal group just might be Madame D.'s church.

October: All Hallows' Eve and All Saints Day

LEAVES

"You're not living in Paris anymore, so don't be a Scrooge. You have to buy candy for Halloween."

Sheena was worried we would forget.

October 31 in France is not the event it is here in the U.S. The Hulk, with an unbuttoned shirt and the chest hair of an ape, took my money at Starbucks®. The Grim Reaper delivered a cup of brew while an angel asked me about my future. I was beginning to feel insecure. Another reaper drifted by the window, sickle in hand, while a witch slipped by on the other side of the street.

How could I forget? Weeks before October 31, costumes fill every spare inch of American stores. Parents spend All Hallows' Eve Day decorating faces and filling candy bowls, then frolicking in the streets with children.

In France, the day after Halloween is a holiday. Chrysanthemums fill every spare inch of grocery stores and florists' shops, bubbling over into fragrant sidewalk displays in the weeks prior to November 1. Families buy bouquets of mums—potted mums, big mums, and button mums, and then spend All Saints Day decorating relatives' graves while children play among tombstones. On both sides of the world, the dead are remembered; one side mourns them and the other plays them.

While in Paris, more than Halloween's festive community spirit, Ron and I simply missed autumn leaves. The trees lining the city's boulevards were chosen for their resistance to the sticky, black pollution—pollution that left a residue requiring steel wool and Ron's muscle to remove from the top of my neglected kitchen cupboards. Paris's tough trees deliver a drab autumn. The most striking colors marking our French falls were the fluorescent green uniforms covering black-skinned city workers as they blew away a day's accumulation of brown leaf litter each morning. Here, leaves gather into heaps of golden happiness where children jump, cats hide, and moms collect craft projects—until the rains begin.

Living with Questions

We rushed home from a full day in Portland, eagerly anticipating eating fresh-baked sourdough—an American invention not decently found in France. Notes were taped on our front and back doors: John, the senior pastor at our church in Salem, was sick so our dinner date at McGraths, along with its fresh, warm bread, was cancelled. I didn't think anything of it; it was probably just the flu going around, knocking people off their feet like a regular schoolyard bully.

A month passed; our ruby-red fall turned into a typical gray, rainy, Pacific coast winter. The grapevine whispered unsettling fragments. "Pastor John spent a week in the local hospital...he's home, in better condition...muscle enzymes at three thousand... should be one hundred...doctors don't know why...biopsy..."

John was ambulanced to the intensive care unit at Portland's university hospital. The grapevine shook under the shock of one short phrase: "life-threatening."

Two days later, on a Wednesday, when the last of my piano lessons were taught and the door locked behind us, we walked across the street to the church, weaving between parked cars plugging the surrounding streets. Inside, the church lights were low, dozens of candles lit, a mosaic of the word "Healer" gracing the front. Beauty stilled our worried, heavy spirits. It brought peace into messy souls where questions lay scattered like dirty, discarded laundry. People poured quietly into the sanctuary for the impromptu vigil. We sang. Tears rolled down faces. Lyrics leaped out as though brand new, holding out kind hands of comfort. We prayed, a thousand whispered voices rising and falling in harmony.

Ron was subdued beside me. Withdrawn. I didn't know where he had gone. Someone guided us to pray for John's wife and their seventeen-year-old son. A seventeen-year-old son...I should have put it together.

When Ron was sixteen, he along with two brothers of five and seven, and a sister of thirteen, squeezed into their 1969 Ford® LTD, the youngest bouncing between mom and dad, the second youngest peering over his daddy's shoulder. The dark green sedan followed a farmer's five-ton grain truck transporting their furnishings and lives out of Winnipeg, Manitoba, across Canada's sweeping heartland, to the province of Saskatchewan. Five hundred miles later, they rolled into a village of five hundred—Dad's new parish.

Except for one year in Indiana while her husband did graduate studies, Ron's mom had never before made a home very far away from her tight-knit, ten-sibling clan. Internet, email, cell phones, and cheap long-distance calling weren't yet even a whimsical dream. Five hundred miles seemed so much farther in those days.

What a change. On this desolate prairie there was no family net, no bustling city boulevards, only sprawling, non-stop acres of ripe grain intersected by gravel roads, dusty harvesters, tractors and trucks. It was another world ruled by inter-married farm folk who passed idle winter days repairing equipment as well as visiting and monitoring the neighbors.

By December, arctic winds had swept south into the Canadian prairies, blowing snow into bleak drifts and plunging the wind chill to minus thirty. On a sub-zero Saturday night in January, a night so cold it sucked the air out of vulnerable lungs, Ron turned off the lights and said good night to his sister and little brothers; his babysitting would soon be over. Once his mom and dad returned home, Ron's father left the cozy parsonage to race across the frozen church parking lot to his study to finish preparations for Sunday.

Ten, then eleven o'clock came and Marian gave up waiting for Henry; she went to bed alone. At two A.M. she woke up, worried, the space beside her still empty. Grabbing a heavy coat to wrap around her thin body, she thrust her bare feet into boots and tugged a scarf over her mouth. Hurrying to the church study where light still burned, Marian found her husband. But the man she loved was gone; a massive heart attack had prematurely stolen his life. That same surreal, bitter night, the darkness also prematurely stole Ron's adolescence.

During the Wednesday night prayer gathering for our pastor in Salem, Ron's memories rose with sobering clarity. He understood too well not knowing how John's story would end. He knew how one tragedy could birth a succession of interlinked injuries. Ron's past called out deep, unspoken, groaning prayers for John's family. There were many in our congregation whose history also shaped their fervent prayers. While we prayed together in our warm sanctuary, doctors introduced an experimental drug into John's veins. Brain damage was one of the frightening, possible side effects. We were told John's kidneys and liver were shutting down, antibiotics and essential fluids leaking from his sieve-like vessels. His extremities were cold and blue. The word "coma" hit parishioners hard.

As days passed, I learned of dozens scattered around the parish sending up passionate prayers not only in lucid daylight but throughout the ominous night, wondering if our pastor still lived. My friend was awake from two to four A.M. the same night I laid awake from four to six A.M., the baton of prayer mysteriously handed from her to me for the next shift. I wasn't sure how praying without stopping worked, word wise. Picture prayers worked better for me, scenes of laying John's limp body into our compassionate Father's strong arms as I pled with my heart, looking into God's tear-filled eyes.

Late Friday afternoon found Ron and I creating a black-and-white Paris photo display for the church's bulletin board. On one side of the lobby, an exuberant wedding party excitedly prepared for the next day's grand gala. On our end, a staff member exited the sanctuary where candles were lit and lights were low. Black circles ringed her puffy eyes; I could hear the tremble in her gentle voice. I laid down my glue stick and put my arms around her. John's possible demise was devastating to so many.

"I can't understand why," she whispered. "What good could it possibly do to take John's life? How does this help the kingdom of God?"

There were no adequate answers. Ron put down the stapler to hold an old friend tightly, to stand silently beside her, patient in the pain.

"I'm afraid. I fear he is going to die. How long can his body take this?" A heavy sigh escaped. "His dehydration is critical; at the same time he's gained fifty pounds in fluids." Her eyes filled. "It really doesn't look good. I just don't understand why."

It was oddly comforting to hear a pastor with deep faith, yet with her own profound experiences of grief and injustice, ask "why" with uncompromised authenticity and resistance to tempting, clichéd answers.

Ron's mother weathered a long season of dangling "whys." Marian was left with small children, mounting bills, and no means of support. Ron became his mother's confidant, his siblings' father figure. They moved out of the parsonage five months after their daddy's death.

Boxes were repacked another four months later when Marian remarried. It was a much different service the stepfather conducted, though the chapel and office were again just across a gravel parking lot. Their kitchen and dining room windows now framed a view of the adjacent funeral home. A Narnian winter still shrouded their tattered world.

Like crocuses promising early spring, hope was given to the Salem church by Sunday. The experimental medication was working without serious side effects. John's life still hung in the balance, but he was alive against all odds and conventional wisdom. Only a man who ran ultra marathons could survive—and we all had thought his running was nuts! One wit had suggested group therapy for his marathon habit, or so John had joked in a sermon.

Monday, the impossible was reported: John's kidneys were beginning to function, flushing away fluids, drop by drop. His heart was now working well on its own. The ventilator was removed and his first raspy words brought laughter and happy tears: "I want a pan of brownies baked with love." His extremities were warm for the first time in days. Excitement buzzed; the grapevine was plump with good news.

This last September gifted Ron and me with spectacular summer days for Marian's visit. The garden was toasty, golden in fall's rich sunshine. Marian and her eldest son lounged on the patio among the vibrant perennials, waging another inevitable Scrabble® war as they reminisced. Their laughter wafted into the kitchen where I shuffled pots and pans, deftly avoiding the game. Old wounds were examined over unhurried days, tenderly massaged and kissed with love. It was healing, a sweet benediction to a process that took nearly forty years to mature. We couldn't see God's movement, His mysterious answers, with naked vision. It wasn't until we stood back with the lens of time held up to our searching eyes that we discovered the shape of a miracle.

At present, we lack the lens of time in Salem. As word arrives of John being put back on the ventilator, we courageously resist premature explanations, choosing instead to cling to the hope of God's love being enough to carry us through, no matter how the story twists and turns. Our pastor's kidneys do not continue to improve. His life is fragile. We grieve. We cry out. Prayers rise around the world. And John is given a tracheotomy.

Even the best theology can feel unsatisfactory when the icy fingers of an Arctic wind grip our lives. I find these seasons calling me to soak in a warm daily bath of David's poetry. He dares to ask gnarly questions with unsanitized passion, still trusting God's love to hold him through the barren winter.

> When my heart was grieved, and my spirit embittered,
> I was senseless and ignorant; I was a brute beast before you.
> Yet I am always with you; you hold me by my right hand.
> You guide me with your counsel,
> and afterward you will take me into glory.
> Whom have I in heaven but you?
> And earth has nothing I desire besides you.
> My flesh and my heart may fail,
> But God is the strength of my heart and my portion forever.[4]

November: Jericho Walls

When Ron and I first returned from France, we were asked to speak at West Coast churches most every weekend. We heard people mourn their shrinking churches. We listened to fears of America following in Europe's churchless footsteps. Often, we noticed an absence of adults under fifty. Additionally, although drums replaced organs, PowerPoint® presided over hymnals, and padded chairs ousted wooden pews, these nods to current culture didn't seem to be tearing down the rising walls dividing the churched and un-churched. One doctoral student summed up what we continue to hear from our non-church friends: "Church is bad for my faith."

MY STRONG NAME

"Hey, how are you? Good? Good! Are you good?"

"Fine, thanks." I leaned against the chapel's back wall.

"'Course you're good. That's what the good Lord gives us. Good days, good life, goodness…That's what life is all about. You and Ron have fine, strong names, very strong. Very strong. And there you are serving the Lord in France with your strong names. 'Ron' is…for 'strong,' and 'Lorelei' is for…'strong witness,' and you are a strong witness in France. So there you go."

"Uh, well, my name is German and my German friends say it means 'enchantress.' The Lorelei was a bare-breasted nymph who sang songs from a rock in the Rhine River, luring sailors to their death."

The gentleman was flabbergasted. "But…but…your name means 'strong witness.' I know that."

"Guess it depends on who you talk to." A German friend had sent me a lengthy article on the siren.

The zesty man full of positive cheer reappeared after the service, waving a paperback. "You two do have strong names and I always say people live up to their names. 'Ron' means… 'strong leader,' like Ronald Reagan. Look how strong he was. Lived up to his name, just like I always say. And," he pointed to a definition as he read, "see here, 'Lorelei' means 'alluring,' which means 'strong witness.' See? Right here in this book. Yup, people live up to their names and your name means 'strong witness' and you are a strong witness in France. So there you go."

MY NAME, AGAIN

Ron gave a moving message on grace another weekend. It was interspersed with portions I read from one of my favorite Baguette stories. After the service, someone waited to hand me an offering envelope. It was taped shut. I thought it might contain the honorarium for speaking. Instead, inside the empty envelope was penciled this unsigned note:

Dear Lorelei,

If the original Lorelei had whispered like you did today, the Rhine River boatmen would not have perished. And because you did whisper, and I could not hear, I and others who also could not understand, may well perish. Less drama and more volume may work.

I was hurt. As the pain subsided, judgment quickly followed—as though I have never criticized. Just last week I had to call someone to apologize for my careless words.

"Lord, pull me back from building my own walls of hasty critiques and harsh judgments."

MR. BURLY

Another weekend, another church. We were taste-testing at a church potluck.

A burly man overrode a conversation already in gear. "Hey there, how are you?"

"I'm a little tired today," I admitted.

"Tired! Well! Being tired means you're busy and being busy is what keeps you honest. So how are you going to be honest if you're not tired? That's what life is all about."

I slipped away to breathe in the soft presence of a consultant from Malaysia.

"I'm not a Christian," he explained sincerely. "I am Hindu."

A meaningful conversation began to evolve. As Ron went to find a piece of paper to exchange email addresses, the busy, burly man interrupted our tête-à-tête, blurting to the Malaysian, "Hey, who let you into this country anyway?" Mr. Burly guffawed.

I was stunned. "You can't say that."

"Nah, he knows I love him," Burly replied, laughing. "Hey, who let you into the country anyway?"

I fumbled, ineptly trying to repair a broken conversation.

Mr. Burly, sensing my irritation, explained, "I don't have a prejudiced bone in my body. I'm just teasing." Mr. Burly turned to call to the slender man who was now across the room, "Hey, Gerjzheet, why don't you come to Sunday school? It's only an hour earlier than worship; you can get up."

The polite man backed farther away, a smile pasted in place.

For months afterward I thought, *How could he not know better?*

This week, a soft voice probed, "How often does your teasing blunder into inappropriate remarks and injury?" Only a few days earlier, Ron told me how much my ribbing hurt during an argument over his shoe choice. More bricks, another wall.

My Walls

It was decades before lasting friendships developed outside my whitewashed walls. It only started after I began to see and speak the truth about my own self-righteousness and brokenness. Unfortunately, the wall syndrome still plagues me. When Ron and I arrived home from France, we lingered over long dinners with friends who aren't part of the church.

And then a month passed, two, and then three. We were busy with church events. It was John and Mary DeChurched who called us. After a clean, fluorescent-lit, missionary potluck, we drove to a dim pub to meet them. A band wailed country tunes in a corner. A couple teetered past our table, holding each other upright. Ron grinned at me, then leaned close to shout in my ear, "This is where Jesus would have come after synagogue."

I need connections with the "de-churched." People outside its walls inspire me to hold my beliefs gently and to ask myself, "Jesus' teaching or my preference?" and "Jesus' example or evangelical subculture?"

Marching Around Jericho

There are many anonymous heroes who inspire me by their determined marching around Jericho to bring down walls:

Ron and I bowled with some church kids and their youth pastor who build their Tuesday night gatherings around the needs of teens living in subsidized housing nearby. The church was brainstorming how to love the ruptured families behind their campus, willing to take cues from a wise teen rising from similar ruins, becoming a daughter to one of the church families.

A minister sold his house and relocated to another part of the same city for the sake of building friendships outside the church family. Others sold homes in the suburbs to become part of the low-income neighborhood around their church. This church partners with another from a different denomination to run a free community medical clinic. Over two hundred volunteers from all kinds of church backgrounds come together to offer help.

A couple flew to a remote village in Central America where children have never seen books; they don't even know how to turn a page to find the next picture. With research completed, the couple has returned home and invites friends to delectable dinners—with new purpose. After eating, everyone troops downstairs to construct specially designed books for this tribe.

I walked into a crowded church reception area one evening just before Christmas. Neighborhood parents were waiting to wrap gifts they'd requested but had not actually purchased for their sons and daughters. A handful looked cynical, others uncomfortable, in the unfamiliar church setting. Some didn't know how to wrap presents so patient volunteers taught them the tricks of cutting, folding, and taping.

"Who should we tell our children these gifts are from?" parents asked the soft-spoken woman in charge.

"They are from you. You requested them, you came, you wrapped them for your children. They are from you."

Some people listen to Ron and me with our stories of brokenness without raised eyebrows or pursed lips. Instead, they respond with their own admissions of weakness. There is no subtle air of superiority, something the pursuit of goodness easily breeds. Their humble honesty lightly blows away walls. They are the kind of people someone without Jesus longs to know, the very people Jesus longs to characterize His Church.

Jesus, we can't change unless you walk around our Jericho walls. Come, Lord Jesus.

November: Cordless Mike

The Phone Call

It started with a telephone message. I could hear the voice projecting loudly from the receiver Ron held away from his ear. It sounded like a radio show playing at great length—it was an invitation to speak at an area church conference as well as at the host church's Sunday service. Weeks later, we drove through spectacular mountains dressed in heavy firs, ribbons of fog draping their necks, to meet the pastor who had filled our message machine.

The Saturday Conference

Pastor Mike wasn't inhibited. "Yup, this is my marrying tie." He lifted it off his torso to make the point. "I'm going to have to slip out after lunch. I do more weddings in this town than anyone else. When someone asks if I'm free, I say of course I'm free. Our Lord Himself was available for a wedding. Then they ask me how much I charge, and I tell them it's absolutely free. Absolutely. They ask me what requirements I have and I tell them absolutely none at all. I just ask to meet with them one time before the wedding and, of course, it leads to more sessions. You know, our church is full of people I married; I once asked for a show of hands of how many couples I helped tie the knot—it was amazing."

I didn't need to think of prompts, replies, or dialogue.

Pastor found our lunch table at the conference, swinging his tie as he maneuvered into a chair, interrupting my conversation with the man beside me.

"Can we conduct a little business during lunch?"

Ron and I turned from our neighbors.

After a few words regarding the Sunday services, Pastor Mike continued. "You notice the gloves on the ladies in the kitchens? We have a bunch of certified food handlers. It's a way we can serve our community. That's what our Lord was doing, out and about in the community, doing relational evangelism. Did anyone tell you about the huge steak dinner our food handlers put on here? It was amazing; we had the news people here and got video footage. We invited everyone who represents a community service—Red Cross, utilities, ambulance crews, even the garbage people who shined up one of their big red trucks. Our parking lot was so full, the road service people used those big light-up signs."

He grabbed a quick breath.

"Our motorcycle club parked all their bikes along the fence—that alone was worth coming to see—and directed parking. The city ran a shuttle bus for us. The mayor was here, the town council. It was amazing, really amazing. Spent four thousand dollars on steak dinners, but hey, it's important we're in the community, doing relational evangelism...like Jesus.

"Marilyn and I are driving a bus now, building relationships another sixty hours a week. The football team kinda asked me to be their chaplain; I pray with them before their game. If they're playing an away game, they want Bus 29; that's my bus. I stand at the sidelines during their games. Everybody knows me; I almost drive off the road waving at all the people who wave at me. People come to the door of my bus and ask for prayer. It's relational evangelism, reaching out and touching people, just like our Lord. Of course, the extra cash helps with the house we bought in California."

PRE-SERVICE PREPARATION

Sunday morning, Ron and I decided to leave copies of an earlier edition of this book in a box until after the service. A few had mysteriously walked away from the lobby the day before even though a sign clearly stated their price.

The pastor commented, "We put this table here for your books."

"Uh, thank you, but I want to wait until after the service. Four of them walked away yesterday and I need to be able to pay my printing bill."

"Not around here; didn't happen here." He shook his head. "But you did hear what I said yesterday about our style of hospitality. I've told them, 'If you see anything you want, help yourselves.'"

I stupidly picked up my box and laid out the books on the table. He walked away.

ANNOUNCEMENTS

Bouncy music came from the bright piano; the pastor's pretty wife was a capable pianist. Pastor Cordless Mike stepped onto the platform for the announcements.

"You know, I went to a church growth seminar where they told us to skip the announcements—people can read them in the bulletin. But these aren't just announcements. Jesus told us to love our neighbors. These are events where we love our neighbors, where we share life together."

People were cajoled to join the choir.

"Some of you may say, 'But I can't sing.' That's all right; we'll place you farther from the mic. I sing and they place me far away from the mic. People say my face is a song."

"Do you know we have a Christian daycare center with almost sixty children? It's completely staffed by women; imagine the administration that requires!"

"Did you come to look heavenward? While we do many things here, our primary purpose is to honor Jesus Christ, our Lord. Our Father chose to reveal Himself in the Son, who is also God. Do you find this confusing? I don't find this confusing."

"The scriptures say that one day every knee will bow. The doubter named Thomas called Jesus 'my Lord.' My Lord. Not just God, but Lord. That's higher yet."

It was a bumpy trail of semi-connected thoughts.

WORSHIP

Singing began. People started to clap. Pastor interrupted easily, cordless mic in hand.

"You know, there's a problem with musicians. They're already all warmed up and ready to go when we start. We're not ready yet. Everybody! Get moving! Make a circle…"

I felt momentary panic. Was there going to be some kind of hand-holding circle dance?

"Say 'howdy' to the people around you. Best of all, if you see someone you don't know, be sure to shake their hand and ask them their name. Get to know them! Quickly now!"

People didn't know we were the out-of-town speakers; they descended on us like dogs on bloody steaks. The singing started, and stopped—again.

"What a mighty God we serve!" The cordless mic was evidently not for the musicians to use.

"Amen," the people chorused.

"What a mighty God we serve!"

"Amen," the people shouted a little louder, waking to his call.

"Is He mighty?" Pastor Mike was fully on stage by now.

"Amen!"

"Really? Have you been watching the news? You haven't, have you? 'It's too depressing,' you say. Is God mighty? How many of you will say, 'There are serious problems in my life.' How many of you have heavy hearts? Go on. Lift your hands. Quickly now. Is our God mighty? Doesn't look that way, does it? But the story isn't finished yet. Our God will be mighty. He will save. Amen?"

"Amen!"

"Here we go!" Bouncy music resumed until Cordless Mike suddenly interjected, speaking to the worship leader. "Seth, now you be sure to tell the folk which part to sing when we get to those two separate parts. The first service, people didn't sing out like normal. We can do better. You let us know."

Seth grinned sheepishly. "OK, Pastor."

Pastor Mike stood in the front row, arm beating the air for an invisible orchestra, eyes closed, face beatific.

We were singing, "Spirit, have your way with me," when the pastor climbed the stairs again, thoughtfully this time, a quietness in his step.

CONFESSION

"We've been praying, 'Spirit, have your way with me' because the song is really a prayer. Is He having His way with us? How many of us can say the work of the Spirit is complete in our lives? Church, it's time to do spiritual warfare. How many of you have your spiritual armor strapped on?"

"I used to pray, 'Lord, fix me' and I wasn't fixed. There may be something in us that isn't being fixed, something we struggle with. Perhaps there is sin, so the Spirit can't have His way with us. Anyone want to say 'ouch' to that?"

"Ouch," they responded half-heartedly.

"Jesus taught us how to pray. He said, 'Satan, be gone from here.'"

The piano continued a non-stop underscore.

"Let's confess sin in our life. Is there anything bad you've done? Let's take a moment to tell God we're sorry."

He stopped talking for a few brief seconds.

"How many of you have serious problems? How many of you confessed your sin? Raise your hands high. Wowww! I declare you to be clean. You're free. Go and sin no more."

He descended the stairs and prayerful music resumed.

THE OFFERING

"We came to worship. Well, I'm back to Christmas. You know, the wise men came to worship and they brought gifts. What gifts should we bring Jesus? More than just our tithes and offerings. How many wish those offering bags were bigger? We could give our children to Him because we know they're really His anyways—it would feel pretty good to put our middle-schoolers in there. Quickly now, ushers."

A FEW WORDS

Pastor Mike was back after a brief music respite.

"I'd like to say just a few words. I was in an environment lately—and I won't say where because I don't want people thinking they can't invite me places or they'll hear about it on Sunday—and I saw people huddle and pray on one side of the place, and then get up and walk to the other side where cursing came out of those same mouths. This was done in front of young people. It breaks my heart..."

THE BUSINESS MEETING

"I want to apologize, not the kind of apology where you feel guilty, but the kind of apology you make because you might make guests feel uncomfortable. We have business to perform. Everybody who is an active member, please stand."

Pastor Mike said it was to be a brief, three-minute meeting.

"Doris, will you let your name stand for the nominating committee?"

"No."

"Doris must have a busy life." Pastor picked up the dead ball with ease.

"I have to take care of Kevin."

No one else declined.

At the end of business, Pastor explained, "You may have noticed we used Robert's Rules of Order. Our God is an orderly God. He loves order. When we do this, we honor Him and His ways. Teach me Your ways, O Lord. If anyone has questions, ask them. We are committed to avoiding the appearance of evil."

SPECIAL MUSIC

A woman with long hair tumbling down her back slung a guitar around her neck. As she adjusted her mic, she said, "Come on up, Dick, if you want to play along." A stooped, white-haired man sauntered to the drums. The bass player casually slumped on his chair. She sang with heart, her voice husky, full, and distinct in its authentic style. Everything about her rang true.

As she descended the stairs, the pastor took her hand, speaking into his mic, "And we all know you know the rest of the scripture you used for your song, which is…?"

A confused look of panic swept her eyes; she said nothing. Pastor Mike smoothly covered, quoting the complete verse and reference. From there he moved to prayer for her wayward son, asking personal questions before a rapt congregation.

MISSIONARIES

It was time to introduce us.

"So, Ron, are you an official denominational missionary?"

"Yes."

"All right then! People sometimes call me 'Reverend Smith' because I'm a licensed, ordained minister in the same denomination. It's not just a title; it's my calling. Ron, have you been ordained?"

"Yes."

"Well, then, we can call you 'Reverend Ron Friesen.'"

"Please don't. Just call me Ron."

"'Reverend Ronald Friesen' is what we'll call you. It's not just a title; it's your calling. Come on up, Reverend Friesen."

"Thank you, Mike."

The Reverend sat down, releasing the microphone. Surely his hand was sweaty. His face was tomato red.

At the close of the service, Ron and I were ending with a reflective song when I caught sight of Cordless Mike mounting the stairs. The Reverend interrupted our singing to re-summarize Ron's teaching, adding, "Go and sin no more."

He then transformed the moment into an altar call, asking Missionary Ron to lay his hands on the people who came forward and to pray for them. During the prayer, Pastor Mike glided down the stairs, stood behind me, and laid his hands on my shoulders as I played piano and sang.

He whispered, leaning close, "Please play after the service too. My wife's gone home…with a headache."

L'Hiver—
Winter 2008–2009

December: Christmas with Ron & Lorelei and Band

MAN ON A MISSION

IT WAS A hot afternoon back in August when Ron flew into the house at super-hero speed. The screen door banged behind him with such force I jumped.

"Lorelei, don't say 'no' right away, all right?"

"I'm not making any promises." Parenting has taught me to be cautious.

"I visited a historic theater downtown. Do you remember The Grand?

"No."

"Do you remember where the county courthouse is?"

"No."

"It's right across the street."

"That's not helping me."

It didn't register. But Ron was on a mission. "The theater has been restored; it's not too big, quite intimate. Charming. Has good sound. Reverberant, without a bad echo."

Where was he going?

207

"What would you think of doing a Christmas concert there? Something to which we could invite the community, held in a neutral space. We'll ask our band to play with us…"

"I think it's a great idea."

"You do, really? You'll do it? The owner is intrigued with my idea; she offered the second night rent free."

"Are you kidding?"

"Nope."

"Wow, that's significant."

Ron decided to test his crazy idea on some savvy friends willing to rescue me from cooking dinner. They listened. We had seconds of the complicated tiger shrimp and coconut milk sauté as they asked those astute questions on which business people sharpen their teeth.

Over dessert, Mr. T. asked nonchalantly, "Would you want sponsors?"

"What do sponsors do?" Ron asked.

"They pick up some of your bills."

Ron's a little more cautious than me; he said he would think about it. I said we'd love sponsors—was he thinking of anyone in particular?

Mr. T. was thinking of himself; he was interested in being a sponsor. Just like that, ping, ping, two significant pieces batted their eyelashes at us—a discounted rate at the theater and the possibility of a sponsor. We paid attention to the signs moving into line, and took the leap.

NEIGHBORHOOD RHYTHMS

The vintage house our home church has provided us squats over a cellar accessed by outdoor stairs. The cellar ceiling hangs low over our heads. Narrow, gritty windows hug the top of the wall; they're not even big enough to squeeze my head through. Exposed pipes and fir planks form the ceiling. A musky odor pervades, though it becomes less obvious as hours pass. A clothes washer and dryer, a hot water heater, and a furnace are planted among drums, a keyboard, guitars, and amplifiers.

The dryer's door is left open, its motor roaring, taking the edge off the basement chill. It's the first time I've had the luxury of doing laundry while rehearsing. Tuesday nights our little house on Church Street rocks off its foundation, our band pumping out "Chestnuts Roasting by an Open Dryer." The hum of the dryer and Christmas favorites fills our back alley, where fat possums waddle on overhead telephone wires, pausing to evaluate the latest ruckus.

Ron booked the historic theatre for our Christmas concerts so the pressure to be ready mounts. Yet, it's not so high there isn't time to do impressions of Edith Bunker screeching a carol. Only one musician is new, his eyes so wide with shock he might not return. Our drummer wipes tears from his eyes and says it's good to have me back. The others ask when we'll be leaving.

Our band adds one more layer of rhythm to the neighborhood's musical kaleidoscope. Sundays, the shadows of country dancers are silhouetted in the windows of the VFW hall next door, only an arm's length away. Tuesday afternoons, Irish dancers tap and leap to a live accordion. Thursdays beckon the bingo crowd. Other times, exercise enthusiasts abuse the groaning floor more often than I care to remember. Their perverted discipline drives me to snack and Ron to mock their ecstatic screams of "Whooo-hoooo." Saturdays feature square dancing, the caller clearly heard over the clink of our cooking utensils. Our neighbor on the right beats his drums daily. Sporadic salsa music floats from across the back alley. The last shade of musical color comes from the quirky storefront in front of our cottage. Violin lessons leak through our shared wall; the sounds aren't quite like my Parisian neighbor's cats in heat, but they're close.

Most every weekend we pull ourselves away from our colorful quarter to travel and speak at another church. We've given up putting away our suitcases in the musty basement; they jump anxiously into the bedroom like poorly trained puppies, bumping against our shins and nipping our vulnerable toes, eager for the next outing. We fill their tummies, pull out their leashes, and walk them to the car where they happily look out the back window, on their way again.

DREAMING OF A WHITE CHRISTMAS NIGHTMARE

After three months of open-throttle rehearsals with our drummer rolling his eyes each time I stopped to correct Ron's haphazard storytelling, we were delighted with the results. At the same time, we were not so delighted by other developments.

There were significant pieces needing to come together for us to return to our beloved friends in France. With numerous miracles under our belts, we settled into waiting. We were seeing a pattern of God opening and closing doors and moving impossible mountains. It's a pattern we had come to trust.

The week before the concerts, the sound gear Ron needed to rent was donated. With another little miracle firmly in hand, our waiting became calmer. Just one more week and we would know if people would actually attend our concerts. Three more weeks and we would know if we could return to Paris.

We were in a holding pattern when the weatherman started messing with my mind. He was playing bad news prophet, forecasting not fire and brimstone, but record-breaking ice and snow. I reminded myself how often weathermen are wrong. This was the Pacific coast where it rains whether sun, snow, sleet, or fog are forecast. Surely the weatherman would be wrong. If snow did come, all of Salem would hibernate. We close our schools, cancel church, pull up a chair by the fireplace and wait for the electricity to return as we listen to sirens scream in the distance. Would the bizarre weather forecast really happen?

The weather prophets did not need to be stoned; their predictions came true. The gray and green world of the Pacific Northwest bleached out into pristine white. Trees became sweeping snow sculptures—until their arms broke off. Every twig and blade of grass modeled crisp straitjackets of ice. The Winter Wonderland I had rehearsed all fall arrived in person for a full dress rehearsal.

Practice had been scheduled in our unheated cellar on the first day of heavy ice. It was the bassist who phoned first. "Would you be upset if I told you I fell on the ice and broke my arm?"

My heart sank. Jeff was not just a pretty-boy accessory. "Oh no, oh no, oh no!" This was the worst news yet.

"I wanted to know if you'd be upset. I didn't fall. Just checking!"

The boys arrived with stocking caps, gloves, and down jackets. The music sizzled in our funky cellar while an Arctic blast whistled outside. We were excited; the crazy white couldn't last long. It would surely be gone by concert time. People would come.

The weather did not relent. As I sat by our big front window, staring at the electrical wires strung over our white yard where snowflakes dumped and drifted, I heard God ask if I could let go of ticket sales.

"Maybe, off and on. I need You to help me with that."

In the thickness of the muffled quiet induced by heavy snow, I heard God calling my attention to another problem. I was attaching my worth and security to how many people came. I hate admitting my insecurity. How old am I, anyway? Thirteen?

Our daughter, Sheena, also was distressed. We had hoped to ease her college bill with any profit from the concerts. What could I say that wouldn't patronize her legitimate fears or shut down honest conversation? We were all dangling at the end of an icy wire, waiting on God, wanting to believe we would not be abandoned.

In spite of the treacherous weather, a number of our friends from outside our church circle came. It was new for them to see us making music. One of them stuttered, paused, unable to articulate her thoughts.

Finally, she blurted out, "Ron, I had no idea you could sing. Not like that!"

Previously, I had seen the anonymous glow of two bare elbows leading to fingers firmly planted in ears in the darkened theater while we sang, so I didn't take her praise too seriously.

The weather worsened. Saturday, the day my family drove from Canada through ten tortured hours of blizzard conditions to hear us sing, the heavens released the full fury of the North Pole. The week prior had only been a warm-up—without the warmth. Snow decapitated some trees to half their height. Neighborhoods were marooned on the slightest of hills. Roads became glacial sheets of ice.

After the final concert, I watched a man in shorts casually stroll past the theater windows while Justin ran up and down the oddly silent street, arms extended like wings, flying, cheeks ruddy. Though attendance had not been great and I didn't know if we ended financially in the red or the black, I was strangely content. We had rocked our audiences with the exuberance of Christ's Christmas and cradled them with the inviting spirit of Emmanuel, God with us. We had brought Christmas comfort to some aching hearts and shared a gift of hope with our community. I was so happy.

Then our drummer fell and broke his leg…for real.

January: The Mountain

Reality returned after the glow of our Christmas concerts. We had asked God to move a specific mountain for us to return to Paris. All through our concert preparations we were waiting, collecting patience and courage by recounting God's movement in the past:

- Sheena's enormous school bill was always paid, never late, always enough.
- We found an apartment on our first day of searching in impossible Paris; it even had plenty of windows and was near people who included us in their lives and loved us well.
- We saw people embrace Jesus and baptized a number of them.
- The cost of replacing a broken washing machine was met unexpectedly.
- Justin was able to come from Salem to Paris for his sister's graduation.
- When I asked God in the spring what I could do to address our financial situation, emails began to arrive, asking if I would teach piano lessons even though I was going to be in Salem for only a year.
- In spite of the North Pole throwing its worst tizzy fit in Salem since 1968, we didn't lose our shirts on the concerts.

- We ended financially in the black, even earning some funds to help Sheena with her college expenses.

I count these as no less than God's generous acts. Miracles. If God wanted us to return to Paris, He could move the mountain.

Our future did become clear. There was no movement of the mountain—no miracle. We had our answer, though it was a hard one. I had prayed for God to make things very clear. We had asked the mountain to move four inches. Would we go back if it moved two? How about one? Would we go then? After seeing God open doors and perform miracles for us to be in France, we have learned to wait and watch for His hand, to move when He moves. Our answer was now clear; it was time to let go of our precious church in Paris. We grieved an enormous loss, the loss of our French family.

As our family sat around the kitchen table enjoying a late breakfast after church, Ron sighed and said, "Well, Justin and Sheena, we've made our decision." He paused. "We're not returning to Paris." He was sad; his shoulders slouched. Tears had already flowed when thinking about the conversations that no longer will take place in the cafés near Genesis. We both had already felt the loss. Ron waited for a thoughtful conversation to unfold.

"Does this mean we can get a cat?" Justin asked.

"You said, Dad. You said we could get a kitty if you didn't go back to Paris," Sheena said.

Ron stared at them, shocked, uncomprehending. He'd just torn out his heart, laid it bleeding on the table, and our kids were talking about a cat?

"Dad?"

There was no response.

"Dad! You said we could. You can't break your promise, you know. You're a pastor," Justin said.

Sheena turned to me. "Mom, he said we could, right? Come on, Mom, help us out here."

It was an ambush, one Ron could not understand. He doesn't even like cats.

Today, there is a black and white kitty dashing from one end of the house to the other, sliding across the kitchen floor, paws splayed as he tries to avoid the inevitable crash into the oven. He sneaks onto Ron's lap between workouts. I stroke his velvety head, consoling myself over the loss of the life and dear friends we will leave in Paris. Our kitty snuggles deeper into Ron's surprised arms, a gentle memo of the place where our lives were profoundly changed, for Sheena named him Marcel, the Métro stop that marked our Paris home.

February: Children of the Millstone

BELT BUCKLE TERRITORY

The highway twisted through sprawling vistas of high desert arbitrarily torn apart by plunging canyons. Ron and I poked along through scattered towns where stout brick banks, Western storefronts, and bucking bronco murals tossed further dashes of spice into the country flavor. Tall hats made men out of even the smallest cowboys. Ranchers waved 'howdy' from hefty pick-up trucks. The staccato of cowboy boots ricocheted through wooden fruit stands as tumbleweed blew past. Our weekend speaking engagement had transported us deep into belt buckle territory.

The last time I had seen a super-sized buckle bejeweling a man's midriff, our family was crowded around a café table in urban Paris. The attentive waiter's waistline was two-thirds smaller and the buckle twice as big as the boldest cowboy's. Justin muttered, "If a girl smiled at me like that, I'd ask for her phone number." Then we noticed: the waiter's buckle spelled a blatant, "OPEN." We didn't see any of those in this rural land of sweet apple pie.

We found the church where we were speaking in a golden valley, circled by a halo of snowy ridges. Homemade food weighted the tables at every event. The savvy planning committee knew what kind of insurance policy to buy to guarantee a crowd. Friday night, piles of seductive cookies gave off a rich perfume France has yet to bottle. Saturday morning, the raspberry pancake syrup was definitely addictive.

As I sat next to a high school freshman during the breakfast, her eyes grew bright as she declared, "I want to go to MIT."

"That's a big goal. Our daughter went to a school in Paris where gaining entrance into those universities was a revered, manic obsession. Want a few of their mantras?"

She listened carefully.

"I guess it's a good thing my grades went in the toilet *last* year," she said. "Starting this year, they really count, right?"

"So they say."

"My dad left us last year."

"He didn't want to be married anymore," her mom added faintly.

I searched the girl's vulnerable eyes. So much was unsaid, perhaps unknown. "There are millions who have lost a parent through divorce, but it doesn't make your own pain any less. Grieve all your loss."

She nodded mutely, her eyes filling. It was as though a millstone had ground across her back, leaving a deep furrow of wounds.

ANOTHER BELT BUCKLE, ANOTHER MILLSTONE

The weekend in the valley flew by. It was only three brief days, yet in that time a delicate thread wove itself in and out of a number of significant conversations. It led to a glimpse of many sobering wounds, all acquired during childhood, in these wildly successful adults. I believe God is broken-hearted, even angry, over the holes ground into their hearts during their childhoods, even though their achievements beautifully hide the scars.

Big Bob Bond, one of those successful, overcomer types, was grist for the family mill. His dad often beat him with a belt buckle or, at other times, with barbed wire, depending on his twisted inspiration. Bob's wife, Betty, was shocked when she first met his family. Arriving at their ranch, she saw cattle scattering all over the hillside as father cussed out son with nightmarish skill. In it all, Big Bob learned to persevere and excel where others would have failed. Though he met God at the age of twenty-nine, grabbing onto his heavenly Father's love with great vehemence, tender mercy is a quality Bob displays with difficulty. Some still think of him more as Big Bad Bob.

Much of the weight of his millstone remains, though decades have passed and his father is dead.

Hex, Weye, and Zee

The distinctive thread of the weekend in Belt Buckle Territory brought to mind my precious friend, Zee. Her Eastern European parents grew up in the aftermath of World War II. Her father, Weye, was orphaned as a toddler and her mother, Hex, was given away when three to a childless couple. Hex remembers standing as a little girl in the driveway of her strange new home and running after her mother's disappearing car, calling for her to return. The child's life was shorn of loving arms wrapped tight around her, stripped of bedtime kisses and forced into unpaid servitude in a distant household.

Zee's parents married young and then immigrated far north to a land of heavy snow and deep forests. Hex was predictably tough with her first-born child. Though their daughter never cried, Weye left the house during the random thrashings his wife inflicted. Because young Zee didn't speak her adopted country's language, she appeared slow when she started school. There were no aids for the tiny immigrant now fluent in five languages.

Her parents became pillars in their church, a community of good, clean, hard-working Christians. Yet, no one said anything about the bruises. The unrealistic standards driving the impressionable child were braided with biblical truth. Zee learned to associate love with meeting ever-higher standards. It drove her to excel. Ultimately, it also drove her to "date her mother," so to speak, over and over again.

Zee found men who criticized her work and her beauty, men who took advantage of her needs, and men who demanded she jump over ever-rising bars of achievement. Their charm was only a thin veneer.

"Gentle men are always weak," my precious friend insisted.

"God, who loves you tenderly, is also strong," I countered. "It's how I love you."

"Men like that are spineless."

"Ron isn't."

"He's different."

Zee knows biblical truth thoroughly, but the distance between head and heart is more than eighteen inches—it's closer to eighteen years packed full of conditional, unreliable, earned "love."

I suspect we are all Zees. We are also all Zee's parents. Perhaps that's the reason Jesus said, "If anyone harms one of my children it would be better to take that millstone, tie it around their neck, and throw themselves into a sea."[5]

I deserve a millstone wrapped around my neck.

Recently I took my son's face in my hands and sadly confessed, "Daddy and I gave you this curse of perfectionism; it leaked from every pore of our bodies, though we often said otherwise. If you want, we can walk out of this valley together."

The ongoing process of repenting, forgiving, and making amends—even seventy times seven times in the same day—is the healing hope Jesus offers to the milled and miller alike.

Le Printemps— Spring 2009

March: Visits with Fear

MARCH 31 LOOMS ever closer. It's the day Ron and I will be officially unemployed. We'll be dangling with a big blank page in front of us, our future uncertain. Dangling scares me.

When it became clear we weren't returning to France, I submitted my request. "Not the dangling thing again, OK? God? God! Hello?" The connection wasn't clear. I left several messages, just in case. "Could you deliver something with, uh…long-term security?"

Fear calls me. As March 31 slides closer, fear shows up at my door carrying a large trunk with him. He's prepared to camp out in my living room for a while.

HOME ALONE

Fear's first splashy visit came in the Pre-Cell Phone epoch. I was seventeen, home alone with my twelve-year-old brother. Around midnight, two quasi-friends set a ladder against our two-story house, pulled hoods over their heads, and lurched along on the

219

roof of our front porch roof. They cast hulking shadows on my bedroom wall. When that wasn't fun anymore, they broke inside and made enough sinister sounds to let me know intruders were creeping up the stairs. I fled to my brother's bedroom in a panic, shaking him awake.

"Get out of here. I have a hockey game at four A.M.," he said, rolling over and pulling the covers over his head.

I tried calling the police but my devious friends had disconnected our phone. They snuck out of our house, neglecting to inform me it was just a joke.

THE BIG, BAD APPLE

Fear paid another vivid call when I was traveling with a vocal band based out of New York City. We were rehearsing in a home on the Hudson River for another tour when I remembered I had left my purse in our van, parked in a wooded, unlit area on the property. I pleaded with the guys to retrieve it for me. They refused. Knowing I would have to go to the van by myself, they slipped out a side door and hid under the vehicle so they could grab my legs when I arrived.

THE DANGER OF CHURCH ATTENDANCE

No pranks were involved the third time Fear dropped by to pay a major visit. My baby girl had napped long that December afternoon. She was twenty-two months old. When we finally arrived at church, late, to build wreaths at the evening Advent service, everyone was inside and all the regular parking was taken. I pulled into the back alley beside a big yellow bus and busied myself getting my toddler out of her car seat. Inside the church, Ron was leading the first joyful carols of the season. By the time I straightened up with Sheena in my arms, a man was standing six feet away.

"Put the baby back in the car," he barked.

"What?" I narrowed my eyes, trying to make out his face under the black stocking hat.

"Put the baby back in the car." His tone was aggressive.

"What would I do that for?" I replied crossly, not about to have a stranger tell me what to do with my child. I felt my mother bear face glaring at him.

He waved his gun at me. Though the vacant alley was dark, his weapon caught the weak light of a distant streetlamp. I hadn't noticed the thick revolver. It didn't look anything like Justin's water guns—those were fluorescent orange and neon green. This was scratched. Black. Real. I held Sheena tightly.

"Put the baby down," he ordered.

I was relieved he no longer insisted on putting her in the car. I set Sheena down beside me, expecting her to fuss. Post-nap time was never a strong moment in her day. She stood stock-still, completely silent, sucking her thumb, clinging to my leg and her blanket. It seemed the angel of small children had wrapped his enchanted wings around her; she was freeze-framed.

A strange conversation went on for some time between the man whose skin was badly pocked, his gun waving at my chest, and me, trying to keep him calm and so grateful Sheena wasn't doing anything to rattle him. I finally offered him my wallet, desperately trying to bring about an ending. When he swaggered beyond my view, I staggered to the church door, my knees no longer obeying my brain, Sheena heavy in my arms.

My little girl wanted me to assure her it would never happen again. I couldn't. I vaguely feared I had used up God's miracle quota. He had granted the miracle gift of this second child after six-and-a-half barren years, He had given the treasured gift of good work at Salem Alliance Church, and He had spared my toddler and me from tragedy. My inside-out baseball theology vaguely suggested, *Three homeruns by God and game over.*

House Sliding

When we learned our house was sliding down the hill, just as Ron resigned from Salem Alliance Church, our lives seemed to tumble and dangle arbitrarily. I did more than invite Fear in for a visit. I let him manipulate the blinds on the window of my soul.

In those dark years, I remember staring at the test holes drilled in our back yard. One of them went down forty feet and still didn't hit solid ground. I thought bleakly, *Each one of these small holes could send our family to Europe and back.*

During that painful season of dangling, God hit numerous homeruns—more than three. There was the stunning house legal settlement, Ron's outrageous two-year California worship leading experience (while living in Oregon!), and the timely Court Street Christian Church interim ministry role. There were the sky-high tuition bills for Sheena's schooling in Paris—bills met every April, September, and December four years in a row, never a penny short, never late. We didn't beg for funds or remind people. Funds simply came—major points for God. There was the whole over-the-top, out-of-the-park Paris experience. All of it was simply an enormous grand slam.

However, the last year we lived in Paris, with the dollar softening so severely and unexpected medical problems, we slid into debt. It was early spring when I pleaded with God, "Lord, I don't want to ask for money. I'm capable of working. I have skills. Could You please provide a way for me to earn the money we need?"

An unusual bird I had never heard before trilled exuberantly every morning outside my window all week long. I felt God was singing over me, reminding He was not far away. Then the emails started to arrive. "Lorelei, I know you're only home for a year, but even so, would you be interested in teaching piano lessons?" All except one came from people I had never met. Our debt was paid by November.

God's tangible provisions perch on my piano bench every week and yet, as March 31 breathes down my neck, I battle apprehension. How can I still flirt with Fear, inviting him in for tea, when my pockets are bulging full of miracles? I just do, even as I gratefully book three more new piano students.

TRUSTING LOVE

I spoke at a retreat in the Seattle area last weekend. As I drove north under a blue sky scrubbed clean by frequent rain, National Public Radio droned in the background, seeding glum economic news and forewarning job paucity. It wasn't a good season for job-hunting. Ron was trying to plant tropical flowers on a cold, prairie winter day. We'd already watched a few hopeful buds droop and die. The season seemed to be more conducive to pruning.

In spite of the sunshine, dismal scenarios slid through my mind as I stared blindly at passing traffic. I was about to indulge a little dread when a strong, kind presence gathered my stray thoughts, pulling my heart into a comforting embrace. I turned off the radio as an inaudible voice caught my heart. "Lorelei, you doubted so much during those hard desert years prior to Paris. They were difficult. You questioned my love as you suffered. Now the dangling days are coming in for a landing. Again. With all those miracles blooming in your past, could you trust me this time? It is not my nature to throw you out of the game when you can't hit the fastballs. It is my nature to hit countless homeruns for you, though I will choose when you walk, when you will be carried around the bases, and when the other team will win for a decade or two. Don't be afraid. You have another chance to trust my love in the desert."

I continued north on the freeway through heavy forests of Douglas fir, driving on remote in the silent van. I was almost mesmerized by the message and its strange mercy. By late Saturday night, I had one session left to teach at the retreat. We'd made our way through Moses' misadventures up to the story in Numbers 13 of the spies returning from the Promised Land. Ten of those handpicked leaders spread a toxic report among the people like rats carrying bubonic plague. They massaged fear. Hysteria erupted as their infectious half-truths spread through the camp and fatally blurred Israel's ability to think clearly. The frightened people reinvented their past, re-coloring their slavery years in pastel pinks and sunny yellows as God's out-of-the-park miracles were carelessly erased.

I read and reread the story late Saturday night before turning off the lamp and going to sleep. Sometime in the heavy dark of the chilly night, I startled awake, missing Ron. I snuggled deeper under two heirloom quilts, wondering if the retreat center would mind if just one disappeared.

Then it came to me. Slowly. Gently. Would I choose to repeat Israel's folly or remember who God is? Neglect my list of His homeruns or recite them often? Pet the manipulative messages of fear or grab trust? God lets me choose. Though I walk through a valley of shadows, I choose to fear no evil. God is with me. His rod, His staff, His ways, His love—they will comfort me.

March: My Brain Takes a Ride

SEIZURE

The young pianist I came to watch was exceptional. I hardly breathed as she flew through seventeen pages of Beethoven. Her technique sparkled like fine-cut crystal. When she finished, we left the auditorium to discuss the weird pedal on the piano and all those technical complaints we musicians love to hurl at the feet of the instrument. We were happily chatting with her mom, quite excited by her extraordinary success, when I noticed the shadow of a fan flashing by the side of my head. There it was again—a flashing shadow in my left field of vision. I decided I would sit in the car and wait for it to pass before I drove home.

It was still early for a Saturday morning so I crawled back into bed beside Ron. I tried to rest, feeling vaguely disturbed but not sure why.

"Are you OK?" Ron asked.

"I think so." I fell asleep beside him.

An hour later, I woke. When I opened my eyes, the world had magically multiplied. Everything was double. I squeezed my brows tightly together, trying to bring the lamp and dresser into focus. Still, there were two of everything.

"Are you OK?" Ron asked me again.

"Um, no."

"What's going on, honey?"

"I'm seeing double."

"Should I take you to the hospital?"

"No, no, no. I'll be all right."

All I could think of was the cost; getting medical help was out of the question. Then a sharp pain stabbed my left side. Was this a stroke? Ron leaped to call 911. Just as the dispatcher answered, a seizure commandeered my body and I lost consciousness, my back arcing, eyes rolling back, arms and legs jerking erratically, froth running from my mouth. The short moments I quit breathing did not feel brief for Ron.

Sirens screamed. Five minutes later, five paramedics were crowded around the bed where I lay. Ron tells me I fought with them until he leaned down and whispered in my ear, "Honey, they're here to help you." Perhaps I suspected the havoc they would wreak with their efficient scissors; my best Merino wool turtleneck sweater was cut in three and my favorite French brassiere destroyed by their pragmatic slashes. Sirens wailed as they rushed me to Emergency. I don't remember a single second of the drama.

Medical tests quickly confirmed there was a tumor the size of a ping-pong ball in my brain. After a long day in which life took a major turn we couldn't see coming, Ron wrote this email from my hospital bedside on the evening of March 7, 2009:

It's absolutely astounding what can happen in a short slice of time. It's just as amazing to see how God prepares us. One moment I'm waking up from a Saturday nap next to Lorelei and then the next I'm calling 911. This woman I love so much is having a seizure. In four hours we learn of a possible lesion in the brain. In another two, we're talking about surgery tomorrow (Sunday) at nine thirty A.M. to remove a ping-pong-ball-sized tumor from the back right side of Lorelei's brain. Fortunately, it's well defined and quite near the scalp. How fragile we indeed are. Lord, have mercy.

He then drove home to an empty house. In the desolate hours of the early morning, sleep was elusive.

Surgery

The operating room was available that Sunday morning, so my brain was dissected less than twenty-four hours after diagnosis by one of Salem's very best neurosurgeons. Before surgery, he came into the small room where my precious family and my friend Jane waited. He told them that the evening before, he was waiting for a red light when he noticed two vehicles barrel through the intersection through a yellow light. Though his light turned green, he felt cautioned to sit and wait a few moments longer. As he lingered, a large, heavy SUV came flying through the intersection, ignoring a blazing red light.

Dr. Hubbard looked at my family and said, "If I had gone through my green light last night I would not be performing surgery today. I believe Someone wanted me here this morning."

I was wheeled away, a cherished card from Ron grasped firmly in my hand. An area the size of an index card was shaved on the back of my head. The skin was cut in a large, grotesque C-shape and folded back. The skull section was cut out and set aside. There lay the tumor, right at the surface, all in a purple sack with no tentacles or fingers the surgeon could see. After he removed the invasive ball, chemo wafers were inserted in its place. Ron loves to claim, "For a small extra fee, a compliancy wafer was implanted as well." It was a poor investment; my feisty lobe regains a few grains of vigor every day. The hole in the back of my head was refilled with the skull piece and slim titanium plates were screwed into place to cover the open edges.

It was from the surgery room where my family received the numbing phone call from the surgeon. Everything had gone well, but the tumor was cancerous, and it looked to be aggressive.

I woke up in the intensive care unit, the treasured card from Ron still grasped in my hand.

SUPPORT

Staying in the ICU was rather impressive. The service was unbelievable, not far removed from that in a VIP presidential suite at the Hilton. I didn't even have to leave the bed to use a toilet. The blankets were pre-warmed...ooh-la-la. The stellar amenities were slightly dampened by the required "uniform" that always hung open in the back. This, together with a blanket only thirty-six inches wide, allowed cold breezes to chase away all thoughts of modest sleep any time I rolled over.

While my dear friend kept watch together with my family, a suspicious nurse demanded, "Who are you?" The petite pastor, unrelated in any legal or genetic sense, looked straight at the nurse and said, "I'm her stepsister."

She was permitted to stay.

God surrounded me with kind, understanding medical people from nurses to doctors. He knew the difference it would make to a neurotic "mediphobic" woman like me, someone who passes out while visiting friends in the hospital. The biggest annoyance was the analytical, science-type questions these folk insisted on asking an intuitive, artist-type person who had suddenly fallen into some mutant biology experiment. They kept on pressing.

"Are you dizzy or weak?"

"Is the headache all over your head or only on one side?"

"What's your pain level on a scale of one to ten?"

"I have a hole in the back of my head. How should I know?"

The nurses woke me every two hours to take a small slice of meat out of my finger. They called it a prick. I called it dishonesty. I offered to pick an impressive scab on my hand so the process would register lower on their omnipresent pain scale. They merely scorned my stellar scab idea.

By Sunday night, I was complaining about the pee tube. Of course, it had to be a male nurse with whom I was having this delicate conversation. I begged him to take out the rubber hose, arguing it wasn't working. He insisted on shoving it in farther—one of his very worst ideas. We struck a deal. If I could pee by the end of his shift, the tube would stay out. I politely asked for water.

He had nerve. "No water yet."

He tried to be nice about it, giving some weak medical excuse, but I could see through his game. He must have been an oldest child with a desperate need to always win.

I bargained. "May I have ice chips?" Once he agreed, I put my family to work running for cups of ice as fast as I could melt them in my desperate mouth.

Boy Nurse had another move up his sleeve. He showed up with a bedpan, denying me the relaxed dignity normal people usually enjoy. He was definitely stacking the deck unfairly. Though he seemed to hold all the trump cards, I still deposited a landmark victory by seven P.M.

As I lay in recovery, every kindness melted my heart. Each benevolence was a gold brick in heaven's economy. Teflon-coated emotions were deeply scoured by the trauma. Whenever I heard of an individual or group of people praying for me, I was deeply touched and started to cry. God's goodness was the handrail I hung on to, providing stability and holding up my jelly legs. I tangibly felt love carrying me, overwhelmed by the care of the church family we left ten years ago. It was as though we were never gone.

DISCHARGE

Five days after surgery, I was discharged from the hospital. The sun shone warmly as I walked slowly, cautiously, up the walk to our cottage. A breeze ruffled my hair not covered by the stylish turban wrapped tightly around my head. Then I saw them—a plethora of potted flowers waved cheery hellos from all over my yard. Pansy angels had visited. Their card said they were pulling for me as hard as they could. One of the pots even had a Paris address on it. I soaked the garden well with my tears.

A week passed. Everything was progressing so well, except for a small, itchy rash from the anti-seizure medication. Brain surgery and chemo wafers in the brain make those meds a necessity for a while. Yet, four days later, pre-seizure symptoms returned.

I couldn't find the faucet to turn off the water or figure out how to get my arms around Ron's neck so I could walk. It was difficult to place my hands in my lap. I seemed to be getting in on the hallucinations and groovy trips of the '70s, though without tie-dyed shirts or recreational drugs and with much less hair. I ended up back in the hospital by Wednesday afternoon. It was a very low, frightening day.

Strength tiptoes back into my life stealthily, though not nearly as quickly as I would prefer. I have a little pity cry each morning while Ron holds me and reminds me there will be blue moments and they're OK. Best of all, my precious God tenderly sends much goodness and mercy my way. Like the delicious food arriving on our doorstep each day, teasing my appetite. Like my mom and sister beautifully cleaning our cottage and denuding my fridge of the green, fuzzy science experiments I was unknowingly cultivating.

People are praying passionately even though there's nothing in it for them. How hard it must be to pray when one does not see the havoc wreaked by this weapon on the other side of heaven's gate, when one does not hear, "I owe you a great debt," or does not receive a well-deserved card of thanks. I hang on dearly to these prayers for healing rising from the far-flung crannies of this globe.

Phone calls come from my dear Madame D. in Paris. She sees me at the bus stop where she often waited for me, on our route down Rue de Renne, and on the street where she guided me to the doctor. She prays, prays, prays over my invisible footsteps laced through Paris.

There are so many undeserved, gold-brick goodnesses invested on my behalf. I am believing and accepting—at a new, unexplored level—how deeply God loves me. He is using the prayers, kindnesses, and arms of many to touch my fragile heart and hold me together.

April: Outside the Numbers

MEMO FROM HEAVEN

Talk danced delicately around the grade of my tumor. Its diagnosis wasn't certain—maybe a 3.5, perhaps 3. It wasn't normal so it was sent out for a second opinion. I reassured myself, "At least the tumor isn't a 4. Somehow I can be healed."

The call finally came. My oncologist wanted to see me; the pathology report was now in from Portland. Our hearts sank; we suspected a difficult day lay ahead.

"Yea, though I walk through the valley of the shadow of medical facilities I will fear no evil." I looped the words in my mind as my knees turned to jelly, my stomach flipped, and my nose detected that nauseating odor reminiscent of science labs. The world of doctors, nurses, and laboratory smells has never set well with me. I had a premonition our visit to the doctor's office would suck the air out of my balloon.

"I just want you to know who I am before we start," I explained to my kind doctor. "I don't do well with medical procedures, medical buildings, or medical statistics. I am a worst-case scenario kind of a person with a vivid imagination so, whatever you tell me, please do it gently. And, uh, don't tell me my statistics."

He calmly outlined the plan for chemotherapy by pill every morning, telling me it wouldn't make me sick and it would be the radiology oncologist's fault, not his, that I would lose my hair.

Finally, I asked the one dreadful question. "What grade is my tumor?"

He looked at me quietly, took a second, and without a word held up four fingers. A 4? What happened to 3.5? I was stunned, leaving the room dazed while Ron and our nurse friend stayed to talk statistics.

We drove away silent, both of us reeling with the news. It was a new low. We had planned a coffee date for after the appointment so we had something good to anticipate. A parking space waited for us right in front of the bakery. We walked in and our favorite server was standing behind the counter.

"How are you two today?" She smiled warmly.

My minimalist husband replied, "It's not one of our better days."

She persisted. "Is it the gray weather getting you down?"

Ron said, "No, one of us isn't feeling very well."

"Oh, is it the flu or a cold?"

By now I was right in front of the counter, looking into her beautiful, deep-brown eyes. No one else was around, so I took the leap. "No, I'm fighting brain cancer."

She immediately quieted. "Oh, I am so sorry. I've had breast cancer twice. Who is your radiology oncologist?"

"Dr. Hennig."

"Oh, my goodness! She was mine. She is the very best, ever so kind and president of the tumor board. She will go to the end of the earth to fight for you. May I give you a hug?"

Out from behind the counter came this gentle baker who wrapped her strong arms around me. I felt like Jesus had taken on flesh to hold me for just a minute.

We took our goodies down to the old, small Starbucks® at the end of the block. We used to have so much fun sneaking away from church on Sunday mornings after the first of three services to treat the worship band to a beverage and energy booster—OK, a pastry. Now we sat there quietly, just the two of us. What was there to say? After a few moments, noticing that we sat at the only table for three—one of the chairs was empty—I remembered a time Ron had led worship with an empty chair on the platform to remind us of God's unseen presence. Here it was again, the empty chair, begging us to remember Jesus walking with us. How well our Savior understood our despair, firsthand.

A dark cloak, complete with hanging hood, suffocated my spirit. The morning passed dimly. We sat down for a lunch I couldn't eat. As I opened my mouth, unconscious thoughts swimming below the surface tumbled out to Ron. "I feel like I can't ask for healing anymore. If the tumor was a 3 or a 3.5, it wouldn't seem so risky to ask God for healing. However, because the tumor is... a 4." I stopped to control my tears so I could speak. "I can't ask anymore. If God says no, the disappointment will be overwhelming. So I'll protect myself. I'll also protect God's reputation. If He says 'no' and lets science take its normal course, how will He look?"

I recalled time after time I had given up on praying for the impossible far too soon. My faith had been self-protective, corroded by science.

As I lay in bed that evening wondering how I would sleep, the story of Gideon popped into my mind. It was sent from heaven, hand-picked for my bedtime.

Gideon was on a covert mission. He was grinding wheat in a wine press to avoid detection by Mideonite marauders who ravaged

Israel's world. As flour flew from the wine press, an angel appeared, telling Gideon he was to lead his defeated nation in a war against the superpower. Gideon was afraid. He questioned, he doubted; insecurities surfaced. So the angel used his staff like a blowtorch to light Gideon's sacrifice.

Gideon was comforted for a few days, but as D-Day came closer, worried Gideon asked for more reassurances. God sent them through comforting fleeces and another dream.

On the big day, thirty-two thousand volunteers peeked out from behind Gideon's skirts, trying to count the Mideonites' high-tech, spitting camels replete with intimidating bling. Gideon's men, holding only trumpets and pottery jars, could no more count the camels than they could the sand at the seashore.

Gideon's guys were hunkered around their campfires, biting their fingernails, spreading the word about the vicious camels and their big jewelry, when God pulled apprehensive Gideon aside and said, "I can't work with these kinds of numbers. I don't want there to be any doubt about who wins this war. Tell all the 'fraidy cats' to take off."

Though twenty-two thousand ran for home, God still wasn't satisfied. He caught Gideon's attention again. "You still have too many guys. I don't want anyone thinking victory is yours because of your own power."

God left Gideon with three hundred men. Though Israel was grossly outnumbered, the Mideonites were beaten to a pulp. God beat the numbers. Gideon's team even got to take home expensive souvenirs.

I rolled over in bed to whisper in Ron's ear, "God is outside the numbers," and then told him the short version of Gideon's story. Ron reminded me Jesus was outside the numbers when He fed five thousand men with five loaves and two fishes. There was comfort in that thought as we fell asleep.

Even so, Thursday was dark in every way. It rained. It was cold. In spite of the memo from heaven regarding Gideon, I struggled. Hope was on a slow journey from my head to my heart.

Friday morning began with an appointment at the cancer clinic. The staff usually run on time but that particular morning they were late. As I waited, a man came in, stopped, looked at me, and hesitated. I smiled, wondering if he was someone I should recognize.

He reintroduced himself, adding, "I understand you're going through difficult times."

"Yes. I'm fighting brain cancer."

"I am too."

He asked a few questions. We learned we both had stage four tumors.

"Listen," he told me, "they will tell you all kinds of dire things, but don't believe them. Never give up hope. They would have had me dead years ago."

I don't remember the rest of the conversation. I think I was too shocked by the obvious reassurance God sent me.

It was now time to map my brain, after which a physics team would design how best to fry it. As I lay on a table, a soft, wet, plastic plate was laid on my face and stretched over it all the way to the table.

"Lots of women say it feels like a facial." The techie tried to be positive.

"If that's what a facial feels like, I can't believe people pay money for it."

At first I couldn't breathe. Wet, limp plastic covered my nose and mouth. I knew not to move, not even the width of a fly's leg. As the techie worked, indentations were pushed in at my nostrils and eyes so the fit was exact. Once the plastic hardened into a mesh hood over my entire head, it was screwed onto the table. Next, crosshairs formed by a variety of red laser beams were carefully marked; each time I came for treatment the rays would hit their target within one millimeter from their mark.

When the process was finally finished, I thanked the young man for his kindness, adding he was unusual for a science-kind-of-guy.

"Oh, you don't want to meet the physics team," he blurted. Then he bravely mentioned the unspoken. "I guess this must be pretty difficult."

"Yes, it's been very hard."

"It will probably be at least two weeks before treatment begins. It normally takes ten days just for the physics team to do the math."

"Dr. Hennig told me they would try to squeeze me in within a week as my cancer is so aggressive."

He looked genuinely sad for me.

So I asked him, "Do you believe in God?"

"Yes, I do."

"Well, do you know any Bible stories?"

"I went to Sunday school when I was a little boy."

"Do you know the story of Gideon?"

He shook his head.

One little voice in my head started screaming at me, "Don't tell! Don't tell! If you're a regular science statistic, God is going to look really bad." The other little voice nervously argued, "It's not your fault God sent bedtime story angels to you last night. Go for it."

I recounted the short version of Gideon's story. The doubtful techie was working hard to arrange his face with an appropriate expression. "Well, there are always outliers," he conceded.

It's true. They are the isolated, bizarre data lying outside the clump of collected statistics. If researchers include them, they ruin the math, so they just throw them out. They're forgotten. Outliers. I call them miracles. They still happen. Science ignores them. God creates them.

My doctor has two ex-patients in Salem who had what I have; he can't explain why they have recovered. I can't demand my healing, but I am convinced God calls me to come running to Him with my heart's desire—to be an outlier—believing He can do anything He wants with the numbers.

Each night as I lie in the radiation tube, I recite over and over again a verse given to me by my dear friend, Jane. It carries me through the day as well.

I am the Lord the Maker of all things,
who stretches out the heavens,
who spreads out the earth by myself,
who foils the signs of false prophets
and makes fools of diviners,
who overthrows the learning of the wise
and turns it into nonsense.[6]

April: Maps

In my estimation, maps are not particularly riveting. I prefer words, stories and pictures. Ron forced me to read maps for the first time as we traveled around France. He claimed he couldn't read and drive at the same time. To my frustration, only the name of the next village would appear on the pint-sized autoroute road signs as we whizzed by. There was no mention of north, south, east, or west, just indecipherable, unpronounceable names. I was a frustrated, incompetent navigator desperately searching for little towns I couldn't locate on inaccurately labeled maps showing highway numbers that had been arbitrarily changed. Ron would think I was a drooling imbecile until he pulled over and looked for himself.

This month, I learned a map would be made of my brain. I was hoping for more accuracy than some of our French guides. After all, a physics team would use it to design the best routes for zapping rays through my head without doing brain damage. My cerebral matter was mapped on a Friday. Days passed. Silence. It was now more than three weeks after my surgery.

"Ron, should I be concerned about how long it's taking to get treatment started?"

"Let's wait until Wednesday and then call, OK?"

Ron made the promised call; a technician called back in short order. "Hey, this is really something. Normally it takes the physics team ten days just to do the math, but your wife's results are already back. They're testing this afternoon and, if everything is accurate, she starts radiation at eight P.M. tomorrow."

I wondered if they used a watermelon for testing—if it didn't explode, things proceeded. Though I didn't get to check if the radiologist's maps were more reliable than those in France, I was almost excited to get the process under way.

My treatment plan specified taking chemo pills the same day I began radiation. Before I popped the first pill, Ron read the impressive list of possible side effects and a warning not to touch the contents of the capsule with bare hands should it accidentally open. Though the doctor was confident this medication would not make me sick, my tummy reported otherwise after a few hours. My head felt as though someone had crowded all the furniture to the center; it was hot in there. By noon I was in bed and an hour later, my body's rebellion was in full swing. Yet, by evening, I could make it to my first radiation appointment.

At the clinic, beginners sit through thirty minutes of skin-care instructions before they're radiated for the first time. A pleasant nurse instructed: stay out of the sun, use sunscreen, wrap up carefully, wear a hat. No hot showers, no water pulsing on my head, use only baby shampoo.

There was special cream for peeling, cracked ears. The tube of heavy cream for my imminently bald scalp read, "Protects skin irritations associated with diaper dermatitis and helps protect from wetness." My crown of glory seemed to be headed for more shame than a baby's pocked bottom in an unchanged diaper.

"Do you have a wig?" the nurse asked kindly.

I thought thirty minutes of bald talk and being reminded, again, that my hair might never grow back was the lowest point of my day until the nurse nicely mentioned, "You'll need to go into the radiation room tonight by yourself."

I had been told differently. I wasn't prepared for this.

"What? Ron can't come with me and watch this first time?"

I was shocked as the nurse shook her head. My bravery was mute and numb; I became deaf to the pert, pretty radiation therapist whose thick hair swung down around her shoulders as she walked me down the long hall to the lead-lined radiation room.

"They could at least hire one bald staff person," I pouted silently.

A large sign on the door of the formidable room cautioned, "WARNING! ACTIVE RADIATION!" The door was a heavy, thick steel contraption probably borrowed from a bank vault. This was where I would lie alone on a carbon table, my head tightly screwed down, while radiation rays fried my brain. Much time was taken making a new map, checking and rechecking it against the old map, calling the doctor, and fine-tuning the calibrations. I kept recycling my trio of favorite scripture portions with no way to check which words or lines I was ineptly shuffling like a nervous dealer applying for a job in Vegas. Finally, they were ready.

After twenty-five minutes, including 210.8 seconds of actual fry time, I was set free to run for Ron. We walked outside into the dark night air where I began to cry. It hadn't hurt in any way, but I found it traumatic. I was an alien trapped in a *Star Trek* experiment. We walked around the perimeter of the hospital with its park and beautiful creek, Ron's protective arm strong around me. My crying slowed and stopped until we drove home. When I saw Justin there, my tears started again, the second verse of the same song.

The chemo performance on day two was far worse than on day one. It was the same day I received another email informing me of yet someone else's relative who had died of cancer. It continued to tell me the husband was now happily remarried and asked if perhaps, between battles with cancer, I could come and speak at a retreat.

On day three of chemo, I looked at a new pink pill lying in my hand. It was the same color as the old anti-nausea medication, but much tinier. What hope could something so small possibly hold? After taking it, I felt great. It was completely amazing. It was a turning point.

As we count down the days, marking off each one on the calendar, Ron suggests I think of the medical staff as friends who are there to help me. Now, after two weeks of basking in nuclear rays, the technicians are looking for ways to move along the lady with black curly hair who talks too much. We have so little time to visit.

In this "valley of the shadow of death," there are periods of warm sunshine when my Shepherd leads me to frolic in green pastures and bask by beautiful ponds. I hear from menopausal friends and young moms with crying babies, neither of whom sleep well through the night. They cover me with healing prayers in the wee hours of the night. Friends, even people I don't know, are begging and arguing with God for an astonishing miracle. As I run in this green meadow, I'm enjoying a droopy version of the thinner teenage body I never had. Ron laughs and says he's going to get in trouble for carrying on with a minor.

Other days, heavy waves sneak in unexpectedly. Recently, a doctor responded to my hope with, "Well, we need to be realistic…" Though I held up my hands to stop what more she might have said, I still slowly sank under dark water, inch by inch. I have found one single way to stay above the waterline: It is essential to refocus my hope every morning.

One morning I tried to pray quietly, "Jesus, I believe. Help my unbelief." It was as difficult to get my mind to stop bouncing as it is to stop a six-year-old from jumping on a trampoline. As I persisted in my efforts to stop my impressive mental gymnastics, a picture of Jesus' hands on my wounded head slid into view. I quieted, deeply touched. For some unknown reason, a random thought popped up. I remembered a decision I made as a small child: If I expect the worst, then I won't be so disappointed when my hopes don't come true.

It's a mantra I never learned to abandon. I can vividly describe a worst-case scenario regarding any situation in less than a second. I would qualify for the Olympics in this event, except for my steroid intake. Anyway, as I saw Jesus' hands on my head, I heard Him gently urge, "Give Me your anxieties and your need to protect yourself from disappointment. Give Me this propensity to fear the worst. Trust Me to give you good gifts, even when you have stage four cancer."

Trust is no small thing for me. I'm the girl who routinely reads the last chapter of a book first—if I don't like how it ends, I find another book. Now my illusion of control is being removed; my own last chapter is uncertain. Replacing my fear with trust is difficult because the roots of angst, curling through decades of my life, go deep into my soul.

I began by lifting up my brokenness, crying out, "Oh, Jesus, I can't change me, so I release these flaws to You. Please gift me with your own faith." As I stayed quiet, my "picture" shifted. Jesus, my Healer, put one great, strong arm around my back, holding me close. His other scarred hand held the back of my head where shorn hair and surgery mark me.

Whispering gently, Jesus assured me, "I not only want to heal your head physically, I want to heal the way you think as well. My little Lamb, we'll go together and it will be good."

May: My Pearls

Alternatives to Aging

I recall Ron, Sheena, and I chatting over a late dinner in the corner of our salon in Paris. In the fading evening light, I looked out over the city past my balcony with its myriad pots and plants bringing a touch of jungle to our cement world. Sheena was telling us of another high school assignment, a biology research paper she had just presented in class. She thought I would be quite interested in the results of her extensive research.

"What was your project about?" I asked innocently.

"Menopause."

"Oh. Really."

It didn't turn out to be one of my favorite reports. God seems to have built a large chunk of inequality between the aging of men and women. I was inspired to watch covertly for the dread signs. I checked the mirror, plucked unwanted hairs, monitored freckles (now called "age spots"), and considered natural alternatives to aging.

Now, in the blink of a seizure, I have received news of a natural alternative to aging, one I really don't like. I have a hunger for life, so thirty years of menopause suddenly sounds very good. I ask God for it every day.

The Wolves

There are days I rest content in my Shepherd's arms, trusting His strong love. Other days are much more difficult. When the Shepherd is carrying me through the valley of shadows and the wolves are running, I get anxious. Before I realize what I'm doing, I slip from the Shepherd's arms and land on the back of What-If. The pack turns back to their lair once they've snared me. The brood mother is Fear and she breathes over me as if I'm her child.

What-If paints dire pictures. "What if Ron never finds a job? What if your medical insurance lapses? What if you relapse? What if, what if, what if…"

Sometimes days pass in the Cave of Fear where I can't hear my Shepherd's voice calling my name as He holds out the bracelet of pearls I've dropped. His great hounds, Love and Sorrow, wait patiently by his side, ready to drive away the wolves as soon as I give permission.

"Come back, Lorelei," my Shepherd gently calls. "Come. Wear the pearls I gave you. Let me hold you, my dear Lamb." The Shepherd holds out the beautiful bracelet as He crouches in front of the cave. I grasp the pearls and the Shepherd's enormous hounds leap to drive the wolves away.

My Fourteen Pearls

1. Ron and I had been traveling a great deal on the weekends, yet I was lying on my bed at home when the seizure happened. I was not driving to or from the piano competition I attended that Saturday morning.
2. Ron normally goes out first thing in the morning. He had also been away speaking on his own during the past weekends. But he was home, able to call 911 when my crisis began.
3. I was diagnosed and operated on in less than twenty-four hours—on a weekend. There was no time for the aggressive cancer to grow further.

4. My excellent neurosurgeon, one of Salem's best, paused at a green light the night before, sparing him an accident with a vehicle running its red light.
5. The tumor was right next to my skull, easily accessible, so all of it could be removed without brain damage.
6. The margins were clean; the cancer was in a sack with no visible tentacles.
7. I am healing well from major brain surgery.
8. I was assigned one of Salem's very best radiation oncologists, one who even understands my medical phobias.
9. Two days after the depressing oncology appointment when my bad numbers were announced, I bumped into a man I hardly knew who's had my same disease for quite a few years. He told me to never give up hope, that science would tell me all kinds of dire things, but not to believe them.
10. God gave me the story of Gideon after I first heard the devastating news from my oncologist. It's a story where God defies the numbers and shows His ability to confound the learning of the wise and turn it into nonsense.
11. The math for designing how to "fry" my brain was done in three days instead of ten, so treatment could start quickly.
12. If this had happened after March 31, we wouldn't have had medical insurance due to our unemployed status at the end of the month.
13. Salem Alliance Church holds us tightly in its loving arms; every way we turn we are surrounded with care. Though we have been away from this church for ten years, people are even helping with the astronomical medical costs. They bring us cards, flowers, meals, and groceries like manna falling on our doorstep in this desert.
14. Our mission agency has extended our employment as long as people donate to our support fund. We count it a great gift of mercy.

THE FIFTEENTH PEARL

Just before leaving Paris only ten months ago, a gentle young man gave me a precious gift of fresh-water pearls from his country, the Philippines. I try to wear them every day, reminding me of the fourteen other God-given pearls. I rehearse them over and over to avoid the wolves' snare. Ron calls the necklace my Protestant rosary.

Even so, I slip back to the Cave of Fear more often than I realize. It's an ingrained habit. My gentle Shepherd always comes looking for me. Once I again feel safe in His strong arms, I plead in my best non-whiney voice, "Some more pearls would be reassuring. And... thirty years of menopause would be great."

My Shepherd tenderly explains, "I want to teach you how to live well with uncertainty, to embrace the present moments I give you. No one has certainty. It's an illusion you've lost, my dear Lamb."

I hesitate. This isn't the answer I want, but I concede. "OK, I do need to learn how to flourish in uncertainty, but could I still have another pearl? You didn't give me my hair wish and that was really disappointing."

My Shepherd smiles at me kindly. "Oh, but you've forgotten your most precious pearl. I gave this one to you nineteen years ago. I'd love it if you would add it to your collection."

Understanding dawns slowly and then wraps courage around my heart. Ron and I had wanted a second child for a number of disappointing years. We'd reached a point where doctors said it wasn't going to happen. Perhaps in vitro fertilization would hold some promise, but even then there were no guarantees. We felt directed to abandon medical solutions, stop all medications, and put the matter in God's hands. One thing we knew, the higher the stress, the less chance there was of conception.

That was the year Ron was the music director for our denomination's national conference being held in Seattle. Under his leadership, worship bands, rather than traditional musical accompaniment, were introduced at the general sessions. Progressives met conservatives, with Ron caught in the middle. It was a painful week, yet, with no medical interventions, after almost six years of waiting, with the stress of the conference skyrocketing off the charts, this was the week our daughter, Sheena, began her journey on this planet.

How can I forget this precious pearl running through my life as she calls from college to say, "Hi, Mom, I just wanted to hear your voice. I love you," and then shares her latest writing. It's an essential time for me to recount all the pearls scattered throughout my life. Remembering keeps me safe in the Shepherd's arms.

> I will remember the deeds of the Lord;
> Yes, I will remember your miracles of long ago.
> I will consider all your works
> And meditate on all your mighty deeds.
> Your ways, O God, are holy.
> What god is as great as our God?
> You are the God who performs miracles.[7]

L'Été—
Summer 2009

June: Corinthian Comfort

We were under great pressure,
Far beyond our ability to endure,
So that we despaired of life itself.
Indeed, we felt we had received the sentence of death.[8]

RON AND I counted the days, striking each one off our wall calendar. Forty-two, forty-one, forty…twenty-three… three, two, one, and finally Z-Day (for zero). I eagerly anticipated a surge of life rushing into my lethargic body at the end of daily radiation and chemotherapy. In spite of feeling an enormous weight roll off my shoulders during the last night of nuclear tanning, the Cave of Fear didn't easily release its hold. "Tired" was a grossly inadequate word. Something had sucked away my life force.

I watched my illness drain Ron. He said so little. He rarely complained. He was dealing with more than one blow. There was also the loss of meaningful work, accompanied by the rejection and disappointment associated with an unfruitful job search. What could I do except assure him? He had as much to process as I did.

I could give him the freedom to quit being my superhero, letting him take off his tights and cape.

Shortly after daily treatment ended, a high-contrast MRI was scheduled. My six-year-old self kicked in. "Why do I have to be someone who requires constant cancer checks? I don't want to go back there and have another fire hose shoved up my arm." Tears slid down my cheeks as we quietly drove to the clinic. Ron silently took my hand in his.

As we walked into Salem's new hospital, just open for only one or two days, everything was plush-posh new. It was beautiful, even by hotel standards. A supervisor, smiling with greater exertion than a Las Vegas showgirl, hovered over two women seated at the information desk. She murmured directives, though no guidance seemingly was needed, smiling and nodding at us between each muted command. An overwhelming abundance of niceness oozed over the counter and pooled at my feet. I sighed. Escorted to decorator chairs, color coordinated to perfection, we watched as our guide gestured like a game show host. A grand piano enticed me from a windowed corner.

A nurse called my name, ordering me to undress once we reached privacy. I looked at her and asked, "You need my clothes off to check my head?" After renegotiating, I left only my hat and shoes in the dressing room and followed fully dressed. She threaded through long, sterile hallways to a door leading outside. Since not all the hospital's new equipment was yet installed, I was escorted to a mobile MRI unit parked behind the hospital.

As we walked down the loading dock, construction workers gawked; the urge to stare at this curiously bald woman was irresistible. As I slunk down the ramp, I tried to rehearse all the advantages of baldness: car windows can be open and my bouffant is still unaffected, I have no hat hair after wearing a bike helmet, no one pulling a strand of curly hair from their dinner can look at me accusingly, and I look the same when I get out of bed in the morning as when I go to bed at night.

Once I was in place with the freak orchestral sounds of the MRI playing in my head, a random tear slipped down my cheek. "How do I find something precious in this moment, Shepherd?" I was petulant, certain it couldn't be found.

"Do you hear that?" the Shepherd asked me.

It sounded like jackhammers, though smaller than those heard on the street below our Paris apartment.

"That's the sound of dwarves drilling for gold in the walls of your valley." My Shepherd's eyes were twinkling.

I almost laughed out loud.

The neurosurgeon smiled after reviewing the results. My brain looked good, technically. I might be cancer free. Still, I kicked against the reality of returning every three months for another search, even if I would be hearing dwarves drilling for gold.

Just as I began to break free from the Cave of Fear and gain hope, I stumbled onto more grim statistics about my cancer. It was the most serious, the most fatal kind; the numbers were even worse than I had supposed. Wolves of Fear rushed back in full force, overrunning my valley.

Perhaps this was what Gideon felt when his already pathetically small army of thirty-two thousand was reduced to twenty-two thousand. Just as he got used to that number, God further reduced his odds, leaving him with three hundred to face 135,000.

> But this happened that we might not rely on ourselves
> but on God, who raises the dead.
> He has delivered us from such a deadly peril,
> and he will deliver us again.[9]

Gideon's three hundred men, armed only with sound effects, decimated 135,000 soldiers mounted on camels. It was a miracle only God could orchestrate. I heard this story often as a child in Sunday school, but somehow I had missed the ending. The Israelites enjoyed a land wiped clean of an intimidating enemy. I imagined great parades and grand parties. Gideon called the people together, asking them to bring their gold bracelets and earrings. He melted the jewelry and created an ephod, which the people worshipped as long as Gideon lived. It was a sad return to their original mode of operation. How could Gideon not have seen the error of his ways, especially after God's outstanding work? Wasn't it obvious?

In my arrogance, I once thought I would never do such things. Like Gideon, I, too, blindly reconstruct familiar idols of comfort and control, in spite of all the recent miracles I've experienced. As I am beginning to know myself, I see these Bible stories as a record of human nature—my human nature, not human aberration. Perhaps the return to the hospital every three months will serve to keep me in a place where I rely on God rather than myself.

> On him we have set our hope
> that he will continue to deliver us.[10]

This last week, a distant memory climbed back into view. In May 1985, Ron and I crossed the Canadian border between British Columbia and Washington and drove south for seven hours to Oregon. We eagerly anticipated candidating there for a pastoral position at Salem Alliance Church. We were young, Justin not yet two, Sheena an elusive dream. I had big hair. Ron had a big beard. We fell in love with the church's big heart.

We toured the city for real estate, encouraged by the economic downturn that had left numerous homes vacant and discounted. There was much excited conversation. The leadership wanted us. We were ecstatic, returning home on a high-voltage mix of gasoline and euphoria.

A few days later, the phone rang. The church wasn't ready for us after all. There were some painful realities to first deal with in the music department, they said, before they could hire anyone.

"Don't hang around waiting for us. Look at other opportunities," the church leadership reiterated firmly, giving us little hope.

We were heartbroken. We went back to our short list but those options had lost their attraction. It felt like we were flirting while we loving another. A month passed. Then another and several more. We checked out other churches but felt restrained. We paused, hesitant to act. Our hearts were in Salem.

I was home when the call came from the district superintendent, the kind who always wears a pressed shirt, tie, and suit jacket. He asked for Ron, but Ron was out. So he told me Salem Alliance Church was extending an invitation for him to be their Pastor of Worship and Missions. Screams of joy escaped. I laughed and talked rapidly. My exuberance was unbounded; the careful, correct gentleman didn't know how to respond. We had waited a year-and-a-half for the right door to open. Though it seemed impossible and we couldn't see the way ahead, God put it all together.

Our story of moving to Paris was similar. We had waited six years. At one point arrangements unraveled, but God, while we waited in the dark, put them back together.

After experiencing God's constant provisions in the past, how could I doubt now? But I do. I am like Gideon, longing for the illusion of control my hands-on gods give me. How can I tie my hope to any of them? I am as vulnerable as a rowboat on the open sea. As Ron and I again wait on our Shepherd, space is created for God to be God. Because it is so very hard, I cry with the Apostle Paul, "It is beyond my ability to endure."

> He will continue to deliver us, as you help us by your prayers.
> Then many will give thanks on our behalf for the gracious
> favor granted us in answer to the prayers of many.[11]

Even though there are many lows these days, they've been well punctuated by surprising peace, even happiness. Every time I plead for mercy, something happens. Letters, notes and cards, gifts, calls, hugs—all of them golden bricks of kindness—arrive at just the right moment, again and again, with just the right message. A kind email came from Alaska on a day Ron was battling the blues over his job situation. It told us of the person's awe and gratitude for the respite God was giving Ron. A respite? That was a surprising new twist.

Our church elders prayed for Ron and me this past Sunday morning. By the afternoon, the dark cloud enveloping me due to the latest grim medical information had lifted. I think of St. Augustine's words, "Without God, we cannot; without us, God will not," and

Ted Loder, who contends that prayer opens up new possibilities and avenues for God to act.[12]

I am convinced the prayers rising for us make an enormous difference.

July: Return to Paris

The sign claimed they were still unloading our plane's baggage. After shifting from foot to foot, leaning over our empty cart for an hour, and cruising the baggage carousel to make sure our eyes weren't overlooking the obvious, Ron tried his French to report our missing suitcases. The Air France office at Aéroport Paris-Charles de Gaulle wasn't surprised. "Ahhh, Monsieur Friesen. Your bags didn't make the connecting flight in New York. We'll deliver them tonight, unless you want to wait."

The large T-shirt, mini toothpaste tube, abbreviated toothbrush, and doll-sized deodorant neatly packed into two navy cases were our consolation prizes. We had expected to see Madame D.'s eager face on the other side of customs. By now, I fretted about her extended wait. Would she still be there? Ron and I hurried through the exit passage. The opaque doors slid open, revealing the ropes that hold back the crowd. One lone person, looking like a lioness who had just leapt from her cage into the no-man zone, paced back and forth in the restricted exit area. It was Madame D.

Unable to sleep, she had arrived at the airport by three fifteen A.M., three hours before our jet's wheels touched the runway. Coffee shops weren't open—no problem. The tenacious Madame D. simply joined the Delta staff at the Sheraton, helping herself to coffee and croissants along with crew members. She then patrolled our exit point for four hours before our reunion finally erupted.

Rain had been forecast, but a cloudless blue sky sang a "soup-air" ("superb") welcome. We sat at a sidewalk café and relished a just-out-of-the-oven crusty baguette, savored cafe crèmes and flagrantly ordered seconds. Traffic careened around the traffic circle. Ornately carved stone buildings and frilly iron balconies competed for attention. Madame D. sat quietly beside me, neither of us quite able to believe the other's presence.

We strolled the elegant boulevard, admiring the statues, posing for Ron's camera. I told my French sister of the peace 2 Corinthians 1 was bringing me in the middle of the night. Listening with an odd expression, she asked me to recite the verses again.

"Lorelei, that is the same scripture I sent you in April while on vacation in Brittany."

"You did?"

"I most certainly did. While on holidays at the sea, I felt the need to go to Mass to pray for you. The priest asked if I would be willing to read the morning scripture. When I told him it had been decades since I'd come to Mass and I couldn't remember when to do things, He said he would help me and then gave me this scripture. It's become my rock."

It was my rock too, holding me together an ocean away.

Madame D. drove us to our Brazilian friends' home on Rue de Bac. Wooden stairs with a red Persian runner wound round and round the wrought iron elevator that could only accommodate two people tucked in chest to chest. As we entered the marble lobby, Priscilla and Carlo flew down the spiral flights. Wrapping us in their arms, they grabbed our luggage.

The Brazilians' apartment became our refuge each night after packing boxes in our old apartment or meeting friends for lunch, coffee, and dinner. On our return, Carlo would put down his work, stroll into the living room and call, "Rrron. Come, visit, tell me how your day went. What? You're still packing boxes? You work very hard, you know. Is the elevator working there yet?" Priscilla would leave her oil painting to join the party in this classic Parisian salon with its twelve-foot ceilings.

Mornings began with fresh-squeezed orange juice and spicy, rich espresso coffee from the little machine next to the floor-to-ceiling windows. There was more tropical fruit than we could consume, the result of early trips to the market before we tumbled out of bed. The laughter began as soon as the caffeine started to work its magic. I would turn Priscilla's name into an opera aria while Ron wove ridiculous harmonies.

"Maybe I should sing to you," Carlo suggested with a teasing smile to his beautiful wife, even though his ability to carry a tune is mercilessly gunned down by his family.

"Never. I would have to leave the apartment and the whole building would follow," she said.

He looked at her with such adoration I never would have guessed their marriage once teetered on a delicate edge.

Priscilla grew up in a Sicilian family re-rooted in Brazil's tropical climate. By the time she was fifteen, there was enormous pressure from her family to marry—but not just anyone. An Italian. One was recommended, an older man. A baby arrived by the time Priscilla was seventeen. The marriage was painful, destructive. By the age of nineteen, Priscilla stood in a room ringed with Italian uncles and told them she would not stay married as they insisted. She divorced in spite of their pressure.

Months later, Priscilla drifted down a street, despairing, crying. She looked up and saw a large, lit cross rising above a church. Inside, the pastor introduced Jesus so beautifully Priscilla couldn't resist Him. She was baptized a week later.

Priscilla was getting to know Jesus when Carlo appeared. He told her to cut out the Jesus talk; it was too much, inappropriate. She left Jesus.

Over the years, though living an exotic, privileged life in Mexico, Priscilla and Carlo's marriage began to unravel. In great distress, Priscilla noticed for the first time a church on a road she had used for years near her house. Hopeful, she went inside and heard she could come back to a welcoming, forgiving God.

"Again? Jesus stuff again? Priscilla, stop it!" Carlo was adamant.

This time, Priscilla matched her husband's determination. "Carlo, you can divorce me if you want, but I will never leave Jesus again."

One by one, her family all followed on her journey with Jesus. Carlo too.

Our first Sunday back at Trinity was euphoric. Faces we treasured surrounded us; names we hadn't called out in eleven months christened our lips.

People leaned forward and listened closely as we spoke. Priscilla said they were all crying, though I didn't see any tears. Telling my story demanded my concentration. I did see Sophie whispering French into the ears of some who couldn't keep pace with my amped-up English.

At the end of the service, a young woman introduced herself, saying our talk had meant a lot to her. "You see, my mom had brain cancer." I braced myself for the familiar bad news.

She continued. "I was three years old at the time. I'm twenty-eight now, and my mom continues to do well."

It was a love note fluttering down from heaven.

Every day was filled with meals with dear friends, from fine French cuisine at UNESCO headquarters to crepes in the lively Latin Quarter; from Moroccan tajine in a quaint apartment overlooking a quiet courtyard to Italian pasta on a well-treed sidewalk. We crisscrossed Paris from north to south, memorizing her crooked, crowded streets. Repeatedly we were asked, "Why aren't you coming back? We don't understand. We were not given an explanation."

Writing in Honfleur

During our second week, we slipped north out of Paris to Honfleur, a seaside village filled with old Normandy charm. We walked the ancient harbor and strolled the sea wall, holding hands. Two romantic days zipped by far too quickly. Back through the tollbooths we sped to Paris, picking up Antoine and Sophie to scurry south to Arcy-sur-Cure.

We wandered Burgundy's historic villages while fending off torrential rain. Even the soaking downpour couldn't blur all the beauty. We left in time to travel back for evening church in Paris.

Energetic Antoine finished leading heart-felt worship, the sermon began to unfold, and the hard wooden pew dug into my back. The chapel was clammy and hot; air conditioning is uncommon in Paris. Self-conscious about the railroad tracks carved into the back of my hairless head, I kept my hat on as we sat near the front. Though my parents had drilled me as a child to, "never, never, ever leave a service since that disturbs others," I left to use the toilet.

When I returned, I couldn't figure out where I had been sitting.

"Where's Ron?" I whispered.

Even with numerous people pointing, it still took some moments for my confusion to clear. I crawled over multiple sets of legs, sat down and told Ron I didn't feel very good. As I began to look up and back, craning my neck, Ron wondered what I was trying to see in the balcony. Then it hit him—a seizure.

The service lurched to a full stop as Ron stood up to lay me down—this was definitely more of a disturbance than going to the bathroom. Soon five strapping EMTs stomped in and spent an hour performing paramedic tricks I don't recall. People gathered in small circles and prayed. Sirens blared. The ambulance rushed me to the hospital faster than friends could follow.

The emergency nurse couldn't find my vein for an IV. As the inexperienced girl kept excavating for veins in my arm, I became completely awake, screaming as she dug into my arm like a bumbling archeologist using a dull shovel. A young doctor who had traveled with us from the church gently suggested, "If you tighten the tourniquet, it'll make her vein more obvious."

An MRI checked for any suspicious growth and found me still beautifully clean. A seizure was confirmed. Heavy drugs were given. Little memory of the next three days remains.

Ron says I could only track with him for a sentence before drifting off. My energy and ability to walk fled. I remember opening my eyes and seeing my French family in a circle around my hospital bed, looking so worried.

Madame D. sat on a chair, her blue suit crisp, her brown eyes concerned. Monday, just one week earlier, we had lunched in the Palais Royal's courtyard, Madame D. cajoling the waiter to squeeze us in without a reservation.

"It is not possible, there is no room," he had said.

"Are you sure?" French sister smiled, undeterred.

"I would have to talk to the captain."

"Why don't you let me talk to him?" she suggested.

We hung around the restaurant's entrance, me insecure, Madame D. quietly confident. The captain arrived, the French flowed, hands flew, and, voilà, we were seated at a prime garden terrace table.

The entrée I chose was declared no longer available. Madame D. intervened. "Perhaps you have just a little bit left? She doesn't need a lot because we're making a 'tour of macaroons.' We've only covered the Left Bank and still have the Right Bank to explore." Madame D. began to list all the famous macaroon shops we had yet to visit.

The waiter laughed, completely disarmed. My request was granted.

Palais Royal Monday was well worth repeating. Hospital Monday was not.

Tuesday's flight home was missed. A Trinity friend, one of those international business people with a bazillion air miles, persuaded the airline to reschedule for free, a definite improvement over the five thousand dollars per ticket they had originally quoted. Madame D. arranged for a taxi to take us to the airport on Friday, as she was working in Lille.

Driving to the airport, we chatted with the chauffeur. Did Madame D. know her favorite cab driver's wife had survived bad brain cancer six years ago? I checked both in English and French to make sure I understood correctly. It was another love note from the Shepherd tucked into my pocket as we flew away from the land to which God had miraculously opened doors for our arrival... and then closed just as distinctly.

In Paris Again, June 2009

L'Automne— Autumn 2009

September: Though Ten Thousand May Fall

TEDDY

EACH MORNING I make an iron-fisted mug of coffee, breathing in its brute force with satisfaction. I carry the brew out onto the deck of my Oregon home to a corner with pots of herbs and flowers. The fragrance of basil surrounds a small table waiting for my mug by a comfortable chair.

As I sat there ruminating, a phrase from Psalm 91 danced circles in my thoughts. "Though ten thousand may fall...though ten thousand may fall..." It was logging laps in my head when Ron returned home and yelled, "Hello." He stuck his head out onto the balcony, smiling at me still in my housecoat.

"Hey, what's happening in the world today?" I asked, knowing he likes to read the newspaper first thing in the morning.

Ron looked at me and paused. I'm sure he wondered why I asked that particular day. "You really don't want to know," he hedged.

"Tell me anyways."

He was silent a moment and then stated, "Ted Kennedy died."

"Oh?" I waited.

"Of brain cancer. He had his first seizure a little over a year ago."

"I see." It didn't take long for the ramifications to become clear. "Though ten thousand may fall..." Now its insistent ring was a monastic chant, essential for carrying me through the day.

Though the surgery removing Kennedy's cancerous tumor was pronounced a success, the tenacious disease returned and the Senator died in fifteen months—just as our modern-day prophets and diviners predicted with this kind of cancer. Kennedy's death and the pervasive news coverage provided a dark background to the following days. There was a proliferation of information on brain cancer. Like Eve in the Garden of Eden, I didn't find increased knowledge to bring increased comfort. Ron and I were quiet; we both found Teddy Kennedy's death disturbing.

I think it's far harder for Ron to watch me go through this valley than I can grasp. His grief is complicated by the loss of his father at age sixteen to a sudden heart attack. I have always been Ron's close confidant, but now, how can he share his doubts, anger, and fears without pulling me under? He is often silent, once again taking care of a family's mother at an undisclosed cost to himself. It's the first time Ron and I have held anything back from each other. I'm not quite sure how to navigate these foreign waters.

I was the one who set these new boundaries last March, stating, "I don't want to know my statistics. I don't want to know what kind of cancer I have. I don't want to know the nasty things my oncologist will tell you. It will mess up my hope so badly, I'm not sure it would recover."

I decided to be a grown-up last week and asked Ron the big question, "Was I diagnosed with the same kind of cancer as Ted Kennedy's?"

"Yes."

His grief was almost touchable.

"I'm angry at God again," Ron told me as we headed for bed. "My soul feels brittle and cynical. Where is God in all this? And all of this is so much harder having no job. I want to work."

As summer dusk turned to darkness, I fell into the heavy sleep my medication invokes each night. Ron lay awake, got up, came back to bed, tossed and turned, took a hot shower, and passed the rest of the night in misery. A nasty case of poison oak had erupted on his arm, making sleep impossible. It continued to chase sleep away night after night, welts weeping, burning, and itching. Then it spread. Then the cat Ron never wanted decided to experiment with unsanctioned litter box options.

I had but one small gift to offer Ron. "Whatever you wanted to talk about and couldn't because I said was off limits, I'm OK with that now. You can discuss anything, OK?"

"What makes you think you can handle that now?" he asked.

I know how Ron handles his doubt and despair. Besides debriefing with three men who regularly check on his heart's condition, he drives deep into farm country some mornings to read and pray next to a tiny clapboard church, its steeple framed by an ancient oak grove. A cemetery with listing tombstones is off to one side. It has become Ron's sacred place to wait for God's voice.

Doubt

The past six months have raised piercing doubts, while at the same time have offered new experiences of God's deep love. As I've limped through Tim Keller's *The Reason for God*, two, sometimes three slow pages at a time, a new, timid vine of faith has begun to root in my plowed-under soul. Only now can I say, though nervously, "I believe God has healed me of a deadly cancer." But I still have recurring hesitations...

I'm afraid of being wrong. So I'm working on letting go of my love affair with being right.

I'm afraid of being presumptuous. I watch horrifying news from Mexico, read the list of young military men tragically killed in Afghanistan, and recall mothers who have died much younger than me. What right do I have to ask for long life? My gentle Father reminds me often not to confuse my journey with someone else's. He reminds me of His wide-open arms, inviting me to ask for healing, not because I am deserving but because of who He is. I then remember Jesus already paid the price for my fears, doubts, and all the other reasons I don't qualify for a miracle.

I'm taking tentative leaps of faith many times every day, powered by sticky notes papering the walls of my soul.

STICKY NOTES

Needing a weekend away, we decided to visit friends in Northern California, arriving as evening began to push aside the day. Their son was hanging out with a friend whose dad had just come to pick him up and head for home. One look at my naked head with the red channel carved into its back and the man launched into a story tailor-made for me. His wife has lived through a malicious brain cancer and has nine healthy years behind her.

After the father and son left, our good doctor friend was incredulous. "That boy hardly ever comes to our place, but he was here when you arrived so his father could tell you their story. What a God thing."

They are the third in my trio of first-hand stories of NBBCS (Nasty Bad Brain Cancer Survivors). I often call these heartening miracles to mind.

All kinds of sticky notes find their way to my heart.

Back in Oregon, a woman stopped me while shopping and said, "I like your hair."

I was a little taken aback; women don't usually go for the G.I. Jane look. I simply thanked her and turned to walk away. She caught my arm.

"Is it new?" she asked.

New? What kind of question was that? A new fad from New York? A new style for me? All I could think to say was, "It's cancer."

"I know." Her voice was gentle, her eyes kind, her brown hair swinging past her chin. "My hair is three years old. I had a double breast mastectomy and a portion of my lung removed. We're going to make it. We're going to make it."

I was startled. I hadn't expected to find a sticky note in a Portland store. I wondered if the woman was an angel, but she was standing in line to buy merchandise—I don't think angels are into home decor.

God finds arms from Paris to Portland to deliver His sticky notes.

The day the news broke about Ted Kennedy's death was the same day I arrived at Psalm 91. The paraphrased line, "Though ten thousand may fall...," was another sticky pasted to my soul's wall, reminding me my Father is outside the numbers.

I believe God is whispering to everyone. There are sticky notes littering the sidewalks of all our lives, just waiting for us to stop, read, and then paste them someplace they will be remembered.

L'Hiver—
Winter 2009–2010

December: Journey with Jesus

BUBBLE LOVE

I THINK BACK to the long, narrow hallway of our small apartment in Paris. A youth worker was glowing as she wrapped her scarf around her neck. "I'm so in love with Jesus," she bubbled. She was perky and pretty. Earnest blue eyes shone beneath a darling hat. "And the girls I'm discipling? They've totally fallen in love with Jesus. It's awesome."

I looked at her and thought, *I'm not sure I can say that in all honesty. Perhaps I just don't know Jesus very well. Maybe if I read the gospels, that would change everything.*

So began my campout with Matthew, Mark, Luke, and John. I started with Matthew—what a disheartening beginning. It quickly bolts into the impossible "Sermon For Overachievers." Jesus is not just a little harsh. He's downright severe. I was disqualified before I even made it through the opening chapters of the first gospel.

Matthew rolled into Mark and Luke. Jesus isn't enamored by church people's virtue. I'm a "church people." As in my efforts to play dodge ball, I was disqualified the moment the game began. John's Gospel was supposed to be the book of love. Maybe I would find something endearing there. Jesus read just as strong, like my initial bitter jolt of European espresso.

My first reading of the Gospels didn't sweep me into a bubbly "I'm so in love with Jesus" experience. So I reread them. Jesus was still tough to chew. Where was the grace? Did Paul make it up? Jesus set the bar so high it was even beyond the reach of sanitary saints, published religious authors and high-profile pastors. I made notes in my Bible's margins of things I couldn't do and things I didn't even want to try. Where was the "Jesus meek and mild" of my Sunday school years? Where was, "If you can't say anything nice, don't say anything at all"? Jesus' mother had obviously overlooked that eleventh commandment. I finished the gospels a second time while still in Paris, thinking this wasn't helping my love for Jesus.

It was on my third time through that it struck me how the big picture of Jesus' life revealed a startling profile of grace. He set the bar at an unreachable place so all us churchy people gain the chance to figure out we're not as lovely as we secretly think. Then he gave himself over to power-drunk soldiers to pay the exorbitant price for everyone, from sex addicts to self-righteous moralists and beyond. As I read Matthew, Mark, Luke, and John the third time, slight shimmers of a deep love rippled under the text. This God-man chose to die. Not because I was nice, but because I was naughty. Yet, Jesus was still intimidating.

I decided to give Jesus a fourth round, hoping I would come to know Him well enough to at least like Him. Shortly after beginning again, I got sick. Seriously sick. For the first time, I read the stories of Jesus as an invalid.

Previously, the way Jesus spent day in and day out with ill, deformed, needy, broken, and possibly whiney people hadn't registered with me. The outlook from my bed revealed a gentle, patient man taking time to touch individuals. My eyes watered over every account of healing as I marked them with a highlighter that leaked through the thin pages. I thought about Jesus only doing what the Father told him to do and realized the Son was presenting God's own merciful heart. Tenderness leaped from the pages and dripped down my cheeks.

THE JOURNEY CONTINUES

Five days after brain surgery I was off of all pain medication, headache free. I was home, lying in my cozy bed, our kitty curled at my feet, while my mom and sister bustled in the kitchen with supper preparations. Cupboard doors slammed and the dishwasher clicked shut as I shook off sleep. In the middle of the mundane, Jesus walked through my surfacing dreams. I opened my eyes and there He still seemed to be, standing beside my head. He was so enchanting, so, so…beautiful, so winsome. I didn't want Him to ever go away. He started to move farther from me, down toward my feet. "Come back," I called silently, watching intently. He moved across the end of my bed, fading, disappearing.

"Please don't go, Jesus." Like lingering French perfume still enchanting an elevator long after the woman wearing it disappears, I was left with a reassuring presence so lovely my room was warmed. I knew I was deeply loved by Him.

Over the next months, I continued through the Gospels, wanting to be able to say, "I love You, Jesus," with an honest heart. As I got closer to the end of a Gospel, I found myself resisting the crucifixion story. Jesus' demise was no longer the same familiar account. Cancer had thrust me into the unfamiliar place of also brushing shoulders with death. As I experienced my own intense desire for life, my heart was devastated as I grasped Jesus' passion to live. His death changed the context of everything hard He had said. We don't need His rescue if we don't know we are helpless sinners.

A paradox was taking place in my little bedroom on Church Street. While I was on the brink of catching a windfall of love from Jesus, I still wrestled with doubts about Him. God and Jesus had always come "packaged together" for me. I was disturbed. If Jesus wasn't who He claimed to be, I had no hope. I wrote in my journal and shared it with Ron.

Jesus, if He isn't the Son of God…
Then I am not forgiven of my myriad failings.
Then there is no intimate access to God.

Then God is not Abba, our dear Father.
Then God didn't come to earth to show us who He is.
Then God isn't Triune, enjoying loving relationship as Father, Son,
   and Spirit.
Then I, made in God's image, am not created for relationship after
   all.
Then God didn't direct Jesus to spend most of His scant ministry
   years lifting the underdog, healing the sick and forgiving the
   guilty.
Then God didn't become human, understanding firsthand our
   frailty, walking in our shoes.
Then God didn't die for us, exposing unplumbed depths of love.
Then death isn't conquered.
Then Jesus isn't preparing a place without tears for us.
Then the benchmark is too high to win God's approval.
Then I face impossible judgment, without an advocate.

It's a terrible thing to stand in jeopardy of losing Jesus. Hope
vanishes. All one has left is positive thinking and denial. What
provides a sound basis for that? I turned to Tim Keller's *The Reason
for God* and paid special attention to his chapter on the Gospels.
Vacationing at a friend's home on the Oregon coast, I found Lee
Strobel's *The Case for Christ*. While Ron read Francis Collins' heady
tome, *The Language of God*, I stuck to Strobel's more conversational
examination of Christ. My head was satisfied, my heart relieved.
Still, I breathed repeatedly, "Lord, I believe. Overcome my unbelief."

Am I "so in love with Jesus" now? Love for Him has grown
only as I've allowed His love to first soak into my independent
heart. Touched deeply after imagining myself in the story in Luke
5, I journaled again.

As Jesus teaches, sand and dirt begin to trickle from the roof.
Debris rains down in earnest. Suddenly, sunlight bursts through
into the home's dim interior. It's the first Son roof. Jesus stops
His lecture to laugh, holding out His hand to catch the sand
still tumbling from overhead. He sits, grinning, waiting as I
am determinedly lowered through the uneven hole, not always
level, inch-by-inch, occasionally a heart-stopping foot at a time.

Ying and Jay Lee hold ropes at one corner, my Ron and Jane at another, our family is at a third and people I don't even know are at the fourth. My mattress and I are finally all the way down, right in front of Jesus' feet, where everyone is pressing in to be. I look at Jesus and am overwhelmed by His gentle kindness. His goodness is irresistible, not at all like the repelling pseudo goodness some people parade. It's like pure, cold water on a sweat-soaked summer's day. I keep looking into His eyes and sense His love is as unstoppable as the ocean's relentless waves crashing onto Oregon beaches.

My unworthiness rises as I lie helpless in front of Him. The past quiet months in bed have given space for a clearer view of my soul's basement. I don't deserve to be healed. I look in His eyes and the Teacher doesn't pretend I am worthy. He knows all about my bad-mouthing and the messy fallout as I've vacillated between insecurity and superiority. He sees the resentments I carry. Jesus knows I try to fill my aching holes with achievement. Being better at academics, better at music, better at parenting, better at making my home picture-perfect. Oh, dear, better at spirituality, better at "getting God." He knows my discontent to simply be who He made me to be, neither more nor less. Jesus is well aware of my story's sorry details.

I know I am not worthy of His healing touch. Jesus knows it, too.

He takes my cold hands—they're cold so often—warming them in His. With calm confidence He says, "Lorelei, my friend," and pauses as I absorb the acceptance His friendship implies, "your sins are forgiven."

Really? My ugliness wiped clean? I see it in His tender eyes. He keeps holding my hands as some church elders and prominent pastors mutter, "Who does He think he is? Only God can forgive sin."

Jesus stands. He isn't tall or muscular, but He is unafraid of these influential powerbrokers.

"All right, then. Which is easier, to forgive sins or heal cancer? So that you know I have the authority to forgive sin, Lorelei, get up, pick up your Sealy Posturepedic mattress, and go home."

His voice sends grand shivers through me. His power pulses in my head and courses down my body. Standing, I throw the mattress over my shoulder and walk outside vigorously, good color in my face, laughing, waving to everyone dancing on the roof. I am washed clean by a divine couplet of forgiveness and healing.

Anyone who has been forgiven a lot loves a lot.

Reflecting at the Oregon Coast

January: Season of Tears

We celebrated Christmas in Canada with a keen sense of thankfulness for being together this year, mom having fallen and broken her leg and me with a clean MRI on December 12.

New Year's Day I wondered if perhaps I saw that old black shadow again pulsing in the background, like an overhead fan. It was faint. I wasn't sure; perhaps it was my imagination. I saw it twice the next day and finally told Ron when he asked why I was getting so quiet and withdrawn.

"It's probably just the scar tissue thickening," we reassured ourselves. Perhaps my sensitive head didn't like all the up and down motion while I denuded the Christmas tree. I was told scar tissue would thicken for a year due to the radiation; it irritates the brain and invites seizures. The next day I didn't have any episodes; the following day there were three. I counted while they lasted—to fifteen. A few days later they extended to thirty. I called my doctor, who immediately increased my seizure medication. What a relief. The fan episodes were behind me.

On Tuesday, January 19, Ron was substitute teaching. The flashing shadow returned and, after six minutes, I gave up counting. Instead, I went to the phone and called my doctor over the lunch hour, leaving a message on his machine. I called my church and urgently asked for my friend, Jane, even though she was in a meeting. Somewhere in that sprawling complex, she picked up the phone.

"Jane, I'm having an episode and it's not stopping. I'm scared. I'm even seeing a kaleidoscope around the periphery of my vision."

She didn't hesitate. "I'll be right there."

I was frightened.

When Jane arrived, she asked if I had talked to a real, live person at the doctor's office. I hadn't. "Call again," she told me, "and get a real person." It was the lunch hour but, for some reason, the answering service put me through.

I heard the nurse's voice. "The doctor is in surgery so I can't do anything, but I think you better go to emergency and they'll give you an MRI."

"Emergency? What am I going to tell them? That I see a shadow?"

Five minutes later, the nurse called again. "Hang on, Lorelei, the doctor has called twice from surgery. It will be much less expensive for you to have an appointment so he's managed to get you in this afternoon for an MRI at the hospital. He's going to do a 'wet read.' Don't leave the hospital until he talks to you."

Since the appointment wasn't for another three hours, we had time to go and choose new glasses for Jane. It was so much fun. The shadow and the kaleidoscope were gone. I got to make fun of Jane trying frames that rimmed her eyes in red; she looked sick. We laughed, just like always. Then off to the hospital we rushed.

This MRI experience was so different from my first. I was asked if I wanted someone to come with me. Come with me? Of course! The biggest weenie in the world never wants to be alone in a medical experience. They even let me have the nurse who gave the best injections. Through the long MRI, Jane held my ankle, stroking it a little bit once in awhile—quite something for a tough little British woman.

It was finally done. God, my Shepherd, stayed large and close beside me; I truly was not alone.

We were ushered to a seat near a phone in the waiting room of the hospital. "The doctor will call you here. You're to wait for him to call."

I heard a voice say my name. I looked up. There was my beloved neurosurgeon. "There's a definite tumor above your right ear, Lorelei. Oddly, it's separated from the tumor bed. It's quite distinct."

"You're sure it's not scar tissue?" I asked, not able to digest the news.

"No, it's not. It's definitely a tumor." He asked me to come to his office the next day at noon so he could go over the films with Ron and me.

Our son, Justin, wanted to come along; he couldn't concentrate on his work. The three of us went to the doctor's office and heard news worse than I originally heard. There was another tumor as well, deeper below the original tumor bed, deep in my brain. There was white edema on the tumor bed. It could be scar tissue; it could be another cluster of tumors. They couldn't know for sure without cutting me open, but that really wasn't too advisable now that we knew there were definitely two new, distinct tumors to fight.

We were stunned—devastated. Questions exploded. Where was the miracle? Why hadn't God done anything? Cancer had returned even faster than the oncologist expected. He, too, was very disappointed. Where was my God "outside the numbers"? I wasn't outside the numbers; I was at their bottom.

I had to ask myself if I still loved God and believed He loves me even when He doesn't meet my expectations. Do I love Him when His ways are not my ways, when my great hope for healing hasn't materialized and seems so fragile?

Following our devastating news, it's almost impossible to sense God's love. Yet, it surfaces again as the old routine of wakening early in the morning resumes. Down the stairs I come to make my coffee. I let in Marcel, my cat, who curls up on my lap. I pull out my precious Psalms that speak so poignantly to my heart. It's in these quiet hours I sense my Shepherd is still here, still cradling me in His arms, still assuring me He will never leave me or stop loving me.

I have some hope for continuing to live. I start treatment on Wednesday. It's a chemotherapy that cuts off the blood supply to the tumors. In some people, the tumors have actually shrunk, though not disappeared. This has the potential of extending my life for some time. I may lose my hair. I'll probably get steroids to reduce the swelling in my brain, making my face fat—like Darth Vader's, without his helmet. So today I enjoy my nappy hair immensely.

This has been so hard for my little family. Sheena and I call each other every day. I wonder how she can keep on studying at university.

Tonight, I laid my head on Justin's shoulder and cried.
"Oh, Justin, I wanted to rock your babies."

"And I wanted you to know my wife," he said softly, tears slipping down his cheeks.

"Well, you better get busy then, Justin. Meet her, marry her, and get her pregnant quick!"

"MOM!"

"Mind if I take applications, honey?"

He laughed. I'm getting away with a lot now!

I worry for my dear Ron. It all hit him hard while I was away speaking at a women's retreat this past weekend. He wept as he slept alone in our bed, catching whiffs of my perfume. Once home, I saw something new that had been birthed in him. He told me that as he showered Saturday morning, these words welled up from deep within: "I will not give up. I will not curse God and die. I will turn to him for life."

May I have the courage to do likewise.

Le Printemps—
Spring 2010

May: Walking with Job

TREATMENT

WITH CHEMO DRUGS flowing thick through my head and anti-seizure meds slowing my brain's activity, I feel overwhelmed in choosing which threads of my story to pick up. My brain now has difficulty organizing my thoughts. I wonder why writing has lost its joy. I have come to realize that each time I sit down to write I'm rehearsing the darkness invading my life. I can't find much laughter in my story.

Treatment after promising treatment has failed for me. The highly invasive tumor in my brain has resisted three different efforts to stop its vigorous growth. Instead, it sprinkles aggressive cells throughout my brain like white twinkle lights on a Christmas tree. The clinical trial I entered in San Francisco has worked for 30 percent of participants, but I'm not part of that percentage.

As Ron and I sat people watching at a Starbucks® in San Francisco, processing the shattering news that the latest treatment had also failed, he walked to the counter for a refill.

The cashier asked, "Excuse me, I don't mean to meddle, I'm really sorry for asking, but is that lovely lady your wife?"

"She is," Ron replied.

"Oh, that's so good to see. There is so much love and tenderness between you."

How wonderful for Ron and me to have time to tie our knots of love as tight as we can. We remind each other often that love lasts forever. It will be there to enjoy for all eternity.

"I'll be waiting for you eagerly, right by the gate," I tell Ron, hardly able to believe I have to go somewhere without him.

"Lorelei," Ron reminds me as I become tearful about being separated from him, "my love for you is but a faint shimmer of Jesus' love for you. You won't be alone or unloved for one second."

Ron and Me in Lighter Times

THE TOAD

I sat outside the video rental store waiting for Ron. As I wondered if Ron was searching for yet another music documentary, I watched a little boy hop outside with great enthusiasm, his DVD tucked under one arm. Passing my car, the bouncing boy bumped into my vehicle, then into the next.

"You keep that up and there won't be any movie for you," his mother screamed. His dad bellowed something else as their energetic toad hopped into their van. I imagined God longing to bend down from heaven and swoop him, me, all of us, up in His great arms to carry us off to paradise. It suddenly struck me: Death is just a comma at the end of life's sentence, not a period.

UCSF Medical Center

Back in March, when all hopes of treatment in Salem had failed, Ron found further help for me in San Francisco. The UCSF medical tower had an extraordinary view of the city. Floor-to-ceiling windows framed a spectacular scene, helping me forget I was in a medical facility and keeping my fainting tendency to a minimum. A historic church capped a small mountain in the foreground. A park sprawled below. The Golden Gate Bridge poked above distant, rolling hills. It wasn't hard to be distracted from the reason for our coming by the city inhaling and exhaling below.

My doctor looked as though she should be buying Clearasil® at Walgreens® (not a comment on her skin condition, only her age). From her we learned my left peripheral vision is intermittent, my compromised brain processing that information quite erratically. That's why I walk into couches and body-check startled people in airport concourses.

When I walk, Ron firmly holds my hand; the tumor's location interrupts my ability to decode direction or find my way. I stumble on stairs and consistently bump into doorposts on my left. More disconcerting are the visual illusions that happen so unpredictably. Shadows flash as though a helicopter is coming in to land. One awful day I couldn't feel my left hand. I wonder if death will be a gradual loss of all my senses.

God's Love

There have been times of late when I can't find God's love. It's like groping for a railing in the dark on steep, shaky stairs. I'm fairly sure the railing is there, but where? It was easy to find in years past, when shadows were few.

It's enormously comforting to read Job's unedited feelings and thoughts. His "blog" is truthful, sometimes caustic, as he navigates brutal disappointment with God. There is great authenticity in his responses to God and to religious people around him. He refuses to be squished into their "proper" responses. What a comfort to read that I'm not the only one who struggles to find God's reassuring presence.

> If I go to the east, he is not there;
> If I go to the west, I do not find him.
> When he is at work in the north,
> I do not see him...
> But he knows the way that I take.[13]

Solutions for Job

Job's friends push formulaic solutions and religious platitudes. When religious platitudes come my way, Ron comforts me, saying, "There's truth here; it's just bad timing."

Job's friends are shocked by their friend's honesty. He accuses God of "uprooting his hope like a tree." As his friends do their best to admonish his disappointment with God, Job doesn't stop being authentic. He resists the temptation to pose as a spiritual superhero.

It's uncomfortable to be present with anger and disappointment. We don't know what to say. The urge to fill the space with answers seems so strong, so right.

Job shouts at his advisory friends, "Clap your hands over your mouths."

Even God Himself doesn't offer Job a solution. He's left with mystery.

Solutions for Ron

I'm a hypocrite. Like Job's friends, I am addicted to giving advice. Years ago, Ron was counseled to control his cholesterol. I knew exactly what he should do. I bought books with grandiose promises. He was less excited about the low-fat/no-fat program than I was. Instead of ice cream, I bought non-fat, frozen yogurt. Far from the table where Ron could not read the incriminating label, I quietly served up a delicious scoop of the frozen white water, whipped into a look-a-like impostor.

"Mmmm, this is good," I raved.

Ron took a bite, then a second. "What is this?"

I tried to look innocent. I should have worn a less modest blouse.

"Could I have the chocolate sauce please?" he asked when I didn't respond.

"Ron, the chocolate sauce is high fat. Look at me, I'm enjoying my ice cream."

"Good for you. I need chocolate sauce." He got up from the table and began searching for the sauce. It wasn't where he remembered leaving it. I may have moved it.

At cafés, if he ordered fries with his burger, I would politely question, "Really? You're choosing fries?"

He'd give me a look and I'd lie. "I'm just asking a question."

"I'm just having an exception." He'd lie too.

Our family loves homemade salsa, a treat difficult to enjoy without high-fat tortilla chips. No problem—I discovered non-fat chips. Even under several inches of potent salsa cloaked in heavy garlic, the flavor of the foam triangles was unforgivable. Books assured me I could make my own delicious low-fat corn chips. They lied as well.

I decided to try to stop advising Ron; he couldn't tell that I had stopped. Our kids took up the challenge where I left off, but with less politesse, more gusto.

When we moved to France, I completely gave up since, there, butter and cream are the two major food groups. I learned to love them both—they've given my culinary arts quite the boost.

SOLUTIONS FOR LORELEI

I have also been advised. Eat puréed asparagus. Read these books. Claim these promises. Pop these vitamins. Breathe pure oxygen. Eat seaweed. It appears there is a discount on snake oil these days.

I have been interrogated.

"Do you juice?" one woman asked.

"I eat lots of raw vegetables and fruits."

She came closer and closer to my face as I backed against the wall.

"But do you juice?" she continued.

"I eat raw carrots, apples, oranges, spinach, broccoli and..."

"Do you juice?" she pressed.

"I'm a vegetarian of nineteen years," I protested.

I was trapped in the church kitchen without a juicer.

To Speak or Not to Speak

What could people say, you might wonder. How about offering a silent presence, even though silence is an uncomfortable, though important, grace? Standing beside a person in pain without answers and giving them permission to be angry is a great gift.

God showed up for the man who was honest and angry. Our Father inserted an entire book in the Bible, with its main character modeling authenticity while facing overwhelming disappointment. Job has helped me to articulate my elusive anger buried beneath decades of trying to be a "good" girl.

Jesus' advice was to "mourn with those who mourn." I like that a lot.

It's OK with my Abba if I mourn and wail. I believe He weeps with me and will show up for me one day, just as surely as He did for Job. Though it's hard to find Him right now, "He knows the way I take."

My parents and dear children have loved me well through the overwhelming pain of these last days. Not one word of advice, just a tender, gentle stream of steady, reliable love. Ron's love for me is constant, even on my weepiest days. If my dad and my husband love me this deeply, how much more will my Heavenly Father and his Son love me? Somehow it will all be OK in ways I cannot see, even though I'm leaving those I love the most.

In the middle of Job's agony he bawled, "I know my Redeemer lives." Later he courageously shouted, "Though He slay me, yet I will hope in Him."

God, give me the strength to hang on like Job, with both authenticity and faith.

What's next? That's the hard part. Today, with tears streaming down my face, I read a small chapter titled "Befriending Death" in *The Dance of Life* by Henri Nouwen. I still have much to learn to die well. It helps enormously to be loved.

So I wait, looking for every little sign of God's love.

L'Été—
Summer 2010

July: Alive on Planet Earth

CHANGE

MY FRIEND JANE and I were excitedly going out for coffee when she said, "Are you OK?"

"I'm not sure."

"Do you need to go home?"

I really didn't want to go home—fresh coffee was on the horizon. But home I came, managing to make it up the stairs to our bedroom. A little later, as I was moving around, Ron heard a crash. He came running upstairs to find I couldn't walk; I couldn't use my left arm and hand. My left side had given way.

It was a hard day.

Then came the phone call. As Ron answered, I could tell it was from Paris. Coming down the stairs, he handed me the phone. I shook my head and refused it. He handed me the phone anyway, crossing all my boundaries. He asked forgiveness later, saying he knew I would want to hear from Sebastien, our friend with the beautiful Colombian accent.

"Oh, Lorelei," Sebastien pled, "don't give up hope."

Then, out of the blue, he began to quiz me.

"Do you have any ideas on how I can propose?"

"What?" He was so far removed from my weeping.

"I would like to propose to my girlfriend. Do you have some ideas?"

Seriously? Did he not remember why I might be crying? Of course he did, and like any good romantic Colombian, he knew a little talk regarding romance could take a weepy girl a long way out of the shadows into joy.

"How about you wire a ring in the middle of a flower in a bouquet?"

"Well, I'm going to be walking all over Paris with this bouquet."

"Parisians are such romantics," I said. "The French are such suckers for romance. Take it in to a florist and they will make it work. Then take your girlfriend for a ride on the Seine River, but not on one of the large boats seating hundreds of tourists. Isn't there a boat for just two?"

"They don't exist."

He continued, discussing possible dinner plans. "You know the beautiful, small restaurant overlooking the plaza at Trocadéro. You can see the Eiffel Tower there—it's very romantic. But the table seats eight."

"That's not romantic," I argued. "You'd better invite some friends if you don't want to be sitting with strangers."

"They won't come because it's eighty euros a plate. I thought of a place where the chef will guide us in making our own meal."

"Boat ride, ring in the middle of flowers, romantic dinner—sounds enchanting!"

Weeks passed before I heard from Sebastien. When he did call, I asked if his girlfriend said yes.

"She said, no," he reported.

He was joking.

GIOVANI

We heard that Sebastien's friend Giovani had arrived in Seattle. After becoming a believer in Paris, he had three projects in mind.

First, be baptized—Ron baptized him in an inflatable wading pool in the church fellowship hall. Second, go to Florida to see his brother and then to Colombia to see the rest of his family. His brother was the first to embrace Jesus, followed by many of the extended family. Third, go on a silent retreat in the Pacific Northwest—the retreat was now complete. So Ron and I drove up to spend an afternoon with him in Washington. We shared much joy—and many tears.

"This is so hard," I said.

"Don't give up," Giovani replied. "We will not stop praying. We will not stop praying."

It was very precious.

HOSPICE

I was hanging onto Ron's neck to make it to the bathroom. Seeing me use him as my sky crane, a nurse friend immediately said, "You are going to need hospice."

To me, the word spelled death. Hospice only comes to those who are dying.

During the initial hospice visit, I distinctly overheard a nurse say, "When someone slips this far so fast, there's no coming back. She could be gone in a week."

A few days later, a "comfort" package arrived on our doorstep, complete with needles, morphine, and other barbiturates to ease the process of dying. Steroids were prescribed, and for some mysterious reason, I responded remarkably well to them. Not everyone does.

In spite of the growing tumor, I regained use of my left side and began to walk again. However, when I sat down and tried to play the piano, I heard sobs coming from the kitchen as Ron said, "Oh, so much loss." My hands couldn't figure out the keys—they couldn't do what they once did so easily.

I kept hearing Sebastien's words. "Please don't give up, Lorelei. Please don't lose hope. We are not ceasing to pray."

FRIENDS

Ron had previously scheduled an evening of healing prayer for Friday of that week. I asked him if he was going to cancel it because I was so far gone. It appeared I had one foot in the grave.

"No, we're not going to cancel it," he said. "We need this more than ever. We're not going to give up praying."

Many others said, "I cannot stop from praying." It was a unison chorus that we kept hearing. It made me wonder if all the Baguette readers over the past years were raised up for such a time as this.

I pictured my Shepherd and I walking together. He was carrying me out of this difficult valley when, all of a sudden, the camera angle changed. I saw we weren't alone; there was a whole crowd of people following us with their prayers. We were surrounded.

I'm not alone. I'm not abandoned. Many people are praying, carrying me and my family in their prayers. They are weaving a powerful braid of love that keeps me safely on the road.

FUNERAL PLANS

I was reminded of how close I was to death when, just two weeks ago, as I was resting on the couch, hospice called again.

"Is Lorelei cognizant?" they asked Ron.

"Yes, she is."

"Have you made arrangements for the funeral?"

"No."

"How about a funeral home?"

I heard Ron say, "City View."

It seemed a reminder that I was already gone.

Yet, each morning I wake up with the gift of life. Today, I am resting in God's arms. I get to embrace my family and continue enjoying the very, very good gift of life.

PEACE

We made trips to UCSF where medicine gave me everything it had to give. It couldn't turn the tide; they didn't give me long to live. Yet Jesus is doing something mysterious in me—I've made my peace with death. It's still an exhausting place to be, especially for the family. Ron isn't sure if he is getting ready for his wife to live, linger, or die.

> But you are a shield around me, O Lord, my Glorious One, who lifts up my head.
> To the Lord I cry aloud, and he answers me from his holy hill.
> I lie down and sleep; I wake again because the Lord sustains me.
> I will lie down and sleep in peace for you alone, O Lord,
> make me dwell in safety.[14]

Epilogue

All Is Suddenly Hers

THE EVENING OF August 19, 2010, began with Lorelei and I sharing a delicious pasta meal at home in the warm summer air. It was too early to go to bed, so I suggested going for a ride into the countryside in the car I had just bought for Sheena's use at college. As we enjoyed the setting sun, little did we know that the sun was also setting on her extraordinary life.

After stopping to enjoy some soft ice cream cones, we returned home. Justin came by, sharing a few laughs with us over the antics of Marcel, our cat, before he helped carry Lorelei to our upstairs bedroom for the night.

I woke at two A.M., hearing Lorelei experience a very severe headache, the pain of which took several hours to get under control. By four A.M. she was sleeping soundly, and by eleven A.M. she had slipped into a coma. I called some close friends who tearfully gathered to say their goodbyes, pray, and offer their loving presence. Then, just before one P.M., August 20, 2010, surrounded by Justin, Sheena, and me, Lorelei peacefully left her weary body behind to be with her God.

During the following hours, numbed by the shock of my great grief, I was reminded of a hopeful prayer by Ruth Harms Calkin as I emailed people to painfully inform them of Lorelei's death.

> Oh Lord, may I believe in the darkness,
> When all hope has vanished,
> When waves beat with fury,
> And no star lights my sky.
> May I believe without feeling,
> Or knowing, or proving,
> 'Till one shining moment,
> When you shatter the darkness
> And all I believed for is suddenly mine.[15]

I also wrote my dear soul mate a final note.

> Tonight, my sweet Lorelei,
> As I cherish the love we shared,
> May you cherish all that is now yours
> From the One who made our love possible.
> — Ron Friesen

Appendix

How We Ended Up in Paris

RIGHT DREAM, WRONG PLACE, WRONG TIME: 1998–2001

THIS IS A long, complicated story full of unexpected pain and cul-de-sacs. It began when Ron resigned from a fulfilling "top-of-the-line" pastoral position at Salem Alliance Church. He felt impressed by God that his work there was finished. Unlike many pastors' resignations, there weren't any angry mobs involved; in fact, all was going extremely well. I was devastated. I loved our life with its security, comfort, and steady paychecks. What more could a woman want? I told Ron it wasn't enough to know what he wasn't going to do; I needed to know what he would do. He wasn't sure of the second part of the equation, only of the first.

Ron had a dream of shaping a church marked by grace and the embrace of the arts in significant new ways. It seemed such churches weren't interested in hiring people our age. Ron was close to the "forty-five-year-hump" and only Wal-Mart® was hiring seniors.

Developing a new church plant in Portland, Oregon, with our denomination seemed a creative solution. We nervously ripped up our roots and transplanted our family to the big city where door after door winked promisingly at us, only to slam shut. Even more discouraging was the growing, unrelenting grip of burnout that was strangling Ron; it finally pushed us to dismally call our band of friends together to move us back to Salem.

Shame taunted our dejected hearts while Justin and Sheena vacillated between embarrassment and relief. We weathered the inevitable comments like, "I knew you'd be back but I never thought it would be this soon." Or, "Sooo…you're back" (uneasy laughter). "I guess you've learned a lot of lessons" (more forced laughter).

After another one of those "lessons" comments, I curtly responded, "I have no idea what those lessons might be." When I feel defensive, I quickly lose the few diplomatic cards I own and slap down something brusque instead. There was an awkward pause, and then I was asked if I would like a gig playing at an office Christmas dinner. I felt like such a jerk.

During this painful period, our house was diagnosed to be sliding down a hill; we became embroiled in a costly legal affair. We considered other pastorates. All options required uprooting our kids, but we sensed this was not the season to transplant them again. There was also the albatross house hanging around our necks—it was not sellable. Now there's an understatement.

We were given the opportunity to lead worship part-time at another church in town, something that definitely helped make ends meet. Then, incredibly, a church in northern California contacted Ron about flying down each weekend to be their interim worship leader. As one fellow frequent-flyer told him one pre-dawn Friday morning, "Wow, that's quite the gig!" For two years it more than paid the bills, kissed us with the kind of friends you want to keep forever, and allowed Justin to finish high school in Salem. We toyed with the idea of living in sun-filled Redding, but somehow sensed God whispering, "This isn't for you." There it was again, the message of what we weren't to do without the accompanying comfort of knowing what we might do.

All the while, our house was creaking down the hill at a glacial pace. Our next-door neighbor was developing a new cottage industry—dealing drugs to clients who crawled out of the wood-work each night. In the same overwhelming period, I discovered a suspicious lump on my breast, one that took six weeks to be diagnosed as non-threatening. Then a bully pinpointed Sheena as a favorite target at school, eating her for lunch each day. To top it all, our cat developed an obstinate, expensive case of ringworm.

I didn't handle those desert years well. I wondered how effective prayer really was. I told my friends if this was what it was to be loved by God, I wasn't really interested. I wasn't sure if I was joking or not.

After three emotionally traumatic years, the lawsuit regarding our sliding home was finally resolved. It was the morning after Ron flew home from leading worship at a conference in Thailand.

"You're damn fools," the judge screamed when we refused to accept less than one third of our home's market value during arbitration.

"This just isn't right," we insisted.

"It has nothing to do with right and wrong," he snapped.

Our coffers were empty; we felt like David with no stones for his sling, facing a towering, well-armed Goliath. Yet three days later, the other party unexpectedly called with an offer to buy our home at close to market value. People, particularly lawyerly types, were amazed at the outcome.

Every bill was paid during those traumatic years. Some financial resources could be reconstructed; others remained a mystery. Checks showed up in the mail or were passed anonymously to us at church. Groceries arrived by the bagful; meals were left on our doorstep; a turkey appeared at Thanksgiving (carried, not ambulatory). We were free of a wearisome financial burden. Justin had graduated from high school. We were euphoric.

With great expectation, we asked again, "OK, God, what's next for our lives?"

There was silence.

"God? Do You have meaningful work for our lives?"

Still, only silence.

People asked what we were doing. We said, "Waiting."

We got a lot of strange looks. Who waits nowadays?

RIGHT DREAM, RIGHT PLACE, WRONG TIME: 2001–2002

The summer after we sold our home, while we were leading worship at a conference in Colorado, someone suggested we check into a staffing need with Trinity International Church in Paris. After visiting France in the fall, we fell in love with the kind of people who collect in an international setting. It seemed our original dream of a grace-full, artsy church was to be fulfilled in another city beginning with "P"—Paris, not Portland.

Though unprecedented, our denomination agreed to fully fund the first year, decreasing the support incrementally as the church grew over the following years. We were ecstatic; the needle on our compass had come to rest and life became filled with exhilarating plans for a move to France. Until... sigh, the Gulf War began and American charitable giving plummeted. All new denominational projects were cancelled, including ours in Paris. Time for more Alka-Seltzer®. As the old ad says, "Plop, plop, fizz, fizz, oh, what a relief it is." We'd felt the plop, we'd seen the fizz—where was the relief?

My heart cried out to God with naked, unreserved honesty. "God, why don't You do something, or are You less powerful, less involved, than I once thought?"

We called our private music students and asked them to return for lessons in the fall. Ron went back to job hunting and I returned to my obsessive worrying, a habit I'd honed with fine skill since we first braved the miserable waters of uncertain paychecks. We were back to waiting and I was tired of being tested, weary of tasting desert sand.

Our piano students were a reliable oasis of income and sweet friendship; how deeply I prized this loyal collection of families sticking by us through shifting hope and despair. Still, I wondered where God was and why He didn't come through for us.

The arrival of spring brought new prospects on the horizon. Ron's interest grew in a college teaching position in Minnesota, only an eight-hour drive from his Canadian prairie family. It looked very promising—the kind of challenge on which he would thrive. Ron made the short list of candidates so we were flown to the Midwest for a whirlwind weekend of interviews, salary discussions, and high hopes. Then the chatter abruptly died and, after ten days of silence, our answering machine informed us a decision had been made not to hire anyone. Again, we heard a door shudder shut.

"Hello? Father God? Are we on our own out here?"

No answer.

Would we be teaching piano again in the fall in Salem, or would we be moving? What to tell our anxious, inquiring students? After interviewing in British Columbia that summer, Ron decided to take a music pastor position there. My parents were ecstatic; we would be back on the Canadian side of the border, only three hours from their home.

In BC, our purchase offer was accepted on a romantic cottage in a wooded setting. In Oregon, an exciting offer on our Salem home fell apart. After forest fires destroyed 250 homes on the edge of the community to which we would be moving, the house we offered to buy suddenly was taken off the market. Renting, rather than selling, had become very lucrative. Nothing else, both suitable and affordable, could be found in the "post-fire" market.

After a second purchase offer for our home fell through, Sheena begged us to let her start middle school in Salem until the house was truly sold. Ron began his work in Canada without Sheena and me, living alone in a deathly quiet apartment above a funeral home, coming home for a few days every two weeks or so.

RIGHT DREAM, RIGHT PLACE, RIGHT TIME: 2002–2006

It was a bright, crisp September day. Ron was home from Canada. Answering the phone, he heard a welcome voice from Paris. It was the lead pastor at Trinity International Church.

"Is there any way we could put this plan back together?" Fred inquired.

Hope sprouted wings and took off flying. There was no hesitation. Yet what about Sheena? Hope hesitated. What about her schooling? The French philosophy of education seemed rather negative, fear inducing and shame based. We also knew neither she nor we would thrive in a boarding school situation. Either option would cost us a precious daughter. The only other alternative, the American School of Paris, was extremely expensive.

Within ten days, our denomination reinstated its original financial plan. We now had to decide if Ron should resign from his new ministry role. Ron talked to people he respected deeply and who knew him well. All of them agreed; though this was an unusual and awkward situation, it undoubtedly had God's fingerprints. It was a custom-made opportunity using all of who we were as people.

Ron talked with his superiors in BC. The response of both the senior pastor and the church administrator left Ron without a doubt—it was God Himself opening the doors for a move to Paris. Ron resigned; our home sold almost immediately. Christmas Eve found us crawling blindly through the foggy mountain passes of BC into the next leg of our journey.

It was January. There were seven full months before our move to France. How could we keep our boat afloat until we left? I felt frantic, even though God had taken care of us through the whole house-sliding-down-the-hill disaster/miracle, until a parent of one of my music students told us about their church losing their music minister to a moral failure. Could Ron fill in while they searched for a successor? Ron began to whistle again as he worked with this appreciative church body. Sheena contentedly completed her middle school years in Salem, something for which she had begged God two years earlier.

I continued to stress over money issues—it's definitely a fly in my ointment. Fortunately, Ron's ointment doesn't have the same particular bug; either he has his feet more firmly planted on solid rock or he does less shouting. I'm not saying my guy doesn't have flies in his ointment; he just carries a different breed than I do. Sadly, they aren't mine to dissect or divulge.

I was the one who was overwhelmed with how much money we would need to raise, so I turned to my trusted tonic: a quiet place, a good dose of the Psalms, and my journal. I had just put the period on the sentence, "I want to let You be the rock I rest on," when the phone rang. It was a businessman living in Paris, attending Trinity, who told me his family was moving back to the U.S. that summer. He was offering us their kitchen cabinets, washer, dryer, fridge, stove, TV, stereo, iron, vacuum, phones, etc.—all only two years old.

When I asked how much this would all cost, he responded with, "Nothing. We believe God wants you here." I didn't even know we needed cabinets. I sensed God saying, "Trust Me. I'll take care of things you don't even know you need."

One issue remained. What about the enormous amount of money needed for Sheena's schooling? Was it even right? "How much is she worth?" someone asked us. "Just put the need out there and see if God opens the door." Then, too, would our denomination approve? Permission was granted.

We learned the school usually requires the entire year's tuition to be paid by June, before the school year even begins. This was definitely not the twelve-month installment plan we were anticipating. "Oh, God, this just isn't possible... is it?" Surprisingly, the school agreed to let us have until December to pay it all. We didn't know how twelve months of fees could be raised in six months, but by this point in time, I was catching on to a new, revolutionary "shut-up-and-look-less-stupid" policy. As it happened, all the money for Sheena's exorbitant school bill was raised by December.

Door after door swung open before us. We found an apartment in Paris on the first day we looked, despite the page-long list of hopefuls who competed for the same space. We had enough money to ship a twenty-foot container full of our furnishings to Paris. Within a month, our French neighbors had honored us with a home-cooked, five-course, gourmet dinner and had introduced us to their friends, Madame and Monsieur D.

Many times we felt we were walking through automatic glass doors like those in our Paris grocery store, doors that silently swung wide as we ventured timidly toward them. Our second French Christmas, we even found a small '99 Saab® waiting to be purchased on the other side of those mysterious doors.

Most amazing of all was the way God orchestrated another event in the fall of 2006—Ron became the new lead pastor of our church. It's a hope he had seven years earlier, but now it was the right dream, in the right place, at the right time.

Endnotes

December 2005: Christmas Light

1. "I Will Trust Your Heart," song lyrics ©1999 by Lorelei M. Friesen.

February 2006: The Times

2. C.S. Lewis, *Mere Christianity* (New York, NY: The Macmillan Company, 1952), 40–41.

August 2006: Back in the USA

3. See Appendix: "How We Ended Up in Paris."

October 2008: All Hallows' Eve and All Saints Day

4. Psalm 73:21–26.

February 2009: Children of the Millstone

5. Luke 17:1–4 (paraphrased).

April 2009: Outside the Numbers

6. Isaiah 44:24–25.

May 2009: My Pearls

7. Psalm 77:11–14a.

June 2009: Corinthian Comfort

8. 2 Corinthians 1:8b, 9a.
9. 2 Corinthians 1:9b, 10a.
10. 2 Corinthians 1:10b.
11. 2 Corinthians 1:10c–11.

July 2009: Return to Paris

12. Ted Loder, *Guerillas of Grace: Prayers for the Battle* (Minneapolis, MN: Augsburg Books, 1981), 19.

May 2010: Walking with Job

13. Job 23:8–10.

July 2010: Alive on Planet Earth

14. Psalm 3:3–5; 4:8 (paraphrased).

Epilogue: All Is Suddenly Hers

15. Ruth Harms Calkin, *Lord, You Love to Say Yes* (Carol Stream, IL: Tyndale House Publishers, 1976).

For further information about Lorelei Friesen
or to order additional copies of this book
please visit
www.loreleifriesen.com

WinePressPublishing
Great Books, Defined.

To order additional copies of this book call:
1-877-421-READ (7323)
or please visit our website at
www.WinePressbooks.com

If you enjoyed this quality custom-published book,

drop by our website for more books and information.

www.winepresspublishing.com
"Your partner in custom publishing."

CPSIA information can be obtained at www.ICGtesting.com
Printed in the USA
BVOW071557110412

287426BV00001B/1/P